THE AMERICAN LIBRARY IN PARIS INC
Alcum post bellum
ex libris lux
1920

D1349851

The Purloined Punch Line

JERRY ALINE FLIEGER

The Purloined Punch Line

Freud's Comic Theory and the Postmodern Text

The Johns Hopkins University Press Baltimore and London

Printed in the United States of America

The Johns Hopkins University Press
701 West 40th Street, Baltimore, Maryland 21211
The Johns Hopkins University Press Ltd., London

♾ The paper used in this book meets the minimum requirements of American National Standard for Information Sciences—Permanence of Paper for Printed Library Materials, ANSI Z39.48-1984.

Library of Congress Cataloging-in-Publication Data

Flieger, Jerry Aline, 1947–

The purloined punch line : Freud's comic theory and the postmodern text / Jerry Aline Flieger.

p. cm.

Includes bibliographical references.

ISBN 0-8018-4048-1 (alk. paper)

1. French literture—20th century—History and criticism—Theory, etc. 2. Postmodernism (Literature)—France. 3. Psychoanalysis and literature. 4. Freud, Sigmund, 1856–1939—Views on humor. 5. Comic, The, in literature. 6. Desire in literature. I. Title.

PQ307.P66F57 1991

840.9'0091—dc20

90-4513 CIP

For my parents, and for Mark

CONTENTS

Preface ix

Abbreviations xiii

PART ONE Postmodernism: A Case of the Comic

1. Introduction: A Comic Contagion 3

2. Posting the Modern (Casing the Comic) 20

PART TWO Psychoanalysis: Comic Theory as Text

3. Freud's Bottom Line: Jokes and Their Relation to the Aesthetic 57

4. Lacan's Purloined Punch Line: Joke as Textual Paradigm 85

PART THREE Poststructuralism: Comic Text as Theory

5. Outwitting the Dialectic: Comic Negativity 125

6. The Infinite Entertainment: Blanchot's "Unworked" Text 166

PART FOUR Postmodern Aesthetics: The Comic as Postscript

7. Beckett's Aesthetic Play: The Comic Text *En Souffrance* 197

8. Postaesthetics: After the Endgame 235

Notes 261

Select Bibliography 271

Index 281

PREFACE

The Purloined Punch Line is at once a postmodern reading of psychoanalysis and a psychoanalytic reading of postmodernism, each body of theory purloining the other's comic vision. The work is meant to challenge a view of postmodernism that has gained currency through the work of Baudrillard and others, a defeatist vision proclaiming the death of Freud's intersubjective oedipal paradigm in a narcissistic, antisocial age. Reading Lacan's return to Freud as a "purloined punch line," I want to suggest that Freud's profoundly comic vision of human interaction may help us to understand postmodernism as a moment of enhanced social possibility rather than a phenomenon of reaction. For Freud's joke theory, rerouted via Lacan and the poststructuralists, may be read as a postmodern allegory of intersubjective communication, a comic social circuit that links human beings rather than isolating them.

The methodology is psychoanalytic as well as poststructuralist (focusing on the use of pun as *polysémie* or *entretien infini*). In addition, the work proposes a feminist purloining of Lacan's concept of intersubjectivity, recasting the oedipal drama as a comic play of shifting roles rather than as a tragic fate assigned by gender. For the effort at "posting" the modern emphasizes that Lacan's notion of text as circulated letter is compatible with the comic notion of woman as post-Man.

Of course, the texts engaged here—the theoretical writing

of such important figures as Bataille, Kristeva, Lyotard, Lacan, Derrida, and Blanchot (as well as the literary texts of Samuel Beckett)—cannot begin to answer the questions raised by the encounter of Freud's theory with the postmodern sensibility, nor can they even completely represent these questions. But the infectious comic tonality in the work of these writers and others, a playful linguistic contagion that continues to rage on both sides of the Atlantic, does suggest a possible point of articulation between psychoanalysis and postmodernism.[1] Indeed, I want to suggest here that the fundamental attitude of postmodernism may be considered profoundly comic when read through Freud's own "comic" theory of human being.

Part I of this study ("Postmodernism: A Case of the Comic") provides a theoretical overview of the intersection of the comic with the postmodern. Chapter 1 ("Introduction: A Comic Contagion") is a framework, outlining the methodology, scope, and terminology of the study. Chapter 2, "Posting the Modern (Casing the Comic)" surveys the parameters of comic theory past and present, sorts out the current debate on postmodernism, and articulates the intersection between the two bodies of theory, with the help of Baudelaire's classic essay on laughter as modern symptom, as well as Freud's seminal work on jokes and the comic.

The second section of this study, "Psychoanalysis: Comic Theory as Text," provides a psychoanalytic frame for the discussions that follow. Chapter 3, "Freud's Bottom Line: Jokes and Their Relation to the Aesthetic," is an analysis of Freud's work on jokes, read as a parable of desiring intersubjective textuality, while chapter 4, "Lacan's Purloined Punch Line: Joke as Textual Paradigm," deals with Lacan's "return to Freud," his postmodern purloining of Freudian comic theory as a model for his theory of the unconscious and for his understanding of the transference as intersubjective transaction. In other words, I suggest that Lacan's celebrated statement, "the unconscious is structured like a language" may be read as a retelling of Freud's original punch line, "the joke is structured like a dream," and that psychoanalytic theory may in turn be purloined by a feminist analysis of gender.

The third section, "Poststructuralism: Comic Text as Theory," deals with several Continental writers often associated with postmodernism, theorists who have posed a radical challenge to the centrisms of our culture, by exploring the relation between writing and desire. Chapter 5, "Outwitting the Dialectic: Comic Negativity," rehearses a preoccupation common to the work of Lyotard, Derrida, and Bataille: the finding of a comic strategy for getting around the ideology of closure and of dialectic totality. Here I explore several approaches to the question of negativity, with the help of Freud's work on negation, "Die Verneinung" (1925) and of Lyotard's Lacanian reading of that work. In chapter 6, "The Infinite Entertainment: Blanchot's 'Unworked' Text," I deal with the extraordinary work *L'entretien infini,* read as a postmodern, and comic, parable of textuality.

The fourth and final section of this study, "Postmodern Aesthetics: The Comic as Postscript," begins with Chapter 7, "Beckett's Aesthetic Play: The Comic Text *En Souffrance.*" This is a reading of Beckett's comic theater as an exemplary staging of the postmodern "scene of desire," corresponding with Lacan's scene of analysis as exemplified in the Schema L. Indeed, Beckett's scene is an example of comic textuality on at least three levels: as technique (in the use of comic material), as subject matter (*Godot,* for instance, is about prolonged clowning), and as model of human interaction (Didi and Gogo are engaged in an infinite conversation, or "play").

The last chapter, "Postaesthetics: After the Endgame," does not presume to offer anything like a final word on the comic as symptom and scene of postmodernity, but it does look beyond the texts treated to the larger issues and implications of postmodern aesthetics: is postmodernism, as some have suggested, an "antiaesthetic" phenomenon, a militant and engaged worldliness?[2] Or, as other would have it, is postmodernism a manifestation of a kind of hyperaestheticism, a withdrawal from the *real* consistent with the Kantian notion of the aesthetic as divorced from purpose? This may boil down in part to a discussion or definition of the term *aesthetic* itself, and the relation of the aesthetic to the question of gratuity or purpose. Once again, Freud's theory of the aesthetic as excess has provided my point of departure for framing these questions.

The question of this relation may prove to be the most important of all, since it inquires whether the desiring or unworked text—which remains exempt from straightforward utilitarian or dogmatic purposes—may be pertinent to social and political reality. It is one purpose of this book to problematize a false opposition between the aesthetic and the useful so that we may look beyond postmodernism toward the future of human interaction, perceived as an endgame with the comic (but deadly serious) project of not ending.

Yet, before we may postdate the postmodern, we must try to understand it; this is no easy task given the proliferation of debate around the subject. A mere glance at the profusion (and confusion) of material on the postmodern—which serves as the opening to the following chapter—brings to mind Kristeva's characterization of the task of interpretation, cited as one of the "opening lines" of this volume: "It is the critic's task, and there could hardly be a more comical one, to coagulate a meaning on a sea of negativity" (*Polylogue* 40). With this injunction in mind, let us dive into the sea of ideas about the postmodern and the comic, and hope that a sense of humor may help keep us afloat.

ABBREVIATIONS

AA	Foster, *The Anti-Aesthetic: Essays in Postmodern Culture*
BI	de Man, *Blindness and Insight*
BPP	Freud, *Beyond the Pleasure Principle*
DF	Lyotard, *Discours, figure*
DS	Derrida, "La double séance"
EC	Baudrillard, "The Ecstasy of Communication"
EG	Derrida, "De l'économie restreinte à l'économie générale: un Hégelianisme sans réserve"
EI	Blanchot, *L'entretien infini*
ER	Bataille, *L'érotisme*
FS	Lacan, *Feminine Sexuality* (introduction, Rose and Mitchell)
Godot	Beckett, *En attendant Godot*
Jokes	Freud, *Jokes and Their Relation to the Unconscious*
IM	Howe, "The Idea of the Modern"
PMC	Lyotard, *The Postmodern Condition*
PME	Bataille, *Préface de Madame Edwarda*
PS	Kroker and Cook, *The Postmodern Scene: Excremental Culture and Hyper-Aesthetics*
SPL	Lacan, *Seminar on The Purloined Letter*
TD	Beckett and Duthuit, "Three Dialogues"
Three Essays	Freud, *Three Essays on the Theory of Sexuality*

OPENING LINES . . .

We can ask ourselves: just what would be, or what is, the language of the "superior man"? . . . It is the Logos which says it all . . . an expression of logical achievement that is stranger to chance, to play, to laughter. But "man"—even superior man—is disappearing.

Maurice Blanchot, *The Infinite Entertainment*

The slumber of reason is not perhaps reason gone to sleep, but is rather sleep in the form of reason, the vigilance of the Hegelian Logos. To laugh at philosophy is perhaps the form of the awakening.

Jacques Derrida, *Writing and Difference*

Freud's *Jokes and their Relation to the Unconscious* reveals . . . the other side of the regalian power of language—the *pointe*, in fact, where its creative activity unveils its absolute gratuity, where its domination over the Real is expressed in the challenge of non-sense, where humour . . . symbolizes a Truth that has not said its last word.

Jacques Lacan, "The Function of Language in Psychoanalysis"

Freud demonstrated precisely this economy of laughter: it is a discharge with two meanings between sense and non-sense

. . . It is the critic's task, and there could hardly be a more comical one, to coagulate an island of meaning on a sea of negativity.

Julia Kristeva, "How Does One Speak to Literature?"

The riot of carnival, the impudence of inversion, the cackling of iconoclasm: these for historical materialism are moments within, not alternatives to, that deeper comedy which is the joke of contradiction and its pleasurable release.

Terry Eagleton, *Walter Benjamin or Towards a Revolutionary Criticism*

A feminine text cannot fail to be subversive . . . to blow up the law, to break up the truth with laughter.

Hélène Cixous, "The Laugh of the Medusa"

Nothing is funnier than suffering.

Samuel Beckett, *Endgame*

We laugh in order not to cry.

Eugene Ionesco, *Notes and Counternotes*

Perhaps because Lacan was hysterical and histrionic, he saw analysis as akin to theater . . . which I will call high comedy.

Stuart Schneiderman, *Jacques Lacan/ The Death of an Intellectual Hero*

Freud . . . the very name's a laugh.

Jacques Lacan, "A Love Letter"

PART ONE

Postmodernism

A Case of the Comic

1. Introduction: A Comic Contagion

Symptoms

The late twentieth century seems obsessed with "post"-marks, with the notion of aftermath or residue. For after that "exquisite crisis of literature" heralded by Mallarmé, after the surrealist revolution, after the existentialist crisis of consciousness, the work of contemporary writers and theorists persists in reminding us that something is continuing to happen, that (in Beckett's words in *Endgame*) "something is taking its course," not only in the literary text but also in the process of writing, reading, and interpretation itself. And as the opening lines, or epigraphs, of Part I attest, there is something peculiarly comic about the bizarre symptoms surrounding and inhabiting the contemporary text.

The surrealists were perhaps the first to call attention to the ludic quality of a certain kind of modern literature, but they have most certainly not been the last to explore this comic quality of modern and of postmodern writing, particularly in the theory and literature of France. In our own day, post-ing the modern continues to imply dethroning the serious, undermining the legitimate, and, most recently, exposing the profoundly parodic nature of those "centrisms" (logo-phallo-ethnocentrism) upon which the Western philosophical and social order has been constructed. As Jacques Derrida has pointed out, in his debunking of the deadly seriousness of the Western philosophical tradition, the Logos seems to harbor the seeds of its own undoing ("to laugh at philosophy is in fact the form of the awakening" [*L'écriture et la différence* 370]). Something, indeed, is taking its course.

Whether we refer to this phenomenon, this mysterious "something," as the intrusion of desire in language (Julia Kristeva), as the decentering of the subject (Jacques Lacan), as the invasion of discourse by figure (Jean-François Lyotard), as the deconstruction of the metaphysics of presence (Derrida, Paul de Man), or even as the subversion of androcentric language by a "(M)Other tongue" (in feminist theory),[1] it does seem that this pervasive something has a contagious and seditious quality, capable of subverting conventional notions of subjectivity, rationality, and consciousness as it spreads across disciplinary lines, touching philosophy, literature, criticism, the social sciences. Indeed, in the late twentieth century, the boundaries between psychic and real, fact and fiction, literature and theory all seem to have been eroded from within. This is what Maurice Blanchot seems to suggest when he refers to a certain contemporary text as an "unworked work" ("*l'oeuvre désoeuvrée*" of *L'entretien infini*): this postmodern text is undone, done in, out of work, engaged in an open-ended play; fractious and unserviceable, it delights in poking holes ("semes"?) in the seemingly seamless fabric of the Logos.

What better breeding ground for this playful contagion than the homeland of the *cogito:* perhaps nowhere has this peculiar comic erosion manifested itself so persistently and so pervasively, even perversely, as it has in postmodern France. Indeed, the contagion of a certain *désir* functions as the absent center of two intertwined and highly contagious Continental theoretical practices that have now invaded our shores: what has come to be known as "French Freud"—the work of Jacques Lacan and his followers—and what has been broadly termed "French theory"—the poststructuralist work of figures such as Derrida, Blanchot, Kristeva, Lyotard, Foucault, Barthes. (Geoffrey Hartman, with characteristic wit, has referred to the combined impact of poststructuralism and French Freud as "the invasion of America by the mind-snatchers from the Continent.")[2]

For purposes of discussion, we may agree to call this invasion an effect of postmodernism, in recognition of the "post" qualities of the writing in question; that is, its persistence and fractiousness, and its challenge to all precedent, including the tradition of the modern itself. Of course, postmodernism is itself an unruly subject, the focus of much debate, and the subject of the next chapter of this book. For the moment, it may be helpful to refer to an apt formulation of the question by William Kerrigan and Joseph Smith: "In postmodernism the rebound of statement upon itself is not suffered passively or received in embarrassment as somehow silencing, but actively embraced. Discourse has been reconstituted about precisely this instability" (*Taking Chances: Derrida, Psychoanalysis, and Literature,* 1984, xi). In this view, the postmodern is not so much a question of a historical period as it is of an attitude, implying a radical perspective on reading and writing, an openness to what the French theorists call *désir,* and the comic recognition that even when all is said and done, systematized and accounted for, "something" is still taking its course, going its own merry way.

But if the mind-snatchers have taught us anything, it is that naming a symptom does not deal with it; having latched on to the attractive and convenient term *postmodernism,* are we any closer to understanding that persistent *je ne sais quoi* that haunts the late twentieth century work? We might begin by looking for an uncommon denominator in Continental postmodern writing—as represented by the series of opening lines introducing this chapter—in order to seek out that ineffable something shared by these highly diverse intellectual and aesthetic voices, a something that lends a plural and playful quality to these texts, contributing a permeability to suggestion or double meaning. Indeed, for psychoanalysis the literary imagination is precisely the creative faculty that invites invasion or "unworking" by unconscious desire and process; the products of the creative imagination are thus marked by a certain tendency to duplicity, the traces of overdetermination. Significantly, Freud argues (in *Jokes and Their Relation to the Unconscious,* 1905) that the technique of overdetermination characteristic of the dreamwork is related if not identical to the process of overdetermination in joke-making. Thus, even if Freud credits the poets and creative writers with the original discovery of the unconscious, he is doubtless the first to intuit the profoundly comic nature of those shadowy processes.

Freud's remarkable work on jokes thus speaks to the question at hand—the nature of the peculiar something that is taking its course in the postmodern text—by its extraordinary insights into the workings of aesthetic processes as effects of unconscious desire. His later work (particularly *Beyond the Pleasure Principle,* 1920) suggests intriguing associations between comic desire and the repetition compulsion, or even the death-drive, as I suggest in the second part of this study. Even though Freud's comments on "the poet's secret" clearly suggest that a kind of primary process may be at work in all literary processes (and indeed in all human endeavor), it is in the postmodern literary and theoretical text that we may encounter a particularly persistent exploration/exploitation of desire at work (or at play), transforming what Freud calls the dreamwork/jokework into a kind of textplay which, as Kerrigan and Smith suggest, has "actively embraced the uncertainties of discourse."

This work, then, is a parallel exploration of Freud's theory on the comic, read as postmodern text, and a number of representative postmodern texts, read as an implied comic theory. My approach represents an effort at placing several emblematic instances of postmodern writing in an open framework, at once psychoanalytic and poststructuralist. In order to read the postmodern work as a text (as in *textere:* a weaving, heterogeneous inmixing; a fabric woven out of significant gaps between threads of meaning), I have followed Freud's lead, deemphasizing or even disregarding conventional boundaries between the literary and the theoretical. As Freud himself so often does, I have taken the liberty of reading the theorists (Lacan, Derrida, Lyotard, Kristeva, Freud himself) as creative writers and the literary figures (Beckett, Blanchot, Bataille) as critic-theorists. Indeed, in order to apprehend the ineffable and comic "something" as it unravels the postmodern text, we need to follow as many leads, as many textual threads as possible through the postmodern labyrinth; for, like Godot, the comic subject is both pervasive and elusive, ubiquitous and absent, everywhere and nowhere in the postmodern maze.

Method: Treatment of Choice

One difficulty in dealing with this peculiar postmodern contagion, given the slipperiness of the subject, resides in the choice of approach as well as in the choice of cases for analysis. An exhaustive diachronic or historical study would have to begin at least with surrealism and *l'humour noir* (perhaps even earlier, in Postsymbolism, or with Baudelaire's important treatise on laughter) and continue to our own turn of the century avant-garde. Such a systematic chronological treatment is beyond the scope of this work, which is limited to the consideration of a more modest question: what is the relation between the postmodern concept of text (as effect of desire) and the psychoanalytic concept of the comic (as symptom)?

On the other hand, a synchronic, ahistorical treatment of this question would necessarily be unsatisfying, given that the concept of postmodernism certainly suggests a historical moment or sequence and that psychoanalysis itself may be considered a creation (as Foucault has shown) of a particular historical moment.[3] Furthermore, there is no reason why a postmodern understanding of "text" should not be applied to works from other eras (as Derrida, has done, for instance, in his reading of Rousseau). Thus, the following chapter will raise some of the issues, historical and otherwise, inherent in the notion of the postmodern. While I do not want to ignore historical considerations, this study will focus on the specificity of our own postmodern notion of writing, in order to relate that notion with a comic theory grounded in a postmodern

(Lacanian) rereading of Freud's work, transcoding a psychoanalytic theory of the self with a postmodern theory of the text.[4]

An advantage of this kind of transcoding, as Fredric Jameson and others have demonstrated, may be that it allows us to think about our human subjectivity as a textual process, but not in the sense in which the notion of text has so often been misunderstood. (Derrida's famous statement that "there is nothing outside the text," for instance, has all too often been misread as a statement of implosion or impasse, justifying the miring of human consciousness in endless verbal ruminations.) I argue that the use of psychoanalytic theory enables us to read "text" as social "context," an interaction or weaving of human subjects (and this is how I in fact understand Derrida's now infamous dictum). In this spirit, I ask the following question: how does the postmodern writer rely on the purloining of the punch line, the celebration of the impossibility of having the last word, to forge a comic vision of human subjectivity, intersubjectivity, and creativity, a vision of human life as social text?

The question of level or register of analysis is in some ways more difficult than the question of scope. Just where may the slippery postmodern comic be apprehended, caught in the act of unworking the text? Is the unworked comic text simply a matter of modality, related to its self-referential quality and its ironic and critical vision, its refusal to take itself absolutely seriously? Or does this text perhaps represent a philosophical strategy, a way of coping with a frightening vision, undoing some of the anxiety of the postmodern condition? (As Ionesco puts it: "We laugh in order not to cry" [*Notes et contre-notes* 175].) Or is the comic nature of the postmodern text a more local phenomenon, residing in specific instances of comic material (the jokes and gags of writers like Beckett and Ionesco, or the incessant punning of writers like Lacan and Derrida)? In other words, should the postmodern comic be analyzed as a literary mode/technique? Or should it be considered a philosophical symptom of what Lyotard has called "the postmodern condition"? Or ought it be analyzed as a philosophical tactic for eroding traditional metaphysics from within?

Case Histories

With these questions in mind, and again taking a cue from Freud, we could read the ten brief quotations that introduce this chapter as mini case histories of sorts, inviting a kind of free association of ideas on the comic and the postmodern text. These snippets of text face off like small confrontations or conversations, suggesting at least four registers of possible analysis of the comic symptom:

1. as technique (or weapon) subverting the authority of patriarchal or logocentric systems (Derrida laughs at philosophy; Blanchot sees play as a sign of the disappearance of philosophical man; Lacan sees Freud's "joke" as a challenge to the domination of the Real and the rational; Eagleton sees the hilarity of carnival as a revolutionary act; Cixous sees laughter as the disarming arm of feminist thought);
2. as metaphor (or analogy) for *desire,* a representation of the "something" that is "taking its course" (for Eagleton, "deeper comedy" represents history; for Lacan, farce is a metaphor for Freud's psychoanalysis; for Schneiderman, Lacan may himself be metaphorized as "high comedy"; for Cixous, the laugh of the female Warrior is a metaphor for a liberated and joyous female subjectivity, which laughs off the domination of Lacan's Name of the Father);
3. as paradigm or working model (a "structural machine" in the poststructuralist sense of the term) illustrating human subjectivity and human signification as processes of interaction (Lacan has constructed this sort of paradigm in his celebrated reading of Poe's "The Purloined Letter" as a kind of farcical allegory, which demonstrates how language makes its rounds in a comic circuit. Similarly, Lacan's metaphoric formula [Freud = a laugh]—cited as the last of my

"opening lines"—may be read as a kind of shorthand, equating the process of psychoanalytic transference with the model of farce);

4. as symptom or evidence, a sign of excessive desire, a trace or stigma that lives on after all is said and done (Beckett and Ionesco see laughter as a symptom of absurd lucidity; Kristeva posits the comic as a symptomatic spark engendered by the confrontation between reason and nonsense; Lacan reads the punch line like a letter, a stigma to be passed from hand to hand; Eagleton reads laughter as a moment symptomatic of the dialectic of desire, the movement between contradiction and release staged in the work of Brecht).

These four related ways of understanding the role of the comic in the process of textmaking (as technique, as metaphor, as paradigm, as symptom) in turn suggest at least four corresponding levels of analysis.

1. Viewed as technique, the postmodern comic could be studied at the level of individual puns, gags, or jokes by analyzing the jokework in representative texts.
2. Understood as theme or metaphor, the postmodern comic could be analyzed at the level of an entire work or group of works. On this level, the individual gags seem almost like holographs of a larger network. In Beckett's theater, for example, the acts of clowning are markers of sorts, indicating that a play like *Godot* is about clowning-around.
3. Read as a paradigm (the most theoretical level, at which questions of aesthetics are raised), the object of analysis is no longer one text or a group of texts, but is the larger question of textuality itself (what is a text and how does it work?). At this level, we may speculate on how the comic process functions as a social exchange (again, with the help of psychoanalytic theory), which may in turn be read as paradigm for all literary or creative activity. This third level of analysis of the comic—as transactional model for all literary processes—opens to extraliterary considerations,

such as the relation between literature, the comic, and dream; or the relation between the comic and the erotic.

4. Analyzed on this extraliterary level, as symptom, the comic could be considered as coextensive with human *désir*—desire as motor not only of the literary transaction, but of all human interaction understood as a textual inweaving of subjects.

The last two levels are perhaps the most significant, for the study of comic process as textual paradigm—with the help of Freud's fable of the joking process as the circulation of an always "purloined punch line" lifted from another human subject—may open to a consideration of the play of desire and inhibition characterizing all human relations. This in turn suggests the possibility of a sociopolitical understanding of the comic process, read as a symptom of a subversive desire which aims at unworking repression in every sense of the term.

Terminology: The Name of the Game

This multilevel approach to the analysis of the comic character of postmodernism may also prove useful in addressing difficult questions of terminology and register: are the terms *postmodern* and *comic* simply equivalent, and if so, does all contemporary literature qualify as comic? If this is the case, what are we to make of the modern treatment of classical tragic themes by Giraudoux or Anouilh, for example, or even the decidedly unfunny fictional works of Bataille and Blanchot, to name two writers who figure in this study? If we address this issue from the perspective of each of the different levels or registers of the comic in the postmodern "text" (understood both as literary work and as larger social process) the question is perhaps less perplexing. For while the unfunny nature of many "unworked" texts does indeed eliminate them from the first level of analysis—the study of jokework technique—the remaining three levels remain important for reading and interpretation of these, and of any, texts. Cixous's "Laugh of the

Medusa," for example, is not a comic text in the usual sense of the term, but laughter figures there as an important metaphor for revolt as well as a symptom of the human desire that motivates this revolt. Even in the case of the serious works of Bataille and Blanchot, the preoccupation with mirthful disorder as theme seems consistently to exceed the thematic or even philosophical level and invade the writing itself, yielding a curiously unworked textual voice, with a dark and dispersive quality. And this kind of dispersive character seems comic insofar as it opposes what Blanchot has called "the reign of light," the oppressive classical notion of order that excludes "chance, discontinuity, and laughter" (*L'entretien infini* 233). In the work of Blanchot and other postmoderns, then, the notion of the comic seems inextricably bound with the subversive antics of textual desire.

The most difficult question of terminology, however, stems perhaps from what the French call *l'embarras du choix,* the perplexing variety of available terms to describe the evasive postmodern symptom. Why choose the term *comic* to describe postmodern textuality—rather than, say, *ironic* or *playful* or *humorous,* to cite three alternative terms figuring in Freud's work on jokes? Or why not remain with the term *wit* (Freud's *Witz*) or *jokes* (its standard translation)? How about *humor,* the term preferred by the surrealists to designate a certain subversive textual quality? Or, following the lead of the American New Critics as well as of contemporary thinkers on both sides of the poststructuralist theoretical fence (Paul de Man, Wayne Booth), why not use the term *irony* to indicate the literary working of tension and contrast? Putting a name to the symptom will inevitably have consequences for the diagnosis and the analysis, so such questions are not trivial.

I have chosen *comic* as the most inclusive term of this study, then, for reasons both practical and theoretical in nature. The term *joking,* for instance, seems too local to characterize the textual game of writing (the *"jeu de l'écriture"* described by Blanchot in *L'entretien infini*) and is far too tame for the kind of explosive comic transgression that is the focus for a writer like Bataille (*"le rire entier"* of *Mme Edwarda*). But *comic* may have a kind of consensual value for all of the writers who figure in the essays that follow (Derrida, Freud, Lacan, Beckett, Bataille, Blanchot, Lyotard, the "French feminists"), while each of the other terms mentioned above (*laughter, joke, wit, game*) is specific to one or two of these writers. Moreover, the term *comic* has a certain functional flexibility, both in its adjectival use (as in Freud's comic theory, which may imply a theory of the comic as well as a body of theory that displays a comic side), and its substantive use (as either a literary mode—*the* comic—or as a reference to an individual clown or joke-maker—*a* comic). Finally, the appeal of the term has been recognized by Charles Baudelaire, whom I read as a sort of "pre-postmodern" and whose provocative ruminations on the *comique significatif* and the *comique absolu* serve as a point of departure for these essays. As Baudelaire's own comic prose poems demonstrate, the comic may be a mode of writing which is not necessarily funny (and which may even seem frightening or poignant) but which can nonetheless be associated with the kind of clowning or gaming so prevalent in late twentieth century writing. Indeed, I use the term *comic* as a performing metaphor that both demonstrates and generates the process it describes.

These are the general considerations that have informed my choice of an umbrella term in this "case of the comic." But as in any diagnostic move, this general term calls for specification and clarification at various points in the study. Specifically, in the chapter dealing with Freudian theory (chapter 3), I discuss the joke paradigm, rather than the more general comic mode, in part because Freud himself draws a clear distinction between the two terms. (I shall argue that this distinction does not hold up, but for reasons of clarity of reference I have maintained Freud's own terminology when discussing his work.)

The term *irony* poses a more complicated problem, given the prevalence of the term in poststructuralist writing and the decidedly postmodern tendency, since the work of de Man, to link the notion of ironic consciousness with a postmodern understanding of literature. In a sense, the critical vogue currently enjoyed by *irony* contributes to its difficulty. I am inclined to agree with Wayne Booth's assertion (in *A Rhetoric of Irony,* 1974) that "the term has come to stand for so many things that we are in danger of losing it as a useful term altogether" (7). Of course, Booth's response to this crisis has been an attempt to stabilize irony—and along with it, the act of literary interpretation—by reading irony as a kind of pact limiting the available meanings of a given text, with an eye to proving that a text's "embodied intentions" lead us "to go so far" in the act of interpretation, "and no further" (91). For Booth, irony legislates and polices a textual transaction in which both parties, reader and writer, "have confidence that they are moving together in identical patterns" (132). This particular use of *irony,* then, is diametrically opposed to the poststructuralist notion of irony as (comic) contagion—a kind of transmissible fascination with "the uncertainties of discourse" (Smith and Kerrigan). Although it is not my intention to quarrel with Booth, I must point out that his use of irony wants finally to stabilize even Beckett's text, which I have read (in chapter 7) as the very paradigm of open-endedness and instability. Booth's endgame, on the other hand, seems more concerned with "end" than with "game." Indeed, Booth's understanding of irony tends to lose sight of the comic sense of the term altogether, and thus is inappropriate for my focus.

The comic sense of irony is retained in Freud's use of the term, as a subcategory of the general term *comic* ("saying the opposite of what one intends to convey to the person" [*Jokes and their Relation to the Unconscious* 174]). But in Freud's treatment of irony there is a pronounced emphasis on the conscious manipulation of language by the speaker, and a downplay of the unconscious desire that eludes the joker's intention. In Freud's understanding of irony, then, as in his view of humor, the joker's consciousness is girded by the joke process, aided in reality mastery by a conscious triumph over irrational fears. (Humor, for Freud, is a joke concerning one's own death or vulnerability; irony consciously manipulates the denotative power of language whereby the speaker makes clear by an ironic tone that he or she means the opposite of what is said.) Freud would doubtless maintain that the unconscious still has an important role to play in both humor and irony, as in all the "sub-species of the comic" named in *Jokes;* yet, in these two cases, where the ego emerges triumphant, unconscious desire does seem to be muted, if not repressed. In other words, although Freud's use of the term *irony* plays down the importance of the unconscious sources of joking, it is precisely this insight into the "relation of jokes and the unconscious" (Freud's own title) that may provide a point of articulation between postmodern notions of *écriture* as play of desire, and the psychoanalytic theory of the self as a construct of desire.

I have a similar bone to pick with de Man's fascinating treatment of irony as demystified literary language.[5] As Frank Lentricchia pointed out in his critique of the existentialist bias of de Man's work,[6] de Man's notion of irony not only highlights the recuperative and controlling role of consciousness but also risks a kind of paralysis, whereby the superior consciousness afforded by irony may lead to a stymied hyperconsciousness (an endless almost Beckettian contemplation of the umbilical knot [Knott?] of existence). Lentricchia's reading of de Man raises a problem that seems to haunt postmodern consciousness, a problem that is already implied in Baudelaire's theory of poetic consciousness as a heightened awareness (*De l'essence du rire,* 1900). Lentricchia points out that while this kind of ironic hyperlucidity may afford a superior perspective on human life, it may also dead end in an embittered rumination on the ludicrousness and hopelessness of the human condition. This is also a much-discussed issue around the philosophy of postmoderns like Foucault and Derrida (and more recently, de Man): do the politics of postmodernism end in or condone a kind of quietism or solipsism, a paralyzed hyperconsciousness trapped in "undecidability"? What does undecidability mean for politics, and for ethics? Similarly, critics of psychoanalysis (and especially of "French Freud") have argued that the Lacanian "interminable cure" is no cure at all but is merely an exercise in endless self-indulgence. I want to take up these issues, arguing as others have done (Fredric Jameson, Barbara Johnson, Michael Ryan) that a postmodern consciousness—although always underwritten by "unconsciousness"—need not find a terminus in social paralysis. It is in part because of these reservations about the implications of de Man's *irony* that I have preferred to couch my own diagnosis of the postmodern text in other terms.

Selection: Comic Case Histories

What, then, has guided my choice of texts for diagnosis and treatment? (The term *treatment* itself brings to mind the implications of postmodern technology for the processing of language, by its associations with the French term for the word *processing: "traitement" de texte*). First, I have been guided by the simple and serviceable definition of postmodernism proposed by Jean-François Lyotard (*The Postmodern Condition*, 1979), which begins with the assertion that literary modernism represents "the fact that the unrepresentable exists" (*PMC* 78). Moreover, Lyotard considers postmodernism an avatar of modernism, concerned with this same paradoxical representation of the unrepresentable. But he makes the following distinction between the modern and the postmodern: whereas the modern writer, like Proust, "represents the unrepresentable" while remaining attached to the conventions of good form, the postmodern writer, like Joyce, invents new forms that reflect the challenge to "presentability." Lyotard sums up his argument this way:

> The postmodern would be that which, in the modern, puts forward the unpresentable in presentation itself; that which denies itself the solace of good forms, the consensus of taste which would make it possible to share collectively the nostalgia for the unattainable; that which looks for new presentations, not in order to enjoy them but in order to impart a stronger sense of the unpresentable. (81)

The question of the unpresentable—which I ally with the notion of the unconscious and of *désir* as used by such theorists as Derrida and Blanchot—is often a question of interpretation, as is the question of enjoyment, also raised by Lyotard's formulation. I, for one, would not exclude the notion of enjoyment from the postmodern sensibility, as Lyotard seems to do. But in any case, Lyotard's definition is only a convenient guideline; even the writers whom I treat here may be classified either as modern or postmodern depending on how you apply Lyotard's criteria. Freud, for instance, who deals with the unpresentable (as the *non-dit* or the unconscious) but who is devoted to good form in his writing, might be considered a model "modern" while Lacan, the *enfant terrible* of psychoanalysis who delights in forms of expression as scandalous as the unconscious they describe, might be considered a "postmodern." Similarly, Derrida's earlier work, which is *about* desire, might be called modern while his later work, which seems to write desire in highly unconventional forms (such as the divided page of Glas), might be considered postmodern. In any case, all the authors treated here might be said to concern themselves with the representation of the unpresentable and to make use of highly suggestive and metaphoric forms—often comic in tone—remaining open to the incursion of *désir* that they "represent."

This permeability of the text to *désir* as (comic) trope (the subject of Lyotard's *Discours, figure,* 1979) is perhaps constitutive of what Lyotard calls the postmodern attitude. According to Lyotard, this attitude is characterized by an "incredulity toward metanarratives" (*PMC* xxix), and especially two rational philosophical metanarratives: the story of Progress as told in the terms of the Enlightenment philosophers, and the story of Knowledge as told by Hegel. Lyotard stages a postmodern challenge to these metanarratives read as global systems that aim at answering all questions, once and for all, in a closure of epistemological desire. Yet, I suggest that one may radically challenge the dominant cultural narratives, such as the metanarratives of the Enlightenment and of German Idealism singled out by Lyotard, without necessarily doing away with the notion of narrative itself as a fundamental act of human communication. (Indeed, Freud's oedipal scenario of subjectivity might be considered one of the master-narratives of our century, and my own reading of Freud proposes the joke scenario as the paradigm of narrative itself.).

Significantly, the two metanarratives singled out by Lyotard are also challenged by the other postmodern writers who figure in this study: the Hegelian philosophical narrative of dialectic fulfillment (the subject of chapters 5 and 6) in which History finds a triumphant happy ending in Absolute Knowledge, and the related metanarrative of linear progress and emancipation propounded by the Kantian Enlightenment, wherein progress is understood as mastery of the universe through science and the triumph of positivist reason revealing universal Truth. The first Hegelian metanarrative has been challenged by poststructuralist thought as "logocentrism" (in Derrida's work) and as the "reign of light" (in Blanchot's work). The second metanarrative of Progress has been challenged by French feminists like Luce Irigaray, Annie LeClerc, and Hélène Cixous, who have argued that the notions of mastery and positivism are the source of an androcentric epistemology complicit with social Darwinism and confusing the notion of brute strength with the cause of Truth.[7]

Both of these narratives are discussed by Lyotard in *The Postmodern Condition,* and are treated as well in his more recent article "Re-writing Modernity" (*Sub-stance* 54, 1988). (In this later formulation, Lyotard expands upon his discussion of Hegelian and Kantian ideology, opposing the postmodern sensibility to the Classical sensibility as well, and challenging classical notions of linear development.) In the later essay, Lyotard backs off somewhat from the term *postmodern,* preferring to "rewrite the modern" in order to distinguish his own position from neoconservative defenses of postmodernism. Regrettably, in neither essay does Lyotard point out the clear implications of his analysis for feminism. Also, he fails to draw clearly the distinction between adherence to a repressive ideology of

Progress entailing the domination of nature by culture or commitment to a nonrepressive ethic of progress as social change. Yet, I would like to insist on the difference between the belief in the notion of progress as the triumph of univocal Reason or Truth and the belief in social change, lest progressive politics be swept away by the alibi of postmodern "incredulity toward metanarratives."

Lyotard's first essay on postmodernism does not speculate on the relation of Freudian theory to postmodern "incredulity", yet nothing challenges the concept of Absolute Knowledge more radically than does the notion of the Freudian unconscious. The thrust of Freud's concept of the repetition compulsion (elaborated in *Beyond the Pleasure Principle,* 1920) is that human progress has perhaps more to do with the insistence of a shadowy desire (the death-drive) than with the triumph of an enlightened reason. (In the more recent piece, Lyotard does mention the importance of Freudian theory in a revision of the notion of progress, but this brief essay only hints at possibilities of a psychoanalytic understanding of postmodernism.) In any case, the "incredulity toward metanarrative" emphasized by Lyotard is an important characteristic of all the postmodern works that I treat in this study; indeed, it is this same incredulity that may provide the kind of critical spirit necessary to open postmodern aesthetics to political and ethical questions. As Fredric Jameson eloquently puts it, in his introduction to Lyotard's *The Postmodern Condition* (xvii), "This is the moment in which aesthetics gives way to ethics, in which the problem of the postmodern . . . becomes that of one's more fundamental attitude toward the new social formation."

2. Posting the Modern (Casing the Comic)

Beckett's postmodern clown, peering into the abyss of the darkened theater, intones that "nothing is funnier than suffering"; Queneau's Duke of Pigsty (*Duc d'Auge*) surveys the ruins of history from his turret and espies flesh-and-blood scraps of language strewn over the landscape; Genet's criminal alter ego spews out a giddy litany of sacrilegious puns; Michaux's trickster-Everyman "Pen" (*Plume*) embarks on a picaresque voyage across the page; Ponge's poetic objects leap from the page to engage their creator in conversation. And the postmodern reader laughs.

Freud spins the old Jewish joke about two elderly men on the way to Cracow; Derrida spins a whole text out of peals of resonant punning (*Glas*); Lacan dubs the human infant a mixed-up kid, a scrambled "*hommelette*"; Barbara Johnson exposes the underequipped poet, insecure about his literary potency, as "*Mal armé.*" And the postmodern reader laughs. In laughing, the reader enters a comic transaction in which the gag seems to have become not only a preferred literary technique but also a vehicle for criticism and theory; indeed, all this clowning seems to invite a willful confusion between literature and theory, and an inmixing of theoretical fields. The irrepressibly waggish and undisciplined postmodern writing seems to be challenging the very notion of discipline.

If this unruly text will not be disciplined, neither will it be silenced; the "unworked work" (Blanchot's "*oeuvre désoeu-*

vrée") solicits the reader's complicity in an endgame that refuses to end, thanks to a comic underpinning that refuses to be pinned down. In a particularly suggestive way, Maurice Blanchot refers to this textplay as an "infinite entertainment" (*l'entretien infini*), with the French *entretien* acting as a pun and a performative allegory, suggesting at once a *conversation* between reader and writer, an enter-tainment (*entre-tien*) or aesthetic *diversion* of reader by writer, and a *suspension* or hold-up (whereby the reader is enter-tained, held up, stranded *between* beginning and ending). In the same work, Blanchot refers to the contemporary text as a turning point (*tournant*), a diversion that turns back from closure even as it turns away from tradition.

As Blanchot's wordplay suggests, there is something uncannily comic about this whole process. For whether it serves to give voice to an absurd vision or to explode formal and stylistic convention, much contemporary writing—and especially Continental literature and theory—has manifested a penchant for the comic mode, which it enlists in an interrogation and subversion of tradition. The appeal of the comic mode for writers as diverse as Beckett, Ponge, Michaux, Cixous, Derrida, Lacan, Blanchot, Queneau—to name only a few salient examples—would seem to indicate that comic technique readily lends itself to many varied but distinctly postmodern projects (with "postmodern" understood, after Smith and Kerrigan's formulation, as an "active embrace of the uncertainties of discourse"). Indeed, comic technique has been brought into play not only in recent literature and criticism but in theoretical writing as well—poststructuralist, psychoanalytic, linguistic, even philosophical writing, beginning perhaps with Wittgenstein's "language games"—theory that makes extensive use of comic imagery and device in its efforts to "unwork" or "deconstruct" assumptions about language, writing, and knowledge.

Yet in spite of the abundance of explicitly comic material in contemporary literature, theory, and philosophy, it remains a difficult task to pinpoint just what is unique about the use of the comic mode by late twentieth century writers. Could we not say, for example, that Diderot's "abysmal" fiction or that Molière's "tragic comedies"—not to mention "modern" works such as *Hamlet* or *Don Quixote*—are "postmodern" in their "embrace of the instabilities of discourse" and their resistance to univocal reading? In other words, in order to determine what is comic about the contemporary text, one is faced with the doubly difficult task of arriving at a workable definition of two tricky concepts—the comic and the postmodern—and then of determining how these two phenomena coincide.

In this chapter on "posting" the modern, I want to play postman, routing these two questions along a series of detours in order to "return to Freud" (via Lacan's familiar route) in the following chapter. Let us begin with some reflections on postmodernism and move on to a consideration of the comic, in order to read the postmodern text as allegorical letter, a message concerning human subjectivity.

"Post" modernism: An Affair of Letters

> Something has changed, and Faustian, Promethean (perhaps Oedipal) period of production and consumption gives way to the era of networks, to the narcissistic and protean era of connections, contact, contiguity, feedback and generalized interface that goes with the universe of communication. . . . We are no longer part of the drama of alienation; we live in the ecstasy of communication.
>
> Jean Baudrillard, "The Ecstasy of Communication"

Not a simple matter, putting a postmark on the modern. The critical scene has of late, like the post office during the holidays, been inundated with writings of men and women of letters, addressed to a deceptively simple question: what is the postmodern, its sources, consequences, and effects? An approach to the problem begins by wading through the stacks of communications, sorting out all these codes. For any response to the question of postmodernism will necessarily bear the stamp of its sender, the mark of the place from which the question is addressed.

Unless, of course, Jean Baudrillard is right about our era, characterized by the flat and obscene "ecstasy of communication," an orgy of pure information in which the narcissistic self has become a terminal or screen rather than an actor in an intersubjective oedipal drama. Baudrillard warns, for example, that "obscenity begins precisely where there is no more spectacle, no more scene, when all becomes transparence and immediate visibility, where everything is exposed to the harsh, inexorable light of communication."[1] Thus, in Baudrillard's nonscenic scenario—entailing the demise not only of public space, but of any space or dimension whatsoever, since the postmodern scene is flat "screen"—*all* letters are outdated artifacts of social interaction, narrative fossils of nonecstatic intersubjective communication. For Baudrillard, delivery has become not only outmoded but impossible.

Thus, Baudrillard's vision poses a radical challenge to psychoanalysis, and to any social or intersubjective code: can Freudian theory (or the theory of Lacan, whom Derrida has attacked as the Postman of Truth)[2] be expected to deliver a message in the debate about the nature of our era? Or, as Baudrillard and others have suggested, is the reign of Oedipus hopelessly dated, fit to be consigned to the dead-letter pile, taken out of circulation?

My own effort at playing post office has thus far ascertained five zones of postmodern theorizing whose lines may be drawn according to the theorist's position on three fundamental issues: the relation of the postmodern to the modern (is it a break or a continuity?); the relation of the postmodern to the aesthetic (is the postmodern a hyperaestheticism positing nothing outside the text; or is it an antiaesthetic phenomenon, a reaction against the elitism of the modernist aesthetic of "art for art's sake"?); the political implications of the postmodern (is it consistent with a new conservatism, or does it offer a radical critique of representation and reference, whereby conservative ideology may be "deconstructed"?).

While there is nothing even approaching consensus on these three issues, I would like to propose a kind of general classification (a sort of postal code) of definitions and attitudes, each representing a different "post-mark" on the modern.

1. Postmodernism as *reaction* to modernism, a reactionary antimodernism. This is the position, for example, of Jürgen Habermas ("Modernity—An Incomplete Project," 1980), who sees the postmodern tendency in the politics of neoconservatives, a category that for him includes not only the likes of Daniel Bell but also the French poststructuralists Foucault and Derrida. For Habermas, the project of modernism is essentially the project of the Kantian Enlightenment, based in the faith in Reason and implying ethical responsibility—and this project has never been fully realized. Where modernism went wrong, Habermas argues, is in splitting off art from life (that is, from the realms of ethics and of science) and creating a hyperaestheticism that is being extended and exacerbated by the "young conservatives" today (Derrida and company). Modernism's true vocation, Habermas argues, should be the integration of aesthetics, ethics, and science; its still incomplete project of integration is thus the antithesis of a hyperspecialization yielding an elitist aesthetics, comprehensible only to the initiated. Jean-François Lyotard has argued against Habermas's position (in *The Postmodern Condition,* 1979), characterizing that view as a kind of organic positivism and mounting a critique of this totalizing vision: "What Habermas requires from the arts . . . is to bridge the gap between cognitive, ethical and political discourses, thus opening the way to a unity of experience" (*PMC* 72). Lyotard argues that for Habermas postmodernism is a kind of messy mistake, which we could undo, were we only "enlightened" enough.

2. Postmodernism as *denial* or *flight* from modernity. Thinkers as different as Paul de Man ("Literary History and Literary Modernity," 1971)[3] and Marshall Berman (*All That Is Solid Melts into Air,* 1982) have equated a certain modernism, and its consequences (postmodernism), with a failure of the mod-

ern will, a faltering or fading of the virulence of rupture which characterizes the true modern spirit. For de Man, after Nietzsche, modernism is a spirit or value entailing a radical break with the past and even requiring a "forgetting of history" (*Blindness and Insight* 146). Commenting on Nietzsche, de Man writes: "Although such a radical rejection of history may be illusory or unfair to the achievements of the past, it nevertheless remains justified as necessary to the fulfillment of our human destiny and as the condition for action" (*BI* 147). While Marshall Berman would certainly not concur with the apparent antihistoricism of de Man's analysis, he does nonetheless criticize a certain "negative modernism" that is too connected with the past, opposing this negative spirit to an affirmative or true modernism, wherein all is flux, "all that is solid melts into air" (Berman's title, of course, is a quote from Marx). While neither de Man nor Berman actually uses the term *postmodernism* to qualify the weakening of the modern spirit,[4] they both talk about what undermines modernism as a kind of return to the temptations of history (de Man) or tradition (Berman) in response to an impulse of restabilization. Yet, it must be noted that in de Man's case, in characteristically paradoxical fashion, there is a problematization of the assertion of the antihistoricism of modernism. De Man insists that in spite of the forgetting of history required by the modern spirit, it is precisely this Nietzschean rupture with the past that makes historical progress, as renewal, possible (*BI* 162). De Man seems to be suggesting that the postmodern (understood as denial of modernism) could be considered either a reactionary lapse into tradition, or a salutary and progressive "forgetting to forget" (151), which would *refuse* to obscure history from view. As is so often the case with de Man's brilliant and troubling analyses, the politics of his (post)modernism remain undecidable.

3. Postmodernism as *leftover* or *excess,* a kind of ruin or residue of modernism (or even of the entire Western philosophical tradition). This seems to be the gist of arguments by thinkers as different as Irving Howe ("The Idea of the Modern,"

1967)—whose classic approach to socioliterary history might be characterized as a kind of modern traditionalism—and Jean Baudrillard, the theorist of the postmodern as "obscene" or "excremental" culture. Howe's view seems more wistful than apocalyptic—he does not claim that the entire philosophical tradition is at stake, as Baudrillard does. But Howe's implicitly negative evaluation of what comes after modernism stems from his argument that the modern has been an idea of great power, which can find only a pale, parodic imitation in what has followed and what is yet to come ("Modernism will not come to an end; its war chants will be repeated through the decades. For what seems to await it is a more painful and certainly less dignified conclusion than that of previous cultural movements: what awaits it is publicity and sensation, the kind of savage parody which may indeed be the only fate worse than death" [*IM* 40]).

Written in 1967, Howe's prediction seems prophetic, especially when one reads contemporary characterizations of the postmodern as parodic excess, in Baudrillard and like-minded thinkers who have gone so far as to posit the postmodern as "the death of the social" and the disintegration of all forms of social transaction and communication in what amounts to a sort of vast cynical joke. In *The Postmodern Scene* (1986), for instance, Arthur Kroker and David Cook perform an analysis of postmodernism grounded in the theory of Baudrillard, Foucault, and the late writing of Barthes (*the Pleasure of the Text,* 1975). Cook and Kroker write of the parody implicit in the current scene: "What else explains our taking delight in images of a dead society—fragmented bodies and video ideology—signs that at least we know we are trapped in the joke of a cynical history?" (131). About Baudrillard as the theorist of "the ecstasy of communication" and the death of representation, including narrative representation, Kroker and Cook write: "Baudrillard then, is the theoretician of a postmodern power which owes its seduction to the 'imminence of the death of all the great referents' and to the violence which is exacerbated by their last, desperate attempts at representation" (*PS* 115–16). In Cook and Kroker's analysis, which sees the late twentieth century as both obscene and parodic, postmodernism is a bleak and cynical fate, entailing the death of the social and of narrative understood as social impulse, that is, as the desire for textual circulation or communication.

4. Postmodernism as *intensification* of the critical spirit of modernism, or even as a tension within modernism itself. Lyotard is one of the best-known proponents of this view (in *The Postmodern Condition*), which is also characteristic of the work of Stephen Melville (*Philosophy Beside Itself: On Deconstruction and Modernism,* 1986), of Jonathan Arac and the group around the journal *Boundary II* (as articulated in the collection *Postmodernism and Politics,* 1986), and of many of the essays in the collection edited by Hal Foster (*The Anti-Aesthetic: Essays on Postmodern Culture,* 1983). While not dismissing the more disturbing aspects of postmodernism that are the focus of Baudrillard and others, these theorists have preferred to propose a "postmodernism of resistance" (Hal Foster). As Foster writes in the preface to *The Anti-Aesthetic:*

> In cultural politics today, a basic opposition exists between a postmodernism which seeks to deconstruct modernism and resist the status quo and a postmodernism which repudiates the former to celebrate the latter; a postmodernism of resistance and a postmodernism of reaction. (*AA* xii)

As Foster uses the term here, *deconstruction* of modernism does not imply repudiation or even hostile critique; in its largest sense, deconstruction invites the exploration of issues raised by modernism, and an intensification and extension of the internal logic of modernism. What enables a postmodernism of resistance, in other words, is the self-critical spirit of modernism.

Indeed, as Lyotard argues, one might consider a distinguishing mark of the postmodern to be a kind of hyperskepticism, a crisis entailing a problematization of reference and a loss of legitimating authority. Thus Lyotard characterizes the postmodern as a crisis of legitimation ("Simplifying in the extreme, I define postmodern as incredulity toward metanarrative" [*PMC* xxix]). Specifically, Lyotard singles out a loss of belief in two grand Western narratives: the Enlightenment narrative of Progress, and the German idealist narrative of the dialectic achievement of Absolute Knowledge (37). In his comments on the postmodern as a literary phenomenon, Lyotard defines the modern as "the presentation that the unpresentable exists" (78) and suggests that according to this definition, the postmodern is "undoubtedly a part of the modern" (79). Lyotard sees postmodernism as the minor mode of the modern, which, in its "presentation of the unpresentable," works to problematize the notion of good form as well as content. In other words, the self-critical tendency expressed in modernism is turned upon the act of expression itself in postmodernism.

In a similar vein, Craig Owens stresses the compatibility of postmodernism with French poststructuralism—since both problematize the activity of reference—and the relation of postmodernism to its antecedent (modernism), even while insisting that a distinction be drawn:

> The deconstructive impulse is characteristic of postmodernist art in general and must be distinguished from the self-critical tendency of modernism. Modernist theory presupposes that mimesis, the adequation of an image to a referent, can be bracketed or suspended, and that the art object itself can be substituted (metaphorically) for its referent. . . . Postmodernism neither brackets nor suspends the referent but works instead to problematize the referent. ("The Allegorical Impulse," 1980, 79–80)[5]

Of the four positions on postmodernism sketched above—postmodernism as reaction, as denial, as residue, or as intensification of modernism—it is perhaps the position of the theorists of intensification that is the most attractive and convincing. This perspective avoids the resolute and somewhat too-cheery positivism of Habermas, as well as Habermas's rejection of the insights of poststructuralism (evinced by his condemnation of Derrida, Foucault, and others). Moreover, it does not give short shrift to the historical, as de Man's "Nietzschean" position seems to do, yet it manages to avoid the somewhat nostalgic tone of the modern traditionalists, who see postmodernism as a fading of the great modern idea. Above all, it provides a ground for refuting the most savage version of the case against postmodernism, seen by Baudrillard and others as a parodic symptom of the death of the social and the ascendance of an imploded screen-subject. And as Baudrillard would have it, this case against postmodernism is a case against psychoanalysis as well, considered as an obsolete theory of intersubjective human experience and interaction. But I will argue that the reports of the death of Oedipus are greatly exaggerated and that an allegorical or postmodern reading of Freud's own narrative may play a role in formulating a postmodernism of resistance rather than of reaction.

In any case, as even this very brief look at attitudes about postmodernism makes apparent, there is no consensus on the postmodern. Moreover, it is evident that the differences of opinion stem in large part from different views on modernism itself and whether postmodernism represents a continuity or rupture with what has gone before. If any "common address" can be found here, it is perhaps to be sought in the consensus concerning the characteristics of postmodernism rather than in its sources or implications. All the positions outlined seem to show the following issues as central to the notion of postmodernism, or even to define the phenomenon in the following terms: (1) a crisis of legitimation, sometimes defined as a disbelief of traditional metanarrative or a questioning of origins; (2) a corollary problematization of the activity of representation itself; (3) a questioning of the concept of originality, with an emphasis on citation, iterability, borrowings, intertextuality; (4) an emphasis on excess, leftover, residue, or aftermath, sometimes associated with the excess of desire which motivates the act of writing; (5) a ludic, ironic, or parodic quality, corresponding in part to the uneasiness about legitimate or authoritative values. All these tendencies seem to signal a crisis of traditional teleology and an incredulity toward totalizing systems of all sorts. The raising of many of these issues, finally, has been accompanied by a recasting of the notion of human subjectivity along radically new models, such as the decentered subject of Lacanian theory or the flattened, ecstatic screen-subject of Baudrillard's theory.

Many other issues raised by postmodernism remain to be considered—in particular, the question of the status of the aesthetic in postmodernism and the political ramifications of the postmodern aesthetic. But here the focus is on the fifth characteristic sketched above—the ludic or parodic quality of postmodern writing. I suggest that this comic quality may be understood as more than a mere characteristic, or even symptom, of postmodernism; it may be understood as a fundamental property of the postmodern text and of the postmodern notion of what constitutes a text (if indeed a "property" may "properly" be assigned to a sensibility so profoundly critical of the notion of propriety and property). After this initial sorting out of notions of postmodernism, as a preliminary to a more definitive "posting" of the modern, let us try now to close in on the comic, to find a theoretical envelope for the comic mode which may serve as an appropriate background for the postmodern postmark. This wrapping of comic theory comes in three layers: I want first to enclose comic theory in a philosophical package, encoding the comic in Maurice Blanchot's literary theory. Then I want to envelop Blanchot's perspective in Baudelaire's (pre-postmodern) comic and literary theory, reading Baudelaire as a kind of postman or messenger announcing the postmodern crisis of literary representation to come a century later. Finally, I want to insert the whole comic bundle—Blanchot and Baudelaire—into Bataille's theory of eroticism (plain brown wrapper?) so that the entire postmodern package may be addressed to psychoanalytic theory.

Casing the Comic

In *L'entretien infini,* Maurice Blanchot offers an optic on the concept of "the unworked text" (*l'oeuvre désoeuvrée*)—by which he understands a discourse about the instabilities of discourse, very similar to the notion of postmodernity advanced here—which may prove useful in considering the relationship between the comic process and postmodernism.[6] For Blanchot, our current literary moment may be characterized as a playful "turning" (*tournant*) from the tradition of the closed and finished masterpiece, the completed work, to the play of an opened-up, "unworked" text, an infinite literature of desire. In commenting upon this desiring literature, Blanchot relies heavily on the technique of pun, as attested by the many resonances of his title (*L'entretien infini*). In fact, contrasting the unworked text with more traditional literature, Blanchot characterizes the conventional literary work as fundamentally serious in its claim to integrity and accomplishment (in the sense of the French word *accomplissement*, as fulfillment, triumph, and completeness): "the masterwork is the expression of logical fulfillment [*parole de l'accomplissement logique*], impervious to chance, game, laughter. . . . a continuous speech, without gaps" (*EI* 233). But the mode of expression of the unworked text is anything but serious, since it remains vulnerable to comic fissures and intrusions and is thus somehow more essentially poetic or literary than the "accomplished" traditional masterpiece. For Blanchot considers the unworked text to be the product of a desiring expression called *la parole littéraire* (literary speech) or *la parole plurielle* (plural speech), associating literary expressions with playful double-talk. Thus, for Blanchot a certain literary project is comic in a most profound sense, since he equates a ludic or equivocal quality with truly poetic expression. While declining to be pinned down to a single, serious definition of "the literary," Blanchot seems to be suggesting, through his own overdetermined speech, that a work fails to be literary to the degree that it assumes the author-ized status of signed and perfected product, the property of genius.

In the same work, Blanchot makes reference to three cognitive processes, each associated with a mode of expression or speech: the *parole d'entendement* (understanding); the *parole de raison* (reasoning); and the *parole littéraire* (literary process). These three types of activity amount to three ways of exploiting or playing with difference:

> Identify by separating, *parole d'entendement,*
> Surmount by negating, *parole de raison,*
>
> The literary word [*la parole litéraire*] remains: it surmounts by doubling, creates by repeating, and by infinite restatements it states once and for all, up to the limit of that excessive word where language falters [*dit une première et une unique fois jusqu'à ce mot de trop où défaille le langage*]. (*EI* 505)

All three of these *paroles* depend on difference or interval for their articulation: the first is a function of separation ("identify by separating" [*identifier en séparant*]), the second of dialectic opposition ("surmount by negating" [*dépasser en niant*]), and the third of repetition ("surmount by doubling" [*dépasser en redoublant*]). The first two *paroles* exploit interval, putting it to use, in order to reach an enlightened "understanding" or to arrive at dialectic "reason" (Hegelian Absolute Knowledge). In the third kind of *parole,* however, interval is not subordinated to a worked-out conclusion but remains as a kind of leftover or aftermath, a persistent symptom of the failed attempt at elaborating a final version, once and for all. It does not grow out of the other two types of expression but seems to stand apart—as a kind of post-mark, an unaccounted-for leftover ("*Reste la parole littéraire*").

The similarities of this literary parole with certain postmodern characteristics are evident (this *parole* is a product of aftermath, emphasizing the instabilities of discourse, and producing a crisis of legitimacy), and I will return to the implications of this coincidence in the last section of this chapter. But first, in order to posit three distinct ways of thinking about the comic, let us look more closely at the relation of all three of Blanchot's *paroles* with the comic mode. Whereas the first two *paroles*—understanding and reason—may be associated with traditional explanations of the comic mode, the third literary *parole* seems to elicit the elaboration of a new perspective on the comic, consistent with the preoccupations of postmodernism.

This three-part categorization of the comic process—like my earlier sorting of theories of the postmodern—is the result of the sifting through of a large number of theories.[7] The first sorting yields a clear distinction between two general views of the comic, which emerge in more or less symmetrical opposition and which bear more than a passing resemblance to Blanchot's *paroles* of understanding and reason. (Yet as we shall see, the sorting out of traditional comic theory seems to yield a kind of noncategorizable "leftover" [no zip code?] that must be put aside, as a kind of post-comic.)

I shall call the two mainline comic types the *referential* and the *absolute* comic, respectively—terms roughly equivalent to those used by Baudelaire in his famous study on laughter ("De l'essence du rire," 1855). Baudelaire's theory is a good point of departure for a consideration of the comic for two reasons: first, his two neat categories—the referential and the absolute comic—subsume and reflect many of the theoretical formulations of earlier thinkers; second, Baudelaire himself may be read as an important modern whose work anticipates the crisis of the postmodern age. And in turning to Baudelaire as spokesperson of the modern, I follow the lead of Paul de Man—that important postmodern who grounds his own discussion of irony in the doubling of poetic consciousness described in Baudelaire's essay.[8] At the same time, I concur with Lyotard and others that the germ of the postmodern lies in the modernism of figures like Baudelaire; my reading thus casts Baudelaire in the comic role of a pre-postmodern.

Yet, however modern Baudelaire may be, his essay on laughter does try to limit itself to a relatively clear-cut dichotomy between two categories: the referential comic [*comique significatif*] and the absolute comic [*comique absolu*], categories that may be compared, respectively, to Blanchot's first two *paroles,* serving understanding and reason. However, Baudelaire's essay does not explicitly posit a third leftover or specifically literary type of comic expression that we might liken to Blanchot's *parole littéraire.*

Nor has anything resembling a postmodern comic mode been proposed by other theoreticians of humor whom I have consulted, although some of their theories seem, unwittingly, to open to this third oblique possibility. We begin, then, by looking at Baudelaire's referential comic as an instance of Blanchot's understanding [*parole d'entendement*], and then consider Baudelaire's absolute comic as a process that operates under the sign of Blanchot's dialectical reason [*parole de raison*]. But as we shall see, the last parole, which refuses to be or to have the last word, is perhaps best exemplified by a certain "other" leftover comic mode, a postmodern comic of desire, which actually seems to require the comic mode for its "faltering," "plural," and "reiterated" expression. In fact, insofar as comic language is always overdetermined double-talk requiring the hearer's double-take, one could say that Blanchot's *parole plurielle/littéraire* never expresses itself *other* than comically.

Baudelaire's double vision

> The comic can only be absolute relative to fallen humanity, and that is how I understand it.
>
> Baudelaire, "De l'essence du rire" (986)

Baudelaire's opening remarks emphasize the double nature of the comic mode, stemming from the diabolical origins of the sense of humor, a result of the fall of humankind from divine grace, that primal scission between fallen human beings and the Supreme Unity. After this preamble on the origin of all comic phenomena in duplicity or sin, Baudelaire turns to the discussion of the first comic category, the referential comic [*comique significatif*]. According to Baudelaire, the referential comic is characterized by a transparent and specific reference point that seeks to draw a sharp comparison between the correct point of view of the laugher and the inferior behavior of the ridiculed object. This perspective contributes to the demonstrative or didactic bent of the referential comic (one example, cites Baudelaire, would be the French comedy of manners); this type of comic expression aims at teaching a lesson or making a point, and is above all a comic of superiority. Moreover, writes Baudelaire, the referential comic is civilized and social, clear-headed and prosaic, which accounts for its popularity in France ("the basis of all French art is to shun excess [*fuir l'excessif*]" 987). Yet, Baudelaire hints that the apparently measured and moralistic nature of the referential comic is suspect, for its judgmental nature harbors a tendency to bestial "ferocity" [*le féroce*] and thus provides an insinuation of the satanic base of all manifestations of the comic impulse, even the most pointedly moral. Baudelaire points out that this triumphant laughter of superiority over a fellow being may actually be read as a sign of weakness (980), and he wryly observes that there is no spectacle more outrageous than that of the satanic laugher—who is, after all, a fallen creature—exulting in the downfall of a fellow being (985).

Still, we might say that this first comic mode at least pretends to make use of doubleness or interval to arrive at a superior perspective or a transparent intelligibility. (Baudelaire calls the referential comic "visibly double" [*visiblement double*]—because it clearly shows both its art and its moral—and "transparent" [*ayant la transparence d'un apologue*]—because it is "easier to analyze" and "written in a clearer language" [985–86] than the poetic or absolute comic.)

Baudelaire's referential comic, then, has a great deal in common with Blanchot's first *parole*, that clarifying process of separation and identification or reference necessary to "understanding" ("identify by separating, *parole d'entendement*"). Indeed, for Blanchot, separation is a necessary precondition for understanding, and understanding is in turn a function of visibility ("Seeing supposes only a measured and measurable separation. To see is thus to seize immediately, at a distance and my means of distance [*à distance et par la distance*]. To see is to make use of separation [*se servir de la séparation*]" [*EI* 39]). In other words, understanding is reached thanks to the transparency of interval between subject and object: the serviceable interval serves as the means by which the object is apprehended, appropriated by the subject (Blanchot: "Interval does not obstruct in this case, on the contrary, it permits a direct rapport. Every relation of light is an immediate relation" [39]). Thus, Blanchot considers this exploitation of interval in the service of understanding to be part of the occidental tradition valorizing light and enlightenment, and equating understanding with dis-covery or bring to light.

The referential comic as parole d'entendement

How might Baudelaire's referential comic be understood as aligning itself with this enlightened tradition, equating mastery of the comic situation with an understanding made possible by separation? First, we could say that it is only thanks to distance that the comic object is held in view, objectively grasped or glimpsed in the moment of downfall. (Baudelaire characterizes the laugher's exultation when witnessing another's slip-up as a kind of measurement of the distance between subjective "wisdom" and objective folly: "'*I* don't fall; *I* walk straight; *I* would never commit the foolishness of not seeing a break in the sidewalk'" [981]). Similarly, we could say that understanding any joke is equated with vision and with grasp or possession at the moment the laugher exclaims "I see!" or "I get it!"

If we consider the classic comedy, for instance, we see that all the distances serve an end of understanding. The audience is distanced from the comic object, the fall guy, so that they may clearly judge his fall; they also profit from a bird's-eye view of the comic imbroglio that permits them to "foresee" the ending where an "understanding" will be reached by all (unlike the characters themselves who are too close to the action to see what is happening to them). Even the lovers are distanced, for a time, in a sort of absent rapport that "foresees" their final reunion.

It is interesting to note that this putting to rights by means of distance is also functionally analogous to a common joke technique, which Freud calls "the finding of sense in non-sense," a technique that works because of the ability of the mind to separate, clarify, and identify. And as we have seen, the judgmental nature of these processes of understanding is also related to a staking out process, marking the distance between oneself and the comic victim, the "I, who am still walking" and the "you, who have fallen," because it is you, not I, who have slipped on a banana peel, *over there*. The distance of understanding and the distance of superiority are thus fundamentally related in the comic process. A similar relation is evinced by the conventional punning process, which requires that one of the two meanings be privileged, making the ordinary or correct sense, to which the second aberrant meaning is affixed or contrasted for comic effect. Such referential punning involves a dissection of language, an examination of possibilities with the "right" meaning always clearly in view as reference. In other words, in this type of comic process, distance is required to make sense, and sense or meaning is in turn associated with the giving of value or the conferral of judgment. But in the referential comic, as Baudelaire himself repeatedly suggests, the faculty of reason only seems to have the last laugh (Baudelaire repeatedly problematizes the assumption of the civilized or reasonable nature of the referential comic by linking it with savage ferocity and delusions of superiority). Thus this first comic category—which Baudelaire confines to "the comedy of manners" and the even more judgmental "ferocious comic"—could be extended to include any comic phenomenon that seeks to reinforce apparently reasonable or consensual standards of behavior, and/or works to gird the ego in a sense of confident well-being.

Four general traditional subgroupings of comic theory could be subsumed by Baudelaire's referential comic, and associated with Blanchot's *parole* of understanding. First, there are the *superiority* theories; Hobbes is perhaps the best-known advocate of this notion (*Leviathan*, 1651, vi, i) which emphasizes the triumph of the laugher over an enemy or adverse situation. Second, there are the *contrast* theories propounded by such important figures as Kant (*Critique of Aesthetic Judgement,* 1790) and Schopenhauer (*The World as Will and Representation,* 1819, xiii) who both find that the essence of the comic resides in the dichotomy between two contrasting situations and the ability to adjudicate that discrepancy; in this century, André Breton (*Anthologie d l'humour noir,* 1966) insists on the poetic and liberating potential of these contrasts, or "chance encounters." Third, there is a group of theories that might be called *tool of socialization* theories; Henri Bergson (*Le rire,* 1900) sees laughter as a way of chastising aberrant behavior, and of course Freud's work on the comic (*Jokes and Their Relation to the Unconscious,* 1905) likewise emphasizes the social function of joking. Finally, *economic* or *motor theories*—such as the views put forth by Herbert Spencer (*Essays,* 1901) and Theodore Lipps (*Comic and Humour,* 1898)—see laughter as a release of excess energy when it is not needed to deal with a situation first perceived as frightening. Similarly, Breton's theory sees laughter as energy or spark, while John Dewey ("The Theory of the Emotions," 1894) and Albert Penjon ("Le rire et la liberté," 1893) emphasize the pleasurable relief or sense of liberation afforded by the laughing release. Indeed, a great many theorists have seemed to adhere to some version of this view of the comic as an exultant manifestation of superiority or even as a recuperative process augmenting the "reasonable" grasp of reality and feelings of control of the laugher. For all these theorists, the comic levels off the excessive, contains and punishes the abnormal, and puts the laugher in the accepted, sane mainstream of the *sens commun.*

It is interesting that Baudelaire is the only one of all the thinkers cited above (at least before Freud) to insist on the illusory nature of the feelings of power and plenitude afforded by this kind of referential comic experience. Baudelaire's position, in fact, seems surprisingly modern and is even startlingly consistent with Freud's analysis. Were Baudelaire to have met that other great "comic" thinker, Jacques Lacan, they might even have agreed that the referential comic is a prime example of an Imaginary construct affording the *illusion* of a unified ego—a unity that is always, however, constructed along a psychic fault line (the Freudian *Spaltung*, allegorized by Lacan in his account of the mirror stage). In Lacan's version the ego is an "Imaginary" phenomenon, operating in the Imaginary register (*"L'Imaginaire"*); like one's own image in the mirror, it is an illusory and always alienated identity constructed thanks to the introjected and alien image of the Other. And for Baudelaire, of course, the fault in human subjectivity is equally primal, and the sense of superiority or unified identity is equally illusory, since both are effects of the schism enacted by Original Sin.

The absolute comic: a "poetic" alternative

Now to the first vainglorious laughter of deluded superiority, the prosaic referential comic, Baudelaire opposes a poetic and sublime absolute comic, so named because it seems to approximate the absolute of blissful unity with the Supreme Being, the innocence of humanity before the fall from grace. ("The absolute comic," writes Baudelaire, "being much closer to nature, appears as a unified phenomenon [*se présente sous une espèce une*]" [986]). Whereas the first type of comic expression emphasizes interval and duality as a tool to engender meaning, the absolute comic tries to close the gap between laugher and victim, emphasizing the dissolution of limits between the "I" and the "thou," in a vertiginous sense of connection. This type of comic production is not clearly referential; in fact, Baudelaire insists that the puzzling, almost mystical laughter produced may be understood [*saisi*] only by intuition. The absolute comic is thus poetic both because it is intuitive and because it emphasizes identification with the "other," providing a curious illusion of unity approximating that natural, Edenic state for which the human species feels an incurable nostalgia. This unified and natural type of laughter, Baudelaire asserts, is related to the innocent laughter of children and primitive people.

A brief detour—this is, I think, where Paul de Man goes

wrong in his reading of Baudelaire, equating the seemingly superior poetic consciousness of the absolute comic with modern irony—as consciousness that is aware of its duplicity and which thus has resonances of existentialist authenticity.[9] Certainly, Baudelaire does conclude that the poet, and the poet alone, is capable of maintaining and achieving a lucid double perspective: the poet's vision is a double vision, derived from an awareness of the inescapable duplicity of the human condition, a condition from which the poet himself is not exempt. (Does Baudelaire not dedicate *Les fleurs du mal* to that "hypocritical reader" who is a "fellow being" [*Hypocrite lecteur, mon semblable, mon frère*]?) To transcode Baudelaire in Lacanian terms, we might say that Baudelaire's poet emerges from the misrecognition [*méconnaissance*] characteristic of the Imaginary register, into a sort of full poetic speech [*une parole pleine*] that owes its poetic quality to its superior vision, its awareness of the duplicity of the poet's own most sincere discourse. Irony is then perhaps a poetic faculty in Baudelaire's sense of the term *poetic.* But in insisting on the poetic nature of Baudelaire's doubling as a justification for conflating irony and the poetic (or absolute) comic—also termed the sublime or the grotesque in Baudelaire's essay—de Man glosses over two important points. First, the absolute comic aims not to achieve a superior consciousness, or double vision, but aims rather to cover up such doubleness, to bridge the gap (since it "represents itself as a unified phenomenon [*se présente sous une espèce une*]"). Second, Baudelaire's exposure of the illusory nature of this unified appearance (depicted as a kind of charade or cover-up) is crucial, for it suggests that the absolute comic, like the referential comic, is based on delusion and produces illusion—the *appearance* of innocence, which is every bit as illusory as the feeling of superiority afforded by the referential comic. Baudelaire is explicit on this point: "I have said: *absolute* comic: but one must be careful. From the point of view of the definitive absolute, there can be only joy [*il n'y a que la joie*]. The comic may only be absolute *relative* to fallen humanity, and that is how I understand it" [986]). Even the joyous, innocent laughter of childhood, Baudelaire cautions, cannot be considered exempt from ambition, for children are, after all, flawed human creatures, "Satans-in-the-making" [*Satans en herbe* 985]. Whatever the absolute comic is, then, it is most decidedly not ironic in de Man's sense of the term (as lucid doubling); its vision depends on a perception (always illusory) of an Imaginary oneness.

However, Baudelaire does seem to consider the absolute comic to be a superior form of comic sensibility, for unlike the referential comic, the absolute comic declines to engage in petty games of one-upsmanship. But even this kind of disinterested or innocent quality calls for qualification: like the referential comic, the absolute comic, however "innocent," seems curiously linked to the human predilection for violence. In the case of the absolute comic, however, the violence is no longer wreaked exclusively on the other, the comic victim, but is directed as well against the laugher, who is shaken and twisted by a sort of mad and excessive hilarity. In the referential comic, the sacrifice of the object is witnessed; in the absolute comic, there is a collective or masochistic self-sacrifice.

Baudelaire is not alone in emphasizing this second kind of comic experience; many theorists of the comic have stressed that laughter often resembles a kind of temporary insanity, an uncontrolled paroxysm implying the abandon of an egotistical sense of self. Dugas, for instance (*Psychologie du rire,* 1921), calls laughter a rupture of equilibrium, akin to a spasmodic unchaining of animal life, while Hegel (*Aesthetik,* 1835) considers laughter the entire surrender of all that belongs to self, a universal dissolvant of limits. William McDougall (*An Introduction to Social Psychology,* 1909) has claimed that laughter is so spontaneous and unreasoned as to be instinctual in character, not unlike the entranced paroxysms of love and anger that "carry us out of ourselves, out of reality, and out of sureness of ourselves" (122). It is interesting, if puzzling, to note that these thinkers have painted a picture of the comic phenomenon diametrically opposed to the picture drawn by the referential theorists: in this second vein laughter is seen as irrational, opposed to understanding, reason, judgment, common sense. It is spontaneous and joyful rather than petty; instead of enforcing limits and accentuating separation between laughing self and comic other, it dissolves limits between subject and object. Likewise, in these "absolute" theories, it is not the feeling of equilibrium afforded by laughter that is valorized but rather the feeling of disarray and vulnerability and the pleasure of this heady confusion. Such laughter is likened to a kind of insanity, as suggested by the French expression *le fou rire* as well as by expressions common to French and English ("to die laughing" [*mourir de rire*]; "hysterical laughter" [*le rire hystérique*]). Perhaps most suggestive of all is the expression "to be tickled to death," which emphasizes the potential morbidity in laughter.

As an example of this ruinous and masochistic absolute comic, Baudelaire describes a mimed play, both violent and hypnotic. This spectacle, Baudelaire writes, seems to produce a strange contagious dizziness ("It is really a drunkenness of laughter, something terrible. . . . Vertigo circulates in the air" [989]). In this pantomime, featuring the traditional characters of the *commedia*, Pierrot literally loses his head (by guillotine), and then makes a joke of his execution, cavorting headless around the stage. In other words, the vertigo—the overwhelming "light-headedness" produced sympathetically in the spectators—is the result of the witnessing of a terrible sacrifice, a vicarious death. Overcome by a terrifying and delightful *vertige*, which circulates around the room like a deadly comic virus, the spectators too "die laughing," intoxicated by the poetic and communal absolute, the dissolution of limits.

Baudelaire's description is compelling and serves to emphasize dramatically that the characteristics of the absolute comic stand in categorical opposition to those of the reasonable referential comic. But at least two questions are raised by this clear-cut opposition. First, we must wonder, how can the same phenomenon (laughter) signify two conflicting things at once (girding of self/loss of self)? Second, how "absolute" is this loss of limits, since as Baudelaire repeatedly points out, all comic phenomena depend on limits and stem from an irrecuperable duality? In recognition of these difficulties, Baudelaire himself insists on the relativity of his illusory absolute; while other theorists of the comic, when confronted with these contradictions, have tended to hedge, modifying their theories ad infinitum, ending up at times with completely conflicting theories, comic in themselves. ("Laughter," concludes Dugas, for example, "shows either a defeat or a triumph of reason.") We may admire the ingenuity of such machinations as Freud's proposition that weakness is really a strength (in the overcoming of adversity by humor), or Baudelaire's claim that strength is really a weakness (since laughter is a stigma, a sign of sin). But the indication seems to be that these endless explanations and refinements are kidding themselves, that both the referential and the absolute views of laughter require a kind of cheating or falsification in order to stick.

I would suggest that it is precisely this kind of cheating or covering up of the contradiction inherent in the comic that points to a possible analogy between the second "absolute" comic and Blanchot's second mode of expression: the dialectic reasoning of the *parole de raison,* whereby positivity and negativity, thesis and antithesis find themselves conciliated in the unity of a final synthesis. But to elaborate on this connection, I need to reroute the discussion one more time, this time via the work of Georges Bataille.

Tickled to death: Bataille's comic eroticism

In his well-known work on sensuality and sacrifice (*L'érotisme,* 1957), Bataille insists on the role of cheating (*tricherie*) in human life; he even suggests that a certain trickery is constitutive of what it is to be human. ("Human life cannot follow without trembling—without cheating—the path that leads to death" [161].) This necessary cheating takes the form of an erotic game, which Bataille calls the "desire to falter" [*le désir de chavirer*] between the possibilities of life and death (163), or the desire to "live at the limits of the possible and the impossible" (161). This formulation recalls Freud's concept of the oscillation between the life and death instincts, elaborated in *Beyond the Pleasure Principle* (1920), and Bataille was in fact influenced by Freud. But Bataille's treatment of this same notion is much more sociological/philosophical than psychoanalytic since Bataille is primarily interested in the social sense of the erotic act. His principal argument is that human beings only play at death in erotic abandonment (orgasm: *la petite mort*) without finally abolishing the limits between self and other. Thus, the erotic is a faltering on the "path to death," a kind of cheating that fails either to conserve or to expend absolutely. It is a play of transgression and limit; indeed; Bataille compares the erotic disequilibrium to an incessantly rehearsed and replayed comedy, relying on trickery, on the playing of a comic role ("In order to live sensually, we must play a naive comedy" [267]). It is, moreover, the capacity to play the erotic game—the transgression of maintained limits—that defines the boundaries between what is bestial (mere copulation) and what is human (sexuality). Bataille's main point is that the human erotic game requires a sense of violation—forbidden fruit or play-acted death—in order to be sexual rather than merely biological.

As Bataille insists, erotic transgression may violate the rules of the everyday world where human beings work and interact, but it by no means abolishes these rules; the erotic violation of taboo, law, or convention (a violation or transgression which for Bataille includes the sex act but is not limited specifically to sexual phenomena) is, in fact, the complement of the "profane" everyday world that it seems to contest (72). This complement is a kind of negativity—often of a sacred or festival character—which seems to be outside of and opposed to mundane experience but which paradoxically is an integral part of the very social order that it seems to contest ("Organized transgression forms, with the taboo or interdiction, a whole which defines social life" [72]). In other words, Bataille's eroticism is a dialectical moment of negativity that consolidates the law it transgresses; it is thus subsumed in the whole of social order.

Perhaps this collaboration of transgression and prohibition may serve to illustrate by analogy the connection of Blanchot's second *parole* of reason ("surmount by negating, *parole de raison*") with the workings of the second comic mode, the absolute or innocent comic. Just as the erotic act finally reinstates those prohibitions it appears to bypass or negate, the seemingly mad self-destructive urge toward dissolution of limits in the absolute comic might be considered a moment of negativity in a dialectical process, which ends up serving the interests of sanity and reason. (This, of course, is precisely what is suggested by those theorists who stress that a mad hilarity is followed by a sense of relief and relaxation of tension.) In a sense, the absolute comic does transgress or negate the limited, the sane, and the reasonable, but it is this very negation which helps to define the reasonable by occurring at its boundary. Even Pierrot's comic self-sacrifice, after all, takes place in a theater, at a literary soiree, before a civilized audience (Baudelaire included) who have paid for their vicarious death, their vertiginous pleasure of being tickled to death, as it were, without risk. Pierrot's sacrifice acts as a safety-valve, a channeled transgression, however terrible or all-consuming the experience may momentarily seem. Not even Pierrot dies in this comedy since he is resurrected to take his bow and replay his game before the next complicit crowd.

For as Baudelaire himself points out, in the comic process absolute continuity may never be attained; the failure of the comic to be absolute derives from the very nature of the comic process itself, which is always engendered from a contrast or a discontinuity, a separation or disproportion, and which relies on the perceived discontinuity to produce its effect. Similarly, in the erotic transgression, the discontinuity between self and other is never absolutely abolished short of death itself. If the erotic process, like the absolute comic, works to bridge the gap estranging self from other, it also reinstates the rules it temporarily subverts. Eroticism depends on maintained prohibition for its spicy effect; the comic depends on maintained discontinuity for its punch. And one potent punch line of Bataille's own treatise is precisely this surprise revelation of the character of the erotic as a "naive comedy" depending on playacting, cheating, and roguish tricks (*tricheries*), engaged in by all human beings, who as safe spectators may play at risky masochistic games, just as the lover plays at death in orgasm.

Bataille suggests that we human beings willfully blind ourselves to the necessary complicity between transgression and prohibition, limit and excess, since it is we who are at once "the victims and blind authors of the comedy of transgression" (267): there is no transgression without limit, and no limit that does not invite violation. Just so, "absolute" jokers blind themselves to the permanence of the limits abolished, while "referential" jokers blind themselves to their own vulnerability and implication in the downfall of their victim. In other words, just as dialectic negativity—Blanchot's "reason" [*"dépasser en niant, parole de raison"*]—not only permits but enables a synthesis (the Hegelian *Aufhebung,* rendered in French as *dépassement*), and just as Bataille's erotic transgression assures the consolidation of the law that it surmounts [*dépasse*], just so does the absolute comic—more comic than absolute—enact a transgressive play where the continuity between self and non-self is played at but not played out, in an infinite entertainment. The doubleness inherent in the comic process cannot be abolished or negated away in a naive attempt to provoke vertigo or continuity or absolute finality, but neither can it be maintained as a secure referential distinction between the superior "I" and the inferior "thou," based on judgment or understanding. Both the referential and absolute comic, functions of understanding and dialectical reason, comically self-deconstruct, for they unwittingly work to undermine the security of reference and the accessibility of any absolute. As George Meredith puts it (*Essay on Comedy,* 1898), "No exemption is granted the laugher from the folly of the victim at which he laughs." But even this bottom line must be followed by an afterword, a punch line: absolute folly—absolute masochism or identification with the comic fall guy—is as impossible as is absolute exemption from the fall.

The postcomic: delayed "delivery"

There is perhaps a third comic possibility, comparable to Blanchot's third leftover *parole* that remains after the completion of the work of "understanding" and "reason" ("*reste la parole littéraire*"). This "other" leftover comic, postmarked by desire which refuses to end, would stand apart from the dialectical complicity of the referential and the absolute comic mode. This "other" expression seems to be noticed in these last years of our century, a sort of residue of what Mallarmé called "the exquisite crisis of literature" in modern times; stigmatized and excessive, this other text recognizes and depends on a certain cheating or artifice, that is, on the willful falsification of a realistic or exhaustive project of representation, the traditional goals of literary mimesis. This desiring *parole* manages to cheat by means of its persistent comic voice, its echoing punch line, which like a heckler in the audience, constantly points to the failure of any staged truth or superior perspective. As I suggest in the last two chapters, a striking example of this desiring comic voice is to be found in the work of Samuel Beckett, who makes aftermath into a theatrical scene.

This postmodern comic of desire found in the works of Beckett and others is based, like the *parole littéraire,* on repetition and recurrence; it thus must fail to offer any resolution or *dénouement,* any untying of the "Knott." Caught up in the compulsion to repeat, it provides no exit, and thus relinquishes any claim to healthful or recuperative function. Its only end seems to be a return to sender, the *renvoi* to a new possibility, a reactivation of the game.

Not only is a certain "post fiction" comic, but a certain "post comic" is fictive; a quip is literally a fiction, something fashioned to be told, and thus always a text of sorts, relying on layers of meaning. Like Blanchot's *parole littéraire,* a joke is first told to one or more listeners ("a first and unique time"), and yet is incessantly repeated by that listener and others to a chain of new listeners ("up to the limit of that excessive word where language falters"). In other words, the postmodern fiction, the *parole littéraire* as Blanchot describes it, is always a plural pleasantry, a worked and reworked text. Indeed, Blanchot uses the term *parole plurielle* interchangeably with *parole littéraire;* the literary, in Blanchot's view, is synonymous with a multiplicity of retellings ("infinite restatements") that undercut the serious accomplishment of any one authorized reading.

The comparison of joke with fiction in the etymological sense of something made or wrought is already suggested on a certain level by F. T. Vischer's statement (*Aesthetik,* 1846–1851) that "the universe is the laughter of God"; laughter is a product, by definition severed from source. This also seems to be what Simone Weil means when she calls humanity a joke of God, likening a joking product to that which is stranded, divorced from source. And a certain postmodern text seems to be just such a leftover fiction, divine garbage of sorts, an artifact after the Death of God, stranded from its sources, references, antecedents, and conventions, unworked by a bizarre comic voice, which is perhaps among other things the Freudian unconscious. This desiring voice disperses and overdetermines, insuring that the literary text will be plural, that it will resist integration into totalizing schemes and definitive interpretations.

Moreover, this literary *plurality,* as Blanchot understands the term, coincides with a kind of proliferation of possibility (a key term for Bataille as well, since he sees the erotic transgression as a faltering between the poles of possibility and impossibility). The desiring comic mode, like the erotic transgression, points out that there is no inviolable boundary: every boundary signifies the possibility of its transgression. And since transgression reinstates limit, no possibility is ever final. Or, as Blanchot puts it, death defines the limits of what is possible, but death itself is always before us and hence "impossible" to attain. After all, the "comic" sentence, "I am dead," is impossible to utter, except falsely. A certain postmodern comic mode exploits this impossibility of ending, which it identifies with the infinite proliferation of possibilities from which no final choice may be made.

Comic post-ponement

Thus, this "other" or third comic is a transgressive act that, unlike the absolute comic, makes no pretense of dissolving limits but rather insists on maintaining and even proliferating them so that they may be trangressed again. Therefore, any comic theory suggesting that laughter is not the result of a single act of judgment and comparison, but rather of a multiple movement susceptible to repetition or reversal, would be compatible with this third, nondialectic reading of the comic process. It is interesting to note, however, that the oscillation view is not in itself modern; it is similar to the contrast theories of Kant and Schopenhauer except that it suggests that the comic comparison is repeated again and again. It is already suggested by Plato (*Philebus,* section 48), who observes that in laughter there is a mingling of pleasure and pain and a movement between the two. Yet, this kind of formulation—according to which laughter is produced either by an alternation between two states or by a simultaneous apprehension of conflicting states—is perhaps more compatible with a postmodern perspective than are the two dominant traditional views on the comic process: for it opens from the smug security of the conventional superior-inferior referential comic dichotomy to the possibility that I may be implicated in your downfall; it also suggests that the process is anything but final since it is infinitely repeated. Transcoding Plato in postmodern terms, we could say that this comic perspective makes the question of winning as undecidable as the possibility of ending.

The deflection of final goal is also a crucial part of the erotic comedy as Bataille defines it; the need to postpone the ultimate discharge of energy (in death) gives rise to the faltering rhythm of human life, which Bataille attributes to the desire to lose without losing. This faltering might also be thought of as a refraction, a reflection of desire back and forth between limits or poles, an oscillation of the kind to which Derrida refers in a key image of "La double séance" as "perpetual allusion, without shattering the glass" (*La dissémination*, 1972, 201). All of these references to deferral, hesitation, refraction—including the reference to that faltering of language in excess which reactivates Blanchot's parole littéraire ("that excessive word where language falters" [*ce mot de trop où défaille le langage*])—share an emphasis on the avoidance of untimely ending, and suggest that the comic/erotic/literary pleasure resides not in the endpoint of desire but in the detour by which the pleasurable game is rerouted, like a letter *en souffrance*.

Modern Comic Letters: The Post-Man Cometh

> And thus, infinitely repeating repetition [the fragmentary work], makes it somehow parodic.
>
> Blanchot, *L'entretien infini* (238)

The postmodern author will be treated here as joker and as post-man, always en route, not superior to reality or able to control it, but caught in the process initiated by the fictive work, an infinite entertainment or suspension. In this ongoing game, desire activates the chain of repeated transgressions; never achieving total gratification, this desire always exceeds any one incident of transgression and gives rise to infinite repetitions.

In certain of these comic texts, the bizarre excess that engenders the repetition of formulaic refrain seems to be a manifestation of a compulsive desire persisting after everything seems to have been finished. In Beckett's *Fin de partie*, for example, Hamm's compulsive renumeration of possible versions of his own origins are the expression of the impossibility of ending the game or of elaborating a final version. It is evident that possibility and impossibility are opposite faces of the same coin, a sort of double meaning revealing the joke that infinite possibility or power is equal to infinite failure.

A certain postmodern literary production seems to have gotten that joke and seems bent on repeating it, by exploiting the parodic structure underlying the excessive exercise of capability. Just as a joke's punch line exposes the duplicity of language (its lack of correspondence to a single referent, its ability to name two things at once which indicates its inability to name anything unequivocally), the postmodern comic text often adopts the task of exposing all the possible versions or meanings underlying a single narrative, all the while demonstrating the failure of such an exhaustive project. For example, the narrator of Butor's *Degrès* loses track of himself in trying to exhaust the possibilities of point of view, since he dies in his own novel; similarly, Ionesco's characters are confounded by what he calls the "mechanism of the possible," the uncontrolled proliferation of words and objects.

We can perhaps begin to see why, as Derrida writes, only laughter "exceeds the dialectic," why the comic mode is the process with which "post" literature so often expresses irrecuperable hiatus or inadequacy. Like joking expression, which in its double-talk affirms and negates meaning at one and the same time, postmodern parodic literary expression seems to function paradoxically. Writing of the parodic nature of the *parole fragmentaire* (yet another term equivalent to *la parole littéraire/plurielle*), Blanchot states that this *parole* is an "unidentifiable fragment, unrepresentable, impossible to recognize [which] ruins [expression] by reconstituting it, as a kind of indefinite murmur . . . as a word which is always already spoken, a word always already to come [*parole toujours à venir*]" (*EI* 238).

The parodic murmur, like the fragmentary or literary word, is unsilenceable (is not joking always the most irrepressible when we try to silence it?). Yet, however unsilenceable this parodic *parole* may be, it nonetheless points out a gap in discourse, which we may understand as the inadequacy of language to its referent. Or, in a Lacanian sense of gap as *béance*, we may understand the gap that haunts language as the gaping hole between human need, which may be fulfilled, and human desire, to and for which we speak without any hope of final fulfillment—the unquenchable desire of meaning expressed in the French *vouloir dire*. In Ionesco's theater, for example, this inadequacy is a motor force: the comic cliché becomes a way of speaking without meaning (as when all characters are named Bobby Watson, wreaking havoc with the story line as well as with the process of characterization). Hence the comic mode may be the means by which a certain "post" text elicits and effects its own transgression, speaking with a comic chatter that imposes silence on meaning, since achievement always coincides with a failure of sorts.

The postmodern comic mode is thus consistent with that kind of literary *parole* upon which Blanchot focuses; whereas the traditional masterwork takes itself and its accomplishments very seriously, a certain postmodern venture makes use of the comic process to turn on itself and to produce pleasure from the exposure of its own shortcomings, "embracing the instabilities of discourse." One function of the unworked text, then, is to play the role of trickster (violating "*parole*"?), exposing the trickery which sustains the myth of the finished literary masterwork, and reactivating the literary game in the bizarre hope of not winning. This is perhaps what Blanchot means when he speaks of the "absent work" characteristic of the postmodern era—it's the work that fails to make good, to "*tenir parole,*" violating the myth of *parole* as inviolable honor.

Blanchot's work suggests that the open-ended nature of such works as Beckett's Endgame renders them absent, the scene of a hopeless hope when an ending is always "future" [*à venir*]. Paradoxically, such a maintained hope is a sign of desire, since it is always a function of lack, of maintained interval, where the parenthesis is never closed. For instance, in Marguerite Duras's labyrinthian repetitions, or Nathalie Sarraute's unsilenceable *sous-conversations,* or Raymond Queneau's proliferated exercises of style, "relation between form and content has become infinite" (*EI* 233), in the manner of Blanchot's unworked work.

Blanchot also writes that the unworked/absent work has

overturned the notion of modernity itself, since the term *modern* suggests the culmination of tradition. He avoids (perhaps happily) the term *postmodern*, but suggests that the idea of the modern has turned to "the idea of a more profound rupture" (again recalling the yawning *béance* in Lacanian theory), "signifying the cessation of all that is memorable" (*EI* 594). Such a rupture is performed by means of the plural literary word, which, in its faltering structure, its gaming nature, and its origin in excess, coincides with a certain comic process.

Of course, the equation of the comic process with the postmodern literary *parole* requires that we relinquish the pretension to the masterful position of understanding occupied by the referential joker, just as we must let go of the authorized canonic masterpiece. It means as well that we must avoid the naive temptation of any absolute claim, including absolute nonsense or escape from meaning, which only reinforces the legitimate and the reasonable. It means that the comic process may no longer be reduced to a choice between superior sense and festival madness. Like the absent work, the postmodern comic points to an interstice, a *béance*, which is perhaps no exit but is certainly an opening.

Opening the letter

With the comic now encased in a postmodern bundle (Bataille, Blanchot, Baudelaire), the package is ready for posting, and for its return to sender, the master-joker himself, Sigmund Freud. For Freud's entire work is built on interstice (as lapse, as the unsaid, as the unconscious) and the comic technique of reiteration and overdetermination. In fact, the letter of psychoanalysis (the letter of the Law?) may itself be opened to a comic and postmodern reading, as comic text. In opposition to the theories that see the postmodern as the death of the social, the oedipal narrative may be read as a comic allegory of the condition and possibility of narrative itself—in Barthes's sense of exchange and circulation of messages. Psychoanalysis, in other words, proffers a profoundly agonistic theory of communicative intersubjectivity, with *agon* understood as struggle (and as game) among human subjects.

In the following section, Freud's comic theory is read as the agony rather than the ecstasy of communication, as the profoundly social process of sending and receipt of messages, in the hope that such a comic vision may even open Freud's letter to a feminist perspective (woman as post-man?) on human subjectivity. For in the Freudian master narrative—which I am grounding in his work on comic theory but which could be intercepted elsewhere in its routing—every act of address is postmarked, to assure that no human being eludes the social circuit, that every delivery elicits a response.

PART TWO

Psychoanalysis
Comic Theory as Text

3. Freud's Bottom Line: Jokes and Their Relation to the Aesthetic

In *Jokes and Their Relation to the Unconscious* (1905; hereafter *Jokes*), Freud calls attention to the complex role played by the joking diversion in the workings of the psychic apparatus. For Freud, joking performs an important function of wish fulfillment or release, like the related activities of dreaming and writing.[1] Freud suggests that the joking process performs its function of wish fulfillment by outwitting conscious censorship and hence providing an outlet for inhibited unconscious desire ("In both [joker and listener] the pleasure arises through the lifting of internal inhibition" [*Jokes* 185]). Freud's account of the joke process therefore reveals a great deal about the interaction between conscious and unconscious modes of psychic activity (primary and secondary process), an interaction depicted as a struggle between the work of (pre)conscious censorship and the play of libidinal impulse. At the same time, Freud's work on jokes lends important insight into the intersubjective process of socialization. It is the situation of the joke at the crossroads of the conscious and the unconscious, the intra- and the intersubjective, which makes Freud's comic theory such an intriguing object of analysis and which may perhaps provide a way of thinking about the importance of a certain comic voice in postmodern textuality.

In addition to breaking new theoretical ground, Freud's treatise provides a framework for some of the most influential earlier hypotheses concerning the phenomenon of laughter. In fact, at first reading, Freud's postulation of two categories of joke—the tendentious joke, fulfilling a hostile purpose, and the innocent joke, a purely aesthetic "aim in itself"—seems to lend support to the notion of two opposing and complementary modes of comic expression, analogous to the referential and the absolute comic categories discussed in chapter 2. The tendentious joke seems to bear all the earmarks of the referential comic of superiority, since it expresses a hostile urge directed against a victim (Freud: "By making our enemy small, inferior, despicable, or comic, we achieve in a roundabout way the enjoyment of overcoming him "[103]). In the innocent joke, on the other hand, which Freud considers an inoffensive production aiming only at sheer pleasure and at refinding "the lost laughter of childhood" (236), the reference is less clear. For Freud states that the point of the innocent joke is simple pleasure; thus, just as in the absolute comic of Baudelaire, the humor of the innocent joke ostensibly remains independent of any demonstrable purpose.

At the outset, then, Freud seems to be proposing two distinct types of joking that we could consider roughly equivalent to Baudelaire's two comic categories, with an emphasis on the purposeful character of the first kind, and the innocent or aimless character of the second. But closer scrutiny of *Jokes* reveals the problematic nature of this clear-cut distinction. Indeed, in the fourth chapter of his work Freud himself alludes to the problems raised by a too-strict adherence to his own categories and seems to suggest that in the final analysis all jokes are independent from tendency or purpose, at least when purpose is equated with "vital need" or biological function. And even earlier, in the opening passages of *Jokes,* Freud already distinguishes between useful and aesthetic activities, clearly placing all joking in the latter category: "The aesthetic attitude towards an object is characterized by the condition that we do not ask anything of the object, especially no satisfaction of our serious needs, but content ourselves with the enjoyment of contemplating it. The aesthetic attitude is playful in contrast to work" (10).

This qualification of joking as aesthetic in nature, however, divorced from serious needs or purposes, may work ultimately to undercut Freud's own distinction between tendentious and innocent jokes. The following section-by-section discussion of *Jokes* isolates those moments in which Freud's thesis concerning two joking categories—distinguished according to the criterion of purposefulness—opens to a third reading of the comic process as an aesthetic activity, a play of desire sharing many characteristics both with Blanchot's *parole littéraire* and with Bataille's concept of the erotic. In other words, Freud's work may be "unworked" with the help of Freud himself, and read as an example of a comic text that playfully subverts its own most serious conclusions.

Joking Technique: Undoing the Work of Reason

In the first two chapters of his work, Freud attempts to describe how jokes produce their effect. He begins by reviewing the work of contrast theorists of the comic (Kant, Lipps, Fischer) to explain the stimulus of laughter, stressing the role of judgment in its production and summing up the main thrust of these theories in three concise formulae: the comic is "a finding of sense in nonsense," a "contrast of ideas," or a process of "bewilderment and illumination" (11–15). This choice of theories seems surprisingly conservative, given Freud's stated reason for undertaking the study of jokes (that is, an interest in the role played by the unconscious). For all of the authorities cited stress the role of reason in the comic process, describing joking as a revelatory activity, stemming from the ability to discover hidden truth or to bind "alien ideas" into a unified perception (15). Nevertheless, Freud's own subsequent analysis of the jokework as a kind of veiling, or cover-up, problematizes this initial formulation of joking as a process of reason or unification.

Condensation (comic ambiguity)

After his initial remarks on the work of the contrast theorists, Freud turns in his second chapter to the purely descriptive task of cataloguing observed comic techniques and of showing their relation to the dreamwork processes of condensation, displacement, and regression. The first main type of jokework, termed condensation [*Verdichtung*], is the compression of more than one idea or reference into a single representation (as in the double meaning of a single word used as a pun). This overdetermination is one variation of what Freud sees as the binding or unifying function of joking; it may occur at the level of a simple play on words or on a more sophisticated conceptual plane (as in the technique of allusion in which two ideas are suggested by a single statement). Freud refers to all these examples of condensation/overdetermination as "multiple use of the same material," claiming that these techniques produce pleasure by first baffling or bewildering the joke's hearers and then by subsequently "illuminating" them, in the moment of "rediscovery of something familiar." Freud emphasizes the infantile nature of this rediscovery, drawing the analogy between the infant's joy in the rediscovery of a beloved face in the game of peekaboo, and the listener's rediscovery of something understandable in the moment of illumination when one "gets" the joke.

This analysis would seem to indicate, at least at first reading, that Freud's explanation of joking pleasure is fundamentally and doubly conservative: first, because (like Baudelaire's referential theory and like Blanchot's *parole d'entendement*) it aligns itself with understanding and illumination, emphasizing the laugher's ultimate victory over an initially baffling situation; second, because it describes joking in economic terms, as a process devoted to obtaining pleasure from a conservation of mental energy. (Freud maintains that in rediscovering something familiar, one is spared the mental expense of dealing with something new.)

Yet, Freud's own discussion of joking condensation poses some problems for such a recuperative reading of the joke process. In a later section of *Jokes* (172–74), for instance, Freud states that the joking pleasure is produced by the alternation between the initial sense of ambiguity and the clarity of the moment of revelation of the joke's punch line. But the use of the term *ambiguity* invites comment for several reasons. First, it highlights the joke's reliance on multiple meanings and hence emphasizes the layered and articulated nature of language, acknowledging that words are never simply identical to that which they designate. So, even though Freud sometimes sounds as though he believes in an original transparent and unambiguous language (referring, for instance, to words that "have lost their original full meaning, but which regain it again in the joke" [34]), his position on joking nonetheless depends on the notion of inadequacy and even arbitrariness of linguistic designation, and of the inherently imprecise nature of language, its inability to "keep its word," to hold itself to unequivocal meaning. In other words, comic effect could be understood as either an excess of meaning, resulting from *double entendre* (too much meaning in one word), or as a paucity of meaning, resulting from play with cliché or understatement (too little meaning in a wornout word). In either case, ambiguous language is a sign of the inadequation of word to referent, the desire within meaning, the *je veux dire* that may only approximate what it *wants* to say.

A second issue is raised by Freud's choice of the term *ambiguity.* Is comic language always, as Freud seems to imply, ambiguous expression whose duplicity may be arbitrated by a move of judgment or illumination that recognizes one meaning as finally more correct than the other? Or, as the work of some postmodern theorists suggests, may ambiguity be read in a radically different manner, as a function of the undecidability of a concept or a word? Maurice Blanchot, for instance, maintains that in ambiguous language, opposing meanings are complementary and are capable of being reconciled in a dialectic process whereby one meaning adds something to the understanding of the other (*L'entretien infini* 143–45). This postmodern formulation is already somewhat different from Freud's understanding of ambiguity in joking, whereby a priority is granted to one meaning over the other by the adjudication of the faculty of judgment. For Freud's view of punning language as ambiguous language implies that the faculty of understanding or illumination is capable of performing an ordering task of separation and identification of multiple meanings, as well as determining which is the real meaning and which is the punning meaning, affixed just for fun; while Blanchot's ambiguous language obeys no such hierarchy.

Blanchot distinguishes ambiguity from paradox, suggesting that paradox is another kind of overdetermined expression in which conflicting meanings are "entertained," suspended in unresolved contradiction (*EI* 144–45). Both phenomena obviously derive from the capacity of language (also a shortcoming) to mean more (or less) than a speaker intends. But as postmodern writing shows, it is quite possible for overdetermined comic language to be paradoxical as well as ambiguous; its opposing meanings may resist any attempt at reconciliation or at hierarchical ordering. For instance, Derrida's writing often makes use of this kind of postmodern paradox as one of the favorite techniques of deconstruction. The term *hymen* (in "La double séance") for example, functions as a stand-in for the activity of writing precisely because it signifies both a fulfillment of desire (marriage) and an obstacle to that fulfillment (hymen). Since such "undecidable" paradoxical puns resist the ordering process that would determine which of the conflicting meanings is right, they can be understood only in a series of mental oscillations from one correct meaning to the other; they may no longer be apprehended in a single coherent moment of understanding. (A visual analogy: Wittgenstein's famous drawing of the "duck-rabbit" cannot be perceived simultaneously as both duck and rabbit, but only alternately as duck *then* rabbit.) Whereas joking ambiguity relies on transparence, each new meaning giving a new dimension to the designated object, revealing another face, joking paradox maintains a kind of opacity in which each meaning momentarily and alternately excludes the other. Since the meanings conflict and since they are equally valid, they may be apprehended only in a constantly renewed movement of psychic alternation from

one to the other: meaning is entertained in a conversational volley between the two.

The more traditional referential comic productions (to which Baudelaire attributes a high degree of "transparency") seem to show a predilection for ambiguous uses of condensed language. But a certain "other" comic voice gives full play to the device of *paradox.* This voice is characteristic of the work of postmodern writers like Derrida and Blanchot as well as psychoanalytic theorists such as Lacan (whose entire theory revolves around a paradoxical pun, the double genitive in "the desire *of the Other*") and Samuel Weber (whose recent work plays with the undecidable resonances of the word *knot.*)[2] Indeed, Freud's own concept of overdetermination is haunted by paradox; while condensations may elicit unifying illuminations they may also produce proliferations of meaning, in a vertiginous *mise-en-abîme* that subverts Freud's own "illuminating" explanations.

Displacement: the joker's sleight of hand

The second main jokework technique discussed by Freud is displacement [*Verschiebung*] (50–57), defined as a "shifting of psychic emphasis" (50) on the part of the joke-maker. This shift of emphasis, Freud maintains, serves to disguise the joke's point, allowing the joker to sneak the punch line past the listener, so that the point may be revealed at the moment of maximum effect, with appropriate punch. (Freud's example: "Have you taken a bath lately?" "Why, is there one missing?" The emphasis is displaced from "bath" to "taken" [51].) The technique of displacement, like that of condensation, would at first seem to consolidate the power of the joke-maker since it is the joker who controls the trick of displaced emphasis, pulling the rug out from under the surprised listener and thus demonstrating superior cleverness. But in Freud's treatment of the technique of displacement there are hints of a fissure in the joker's superior facade. First, most obviously, the hearer of the joke is the person who seems to benefit most from the transaction since he or she derives the greatest pleasure from

the joke, in spite of having been taken in by the joker's trickery. In a sense, it is the dupe of the jokework, and not the joking trickster, who seems to come out on top. And a second qualification of the joker's superior stance is elicited by Freud's comparison of the jokework to the dreamwork, which is at the heart of his theory. This parallel emphasizes the role of involuntary forces in the joke's production and suggests that even the most controlled act of joking is still in a sense an admission of unconscious evidence and hence a sign of the limitations of the conscious rational faculty.

The technique of displacement as described by Freud also works on a purely mechanical level to undermine the surface security seemingly afforded by the joking transaction. Freud tells us that the displacement joke relies on automatism in order to make its point: rigid thought patterns in the hearer, which take for granted the direction or meaning of the joking statement, cause the listener to be caught unaware by the joke's punch line. This is an indication that reasonable thought lacks flexibility and that normal psychic patterns can easily be tripped up. In a sense, the displacement sets up the listener's own Freudian slip or parapraxis; caught off-guard, the listener's conscious censorship gives ground to an unconscious inhibited thought since, as Freud repeatedly insists, the joke always has "something forbidden to say." Freud's exposure of the built-in limitations of conscious thought, in any case, helps to undermine his own assertion that joking affirms the triumph of reason in mental processes and indicates that even the most conservative views of laughter may not to be taken at face value as evidence of the triumph of illumination over the unconscious.

Still another flaw in the notion of the primacy of reason in the joking process is suggested by Freud's long digression on nonsense as an example of the jokework technique of displacement. In nonsense, Freud writes, the bewilderment of the joke is not followed by illumination but merely by "the revelation and demonstration of something else that is stupid and nonsensical" (58). In a later footnote, Freud gives this example: "A man at the dinner table who was being handed fish dipped his two hands twice in the mayonnaise and then ran them through his hair. When his neighbor looked at him in astonishment, he seemed to notice his mistake and apologized: 'I'm sorry, I thought it was the spinach'" (138).

This joke demonstrates a favorite device of nonsense: the proliferation of detail literally "diverts" us since it causes us to lose track of any logical point. In Freud's example of nonsense, neither the action nor the explanation of the eccentric diner is demystified, and the hoodwinking of the reason produces a pleasurable confusion. But characteristically, Freud seems unwilling to leave things in this enjoyable muddle since he insists that the mix-up is finally put to rights by the hearer's realization that "this is only nonsense." Freud suggests that the ensuing laughter is generated from a sense of relief that no valid explanation need be sought in this absurdity. Yet, even though Freud does grant the final victory to the faculty of reason—when the hearer mentally classifies confusion as nonsense—he concedes that in the nonsense joke there is a prolonged hesitation during which the mind oscillates between bewilderment and illumination rather than performing a single judgmental move (59). Thus, this discussion of displacement in the nonsense joke at least hints that the obscure side of the joking process, the bewilderment phase, may be as important to the production of pleasure as the ensuing illumination. Like the preceding discussion of condensation, Freud's treatment of displacement perhaps unwittingly raises issues which undercut the assumption that joking affords any sort of definitive superiority for the "reasonable" joker.

The Joke's Purpose: Transgression as Aesthetic Process

In the third chapter of *Jokes* Freud turns from the question of technique to that of purpose in the joke, dealing at length with the difference between innocent and tendentious jokes. This "firm" distinction, however, is built on treacherous ground that proves to be a kind of quicksand undermining the solidity of the notion of comic purpose.

Freud states that the purposeful or tendentious joke (from the German *Tendenz:* aim) is defined both by its content and its intent since it is always aggressively aimed at a comic object. He asserts that the tendentious joke is always a put-down or exposure, hostile or sexual in nature. In fact the hostile or obscene joke, Freud maintains, is always a substitute for a satisfaction of the original murderous or sexual impulse toward the joke's object. Freud develops this important notion of the joke as substitute gratification in a discussion of the difference between "wooing talk"—as prelude to sexual activity, at the service of an explicit biological aim—and "smut," Freud's term for the coarse banter substituted for sexual gratification when the presence of an outsider makes sexual activity impropríetous. The genesis of the obscene joke, the passage from "wooing talk" between man and woman to the exchange of "smut" between man and man, is described as a tripolar transaction:

> A tendentious joke calls for three people: in addition to the one who makes the joke, there must be a second who is taken as the object of the hostile or sexual aggressiveness, and a third in whom the joke's aim of producing pleasure is fulfilled. . . . When the first person finds his libidinal impulse inhibited by the woman, he develops a hostile trend against the second person and calls upon the originally interfering third person as an ally. (100)

Any tendentious joke, then, "makes possible the satisfaction of an instinct in the face of an obstacle which stands in its way" (101). But it is crucially important to note that in each case the satisfaction thus achieved is radically different from the underlying motivating impulse toward murder or sexual violation. It becomes, in either case, a safe substitute pleasure, providing a way for societal beings to play out their hostilities and tame brute impulse: "The repressive activity of civilization brings it about that primary possibilities of enjoyment are now lost to us . . . we find that tendentious jokes provide a means of undoing the renunciation and retrieving what was lost" (101). In other words, the joke is a replay in which civilization compensates for its imposed discontents.

So, the tendentious joke outwits censorship in two ways: first, it masks the underlying urge to hostility or obscenity and then satisfies that urge in an acceptable way ("We can only laugh at smut when a joke has come to our help" [101]). Since the joke is born of deflected desire, it is profoundly social in nature, for it is the entry into society which occasions the repression of libidinal impulse.

Forbidden fruit: the joke as erotic act

This understanding of the joking process as a libidinal transgression of social prohibition suggests an intriguing parallel between Freud's comic theory and Bataille's theory of eroticism as a kind of postmodern reading of transgression. For Bataille, the paradigm of the erotic act is a witnessed sacrificial rite involving three parties: a "priest" who officiates, a victim, and a spectator who experiences a vicarious sense of self-obliteration when witnessing the sacrificial drama between priest and victim. In Freud's tripolar joking scenario one may recognize an analogous configuration: the joker-priest sacrifices the comic victim before the joke's hearer, who derives vicarious pleasure from the witnessed put-down. The third party is the key term in both instances, since "he" (implicitly male in both Freud's and Bataille's account) is the recipient of the erotic pleasure, at least partly masochistic in character (in Freud, the hearer derives pleasure from being taken in or tripped up; in Bataille, the witness plays at loss of self in vicarious "death"). And even in an unwitnessed sexual act, Bataille writes, the woman's role is to remind both partners of the symbolic third party—the absent voyeur who assures that the sexual enjoyment is a guilty pleasure; it is her role to play, coquettishly, at shame. (Similarly, Freud tells us, the offended lady of the joke scenario often "feels ashamed" and even leaves the room when the dirty joking ensures.) She is, then, both victim and witness to her own sacrifice, and thus takes on two roles in this erotic triangular play.

Freud's patriarchal peep show displays a remarkably erotic character, playing out the violation or exposure of the object of desire before a third party who is "bribed by the effortless satisfaction of his own libido" (100). The joke might qualify as an instance of what Bataille calls "ordered transgression," that is, a socially sanctioned erotic act (like sex in marriage or killing in war) which functions as a sort of consolation prize, paradoxically acting to reinforce the civilized prohibitions (around sex and death) that it seems to transgress, by working as a safety valve for excessive desire.

The safety of the joking process, which assures that its transgressive and hostile nature is contained and regulated, clearly also has much to do with the mood of aesthetic playfulness accompanying the joke (Freud: "The aesthetic mood is playful in contrast to work" [10]). For this mood permits the joker to temper the consequences of the hostile jibe with the defense that "it's only a joke." Thus, in a number of ways the civilized phenomenon of tendentious joking recalls not only Bataille's erotic transgression but Baudelaire's referential comic as well. Like the referential comic, which Baudelaire considers a civilized phenomenon masking a ferocious nature, the safe tendentious joke has the capacity to turn "positively cruel (Freud 100). Thus Freud's first category of joke is already a complicated case; though it seems in some ways neatly to correspond to that civilized referential comic category suggested by Baudelaire and others, it also harbors sadistic sacrificial elements, like Baudelaire's absolute comic. Indeed, this overlapping between Freud's categories may heighten our suspicion that Freud's dichotomy between two comic categories is no more tenable than is the distinction between the absolute and referential comic, questioned in chapter 2.

A questionable innocence

In his discussion of the joking purpose, Freud has relatively little to say about the innocent joke because he denies that such jokes have a purpose, insisting that in the innocent joke the pleasure is aesthetic, an "aim in itself" (90), like the play of children. Again, this distinction bears an uncanny resemblance to Baudelaire's distinction between the interested stance of the referential comic and the disinterested or "innocent" stance of the absolute comic, associated with child's play. Presumably, for Freud as for Baudelaire, the only aim of the innocent joke is pleasure. And even though this hedonistic aim could be said to constitute a purpose of sorts, Freud at least seems to suggest that the purpose of mere pleasure is somehow less real or serious than the identifiable aims of the tendentious joke. Even this distinction, however, is problematic since the clear aim of the tendentious joke (the put-down of the butt of the jest) is always already mitigated, deflected from another (hostile or sexual) aim.

And in fact, Freud hedges about the real nature of the purpose in joking; he seems to suggest that the exterior purpose—the basis for differentiation between the innocent and tendentious joke—is perhaps not the essential aim of joking. In a modification of his original formulation, Freud writes that the primary purpose of any joke would seem to be that of pleasure, since all jokes, tendentious and innocent alike, share "the unmistakable aim of provoking pleasure in the hearer" (95). The aim of pleasure, then, since it is common to both types of joke, would seem to be the defining characteristic of joking while the "exterior" purpose of tendentious jokes would be of secondary importance. Indeed, if we recall Freud's definition of the aesthetic as a property of any pleasurable activity not connected with the satisfaction of "serious need"—that is, biological goals or utilitarian purposes—we might say that any joke, of either category, could qualify as an aesthetic product since the primary aim of any joke is not the gratification of biological need but the production of pleasure. In the

chapter on joking purpose, Freud himself substantiates this view:

> If we do not require our mental apparatus for supplying one of our indispensable satisfactions, we allow it itself to work in the direction of pleasure and we seek to derive pleasure from its own activity. . . . As regards joking, however, I can assert . . . that it is an activity that aims at deriving pleasure from mental processes, whether intellectual or otherwise. (96)

Since this depiction of all joking as a gratuitous entertainment divorced from "indispensable satisfaction" here clearly applies to all jokes, Freud's original distinction between joking categories—based on a distinction between the hedonistic aesthetic aim of innocent jokes on the one hand and the "real purposes" of tendentious jokes on the other—must at best be considered a convenient handle for sorting out and discussing jokes rather than an essential opposition between types of jokes.

Even the most tendentious of jokes is always a substitutive satisfaction entailing a diversion from biological goals; therefore, it is no more subservient to serious purpose than is the innocent joke. Conversely, even the most innocent of jokes is in some sense purposeful since, as Freud reminds us, all jokes are based on transgression, on the articulation of something forbidden, and derive their quotient of pleasure in part from the overcoming of censorship. When the violated norm is clearly exterior, as when the joke entails an attack on another person, Freud would classify the joke as tendentious. But every innocent joke always performs a violation of sorts as well, even if the transgressed norm is only, say, the everyday usage of a word, as in the case of a simple verbal pun. When Freud himself concludes that jokes "are in fact never non-tendentious" (132), he seems to be acknowledging that his own categories, however categorical they may appear, are no more than heuristic concepts. For Freud's own treatment of the purposes of jokes "unworks" these categories, demonstrating on the one hand that no joke is untainted or innocent of transgressive aims, of shady dealings with censorship and inhibition, and suggesting on the other hand that even the most pointed (sexual or hostile) aim is designed to miss the mark, since no joke is ever engendered without the diversion of a tendentious desire from its original biological or serious purpose. (If wooing talk ended in successful coupling, no "smutty" joke would be generated.)

A postmodern treatment of a related question forms the core of Jean-François Lyotard's discussion of linguistic transgression in *Discours, figure* (1971); Lyotard considers figure of speech to be the intrusion of primary process onto discourse. Writing about the literary figures produced by condensation—which Freud of course considers a technique of the dreamwork and the jokework as well—Lyotard writes that condensation is "a *transgression* of the rules of discourse" and asserts that this transgression consists in the process of condensation itself, in the violation of the space of discourse by figure. ("To crush signifying or signified unities one against the other, to mix them [*les confondre*], is to neglect the stable spaces [*écartements*] which separate the letters and the words of a text, to ignore the space of discourse" [*DF* 244]). In other words, in Lyotard's reading of condensation, the quotient of wish fulfillment [*accomplissement du désir*] afforded by primary process is attributable not to the content of the literary figure, but to its process. For Lyotard, all modifications of discourse by *désir* (primary process) are textual intrusions of desire, manifested in plastic forms or tropes that rework and unwork the space of discourse, invading the narrative surface by what Lyotard calls "the mobility and freedom of primary process" (245). One could make a related point about the joke: any joke is transgressive, however innocent its content, by virtue of its process alone. Read through a postmodern optic, Freud's "innocent" jokes are compromised, innocent only of explicit motive, indulging in a transgressive play that "aims" at wreaking havoc in linguistic space.

In light of this reading of all jokes as transgressive acts, it becomes possible to extend Bataille's definition of the erotic act to the process of joking, as well as to its content. For this shady business, like the "comedy" of Bataille's erotic act, may always be considered a gratuitous aesthetic process, according to Freud's own rules of the game. Yet, as this reading also implies, the notion of the aesthetic in Freud's sense of the term cannot be confused with purity (as it is, for instance, in the aestheticism of high modernism, which extols the purity of art as disinterested aesthetic, divorcing "art for art's sake" from the dirty business of real life). Freud's aesthetic, on the contrary, is far from innocent, opening to the abyss of sexuality. Indeed, in the *Three Essays on Sexuality* [1905], written the same year as the work on jokes, Freud suggests that it is divorce from biology—and hence from need or purpose—that grounds human sexuality, since sexual desire is "laid on to" the act of feeding, as an excessive and insatiable desire for the repetition of pleasure in excess of biological need. It is this concept of "laying on" in turn that grounds Lacan's distinction between need and desire, underscoring the excessive nature of *désir,* in the oft-cited Lacanian formula: desire equals the excess of demand over need.[3] In this light, sexuality may itself be considered an aesthetic production, with aesthetic understood not as that which is pristine, but as that which is both engendered by and always already deflected from need. If Freud's aesthetic has a bottom line, it is perhaps only that the aesthetic is a bottomless non-linearity, the antithesis of closure.

It is perhaps this aesthetic excess which accounts in part for the attraction that Freud's *Witz* exerts upon postmodern textuality, for Blanchot's "unworked" text, like Derrida's *écriture,* is excessive and paradoxical. On the one hand, it harbors a tendentious quality, an irreverent taste for subversion; at the same time it maintains a certain innocence in its slippery quality, its refusal to be pinned down to a serviceable meaning. The comic, like every aesthetic process, is a paradox deriving from both excess and lack, an excess of desire and of opportunities of its partial satisfaction, and an unbridgeable gap stemming from the irretrievable loss of the original object. The offended lady in *Jokes*—who leaves the room rather than be exposed to locker room humor (100–103)—is perhaps the lost love of our infancy.

The Economics of Voyeurism

In the fourth chapter of *Jokes*, Freud deals with the pleasure mechanism in the joke, emphasizing the paradoxical role played by the obstacle in the joking process. In this section, he sets out to reconcile economic theories of joking with his notion of purpose in the joke by valorizing the role of the obstacle in both cases:

> Laughter is . . . the proof that the psychical employment of the excitation has suddenly come up against an obstacle . . . In laughter, therefore, on our hypothesis, the conditions are present under which a sum of psychical energy which has hitherto been used for cathexis is allowed free discharge. (148, my emphasis)

Freud states his hypothesis more concisely in the following formula: "The yield of pleasure corresponds to the psychical expenditure which is saved" (118). Thus in a tendentious joke, Freud explains, the savings is on the quotient of energy that would have been required to maintain the inhibition, since the repressed thought is released by the joke. Similarly, in the innocent joke, the economic pleasure represents a savings in inhibitory energy because it adopts the "relaxed" and "comfortable" thought-patterns characteristic of infancy.[4] The pleasure derived from these infantile "comfortable psychic procedures," Freud says, flows from following the path of least resistance, a result of a sort of psychic laziness in which the wordplay provides a shortcut between two ideas ("The pleasure in a joke arising from a 'short circuit' like this seems to be the greater the more alien the two circles of ideas that are brought together by the same word—the further apart they are, thus the greater the economy which the joke's technical method provides in the train of thought" [128]).

But Freud stipulates that in spite of the economic attraction of the shortcut of comfortable thought processes, the joke in its most evolved forms will nonetheless opt for detour or long-circuit since its pleasure yield is increased by the placing of obstacles in the path to the final revelation. Freud's statement that the "games founded on this economic pleasure make use of the mechanism of damming up only in order to increase the amount of such pleasure" (122) again valorizes the role of the obstacle in the joking game and emphasizes the erotic nature of the titillating process by which joking prolongs and heightens pleasure (the initial bewilderment acting as a kind of foreplay that serves to heighten the pleasure yield of the illumination). Yet again, it seems evident from Freud's remarks that pleasure is the essential aim of joking: in the joking game of hide-and-seek, immediate gratification is deferred as a strategy to up the ante of the eventual pleasure pay-off.

In other words, the jokework itself acts as obstacle to immediate satisfaction, disguising the joke's point in order to increase the punch of the punch line. The disguisers of joke technique serve another function as well since they act as camouflage, "[protecting] pleasure from being done away with by criticism" (131). Thus, the tantalizing veil of the jokework serves to "promote the thought by augmenting it and guarding it against criticism," making the thought acceptable to the listener. Freud seems to imply that the content of the joke is finally less significant in the production of pleasure than is the process of stripping away the veil/obstacle which has both disguised and protected the underlying thought.[5] We may infer that the tendentious nature of any joke resides in an internal transgressive process; the essential violation is not directed toward an exterior object but toward an internalized inhibition. Thus the joke's manifest point or content is merely the pretext for a pleasure transaction always deflected from direct aim.

In other words, Freud's comic theory, just as in Bataille's erotic theory, the role of the obstacle is crucial to the genesis of pleasure. Moreover, for Freud, the obstacle not only generates the joke but it actually changes the nature of the satisfaction: "Since the aggressiveness is held up in its advance towards the act . . . [it] is no doubt altering its character as well, just as any libidinal impulse will do if met by an obstacle" (99). And the joke itself may be considered as not only a response to the obstruction of desire but as itself a kind of obstacle to straightforward satisfaction since it serves as a disguise for the direct expression of a forbidden thought or impulse. Freud even maintains that it is this recourse to artifice—the "disguised representation of the truth" (108)—that gives the joke its duplicitous character.

Freud's use of the term *disguise* in any case evokes an apt theatrical metaphor, which echoes earlier references (in chapter 1 of *Jokes*) to the joke's forbidden material as a statement masked by the jest or "concealed behind a facade," yet directed to an audience. We recall that Bataille similarly insists on the theatrical nature of the erotic transgression, characterized as "a naive comedy." The antithesis of the natural or the instinctive, erotic pleasure is heightened by a game of hide-and-seek, a disguise of overt desire, as when the woman plays at shame. Similarly, one could argue that like the erotic act, the joke is unnatural, both in its distinction from brute biological instinct and in its paradoxical theatrical nature, which hides and exposes at once. And like the erotic act the joke is always a social function, for the comic exchange is always by definition a witnessed transaction. Indeed we could make a case for a structural or functional analogy between the joking and erotic processes, hinging on the voyeuristic/exhibitionist character of both activities.

Furthermore, the joking process, like the highly theatrical erotic (tripolar) "sacrifice," may be considered fundamentally perverse in character if we understand *perversion* as Freud defines the term, as a deflection from or deferral of biological aim. Freud writes in *Three Essays on Sexuality:* "The perversions represent either (a) anatomical transgressions of the bodily regions destined for sexual union or (b) a lingering at the intermediate relations to the sexual object which should normally be rapidly passed, on their way to the definite sexual aim."[6]

In a later chapter of *Jokes,* Freud again makes clear that the activity of joking, unlike dreaming, is separate from any specifically biological function or vital need (179): "Dreams retain their connection with the major interests of life; . . . they are permitted to occur for the sake of the one need which is active during the night—the need to sleep. Jokes, on the other hand, seek to gain a small yield of pleasure from the mere activity, untrammeled by needs, of our mental apparatus." If we then superimpose Freud's notion of perversity (as that which is not subservient to biological function and which is diverted from reproductive purpose) on the analogous notion of the aesthetic as that which is distinct from "serious needs," we could say that in Freud's view joking is both perverse and aesthetic in nature.

In the case of this comic perversion/diversion, the deflection of desire is occasioned by the presence of the onlooking third party, who, as obstacle to sexual union between the first two parties, is responsible for the perverse turn of events. This outsider in turn derives a voyeuristic pleasure from participation in the joking long-circuit, since "he" (a male in Freud's account) witnesses the exposure of the (female) comic victim. His pleasure is doubly perverse since he witnesses not only the dressing down of the joke's hapless object but also the unveiling in the punch line of a forbidden thought, heretofore artfully cloaked by the jokework.

The Joking Triangle as Social Contagion

Freud's emphasis on the internal workings of the joking transaction by no means implies that joking is asocial in nature; in fact, in chapter 5 of *Jokes* ("Jokes as a Social Process"), Freud insists that the compulsion to repeat a joke to someone else is obsessive in character: "An urge to tell the joke to someone is inextricably bound up with the joke-work: indeed, this urge is so strong that it often is carried through in disregard to serious misgivings. A joke *must* be told to someone else" (143).

This necessary recourse to an audience (the third party in

the joke triangle) seems to be symptomatic of a vague sense of excess, an unfinished feeling: "The psychical process of constructing a joke seems not to be completed when the joke occurs to one: something remains over which seeks, by communicating the idea, to bring the unknown process of constructing a joke to a conclusion" (143). Clearly this conclusion is only a temporary one, since the listener is compelled to retell the joke, becoming the first person in a new triangle, and spreading the contagion to a new third person. So, in the social transaction of joking, it is the third party, the interfering outsider, who acts as catalyst. Not only is this third the recipient of the joking pleasure, but "he" is also a collaborator (Freud: "I myself cannot laugh at a joke which has occurred to me without his help" [143]).

The third person is thus "used" to promote pleasure in the joker (Freud: "I am actually making use of him to arouse my own laughter" [156]). Again, this thinly veiled sexual nature of the "use" of the joke's listener brings to mind the role of the spectator in Bataille's erotic triangular ritual (priest-victim-witness). Likewise, in the sexual triangle par excellence, the oedipal triangle, it is the third (the Father) who plays the role of the interfering party, initiating the child into the social order. And in the next chapter I will suggest that this oedipal thirdness provides yet another way of thinking of the crucial importance of "the outsider" or obstacle, not only in Freud's theory of the comic, but in Freud's entire body of comic theory.

To summarize: in the joke, the obstacle plays at least three critically important and interrelated roles. First, the obstacle represented by the third person (or by the societal norms he or she embodies) initiates the rechanneling of instinct into the substitutive activity; second, the obstacle of censorship or propriety exerts an influence on the joke's form, requiring that the thought be masked or disguised in order to provide a barrier to a short-circuited fulfillment of desire; third, additional obstacles work to increase the pleasure-yield when the listener finally "gets" the joke. The first four chapters of Freud's

work demonstrate that the social nature of the joking process is by no means restricted to useful social aims (of socialization or chastisement, as Bergson and others have argued) associated with the content of the joke; indeed, the more significant social aspect of joking is that intersubjective game in which desire is deflected, modified, and substitutively gratified in response to social constraints, in a social long-circuit. Thanks to the diverting (and perverting?) obstacle, finally, all jokes may be read as gratuitous and aesthetic productions, a form of "developed play" (Freud 179) derailed from a serious train of thought.

Freud's Comic Oversight: Humor and Mimesis

The last chapter of *Jokes,* "Jokes and the Comic," suggests a final way in which the view of joking as a purposeful activity may be problematized. In this section, Freud seeks to distinguish between jokes and the comic, maintaining that the difference between the two resides in the number of people involved. The comic, says Freud, is characterized by two poles or participants, in counterdistinction to the joke's three poles. In the comic the two poles are the laugher and the comic object: no exterior audience is necessary. In other words, Freud is claiming that the joke's third pole, the all-important third party whose presence both engenders the joke and insures the completion of its pleasure-circuit, is absent from a comic exchange which may in fact require only one person ("If I come across something comic, I myself can laugh heartily at it, though it is true that I am also pleased if I can make someone else laugh by telling it to him" [143]). When we laugh at someone's slip on a banana peel, or at our own Freudian slip, we are laughing at a comic situation. When we hear or tell an anecdote, we are engaged in a transactional joke situation.

Freud explains the phenomenon of *ideational mimetics,* in which the laugher draws a comparison between "an observed movement and his own" (193). A comic effect is produced in the observer when the observed movement is not commensurate with the amount of energy that is psychically estimated as necessary to perform the task: "If the other person's movement is exaggerated and inexpedient, my increased expenditure in order to understand it is inhibited *in statu nascendi,* as it were, in the act of being mobilized; it is declared superfluous and is free . . . for discharge by laughter . . . the comic effect depends on the difference between the two cathetic expenditures—one's own and the other person's as estimated by empathy" (194–95). Freud also refers to this process of empathy—whereby one follows the action of the other, psychically imitating it—as "comic lending."

This theory of ideational mimetics is fascinating, in part because the concept bears a striking resemblance to the notion of identification developed in Freud's later work, especially in "On Narcissism: An Introduction" (1914), "Mourning and Melancholia" (1917), and *Group Psychology and the Analysis of the Ego* (1921). In each of these works, narcissism is associated with the introjection of the image of the other. Moreover, this process of introjection is associated with cannibalism and totemic sacrifice in *Totem and Taboo* (1912) in which Freud argues that the powers of the sacrificial totemic animal (or of the Father) are ritually or symbolically ingested. In all these works something like an "ego ideal" is internalized through a process of identification/introjection. Interestingly, the germ of this ego ideal is already in Freud's discussion of the comic, whereby the observed other elicits ideational mimetics or psychic identification. We might even suggest that Freud's ideational mimetics anticipate the Lacanian notion of the narcissistic constitution of the ego, whereby the ego is formed in a process of introjection and identification.[7]

In spite of the intriguing implications of Freud's brief comments on the comic, his principal point—the distinction between jokes and the comic—seems to be based on two fundamental oversights. First, Freud overlooks the importance of the phenomenon of comic lending in the joke process as well as in the comic situation: indeed, a certain lending or identification is crucial to the joke technique of displacement. In the joke, the hearer "follows the lead" of the joker and is thus tricked (by jokework displacement) into diverting his or her attention away from the point of the joke—the punch line that is sneaked past the hearer. When the trickery is perceived ("Have you taken a bath lately?" "Why? Is there one missing?"), laughter ensues. Thus, a distinction between jokes and the comic in terms of the technique of psychic lending does not hold.

But there is a more serious problem with Freud's distinction between jokes and the comic, hinging on a confusion concerning the number of poles or parties involved in each process. This confusion is produced because Freud momentarily seems to forget that the second pole or object in the joke triangle, as he himself defines it, need not be a person but can in fact be any norm that is violated, such as normal linguistic usage. In the case of verbal jokes or puns, for instance, it is simply the everyday meaning of a word that is violated by the jokework condensation, which adds another reference. even in the obscene tendentious joke—Freud's generalized model for the structure of all jokes—the offended lady may really only be a symbol or stand-in for a norm of proprietous social behavior, since she herself is not violated in her person. (As Freud himself suggests, she often absents herself, leaving the room when the smutty exchange between complicit males gets under way.) At any rate, the same three poles figure in the comic process as in the joking process. The person whom Freud mistakenly identifies as the second party in the comic situation—the object of laughter who slips on a banana peel—is really in a situation analogous to that of the joke's teller (pole one in joking), initiating the action that engenders laughter. Like the joke-maker, the comic object is the source (albeit unintentional) of the laughter, the maker of a visual joke; as source and object of the laughter, then, the comic object occupies two of the joking poles at once. But as the notion of ideational mimetics underscores, the second pole—the "butt"—is actually not the person who falls but is rather the norm of expedient behavior violated by the inappropriate movements (the wild gesticulations as the comic object falls).

The third pole, supposedly absent in Freud's account of the comic process, is the person who laughs, because, like the joke's hearer, he or she has been spared a psychic expenditure: "finding" the comic, the laugher gets the laugh for free (exactly like the joker's freeloading audience, bribed by the voyeuristic pleasure of the offended lady's exposure). Freud himself concedes that in laughing at a comic situation, "we are behaving like the third person in a joke, who is presented with the economy without any effort on his own part" (182). It would seem that the only substantial difference between the joke and the comic resides in the intent of the first party to make a joke, as contrasted with the accident of the comic object's slip-up; but even this distinction is qualified by Freud when he states that we can decide to make ourselves or others comic (189 and 199).[8] Freud's primary example of a comic spectacle is the performance of a clown, who certainly acts like a joker, *intending* to produce laughter in the observer.

After wavering on this question of intent, Freud finally settles on a somewhat more satisfactory distinction between jokes and the comic: "Jokes and the comic are distinguished first and foremost by their psychical location; the joke, it may be said, is the contribution made to the comic from the realm of the unconscious" (208). His distinction seems finally to come down to the question of control of the process by the joke-maker. Even this conclusion must be qualified, however, since the notion of control or mastery in any situation where laughter is produced is problematic. It is finally perhaps not important whether the joke-maker sets out to mock a comic victim or whether the joke emerges ready-made, for as Freud himself insists, all laughter is a symptom of unconscious desire and of the fact that reality is always that which is beyond our absolute control.

Comic lending: putting oneself in the other's (oversized) shoes

A related "postmodern" take on Freud's comic theory as a scenario of intersubjective desire is found in Jeffrey Mehlman's treatment of the comic process, suggesting yet another way in which Freud's notion of comic control may be exposed as illusory.[9] Mehlman's reading may be considered postmodern because it emphasizes "the uncertainties of discourse" at the base of the joke process at the same time that it exposes the uncertainties of Freud's own discourse, performing a Freudian analysis of Freud's text. Mehlman's discussion of the comic process—even though it is flawed by the adoption of Freud's own misunderstanding of the three poles involved—proposes a fascinating Lacanian critique of the "illusory plenitude occasionally championed by Freud: the ego" (Mehlman 440). Mehlman's treatment of the erosion of the notion of ego as a whole, rational surface of psychical organism, a concept found in Freud's late work, is based on the comparison of the comic phenomenon of psychic lending or ideational mimetics—the process by which one puts oneself in the place of the observed other—with the model of the narcissistically constituted ego proposed by Lacanians. This concept maintains that the ego is "constituted originally as the introjected image of another" (456) and that the notion of self is thus based on a primary scission/alienation of perspective, the distinction between self and other which allows the mental comparison to ensue.

Mehlman argues that the comic process of lending is similar to the process by which the ego is constituted; the comic effect depends on an analogous identification with the other and an interiorization of the other's image, performed paradoxically thanks to the distance or separation from that other constituted as an object (with whom the laugher may identify thanks to comic lending). Thus, any debasement of the comic other is also made at the laugher's expense since laughter is a function of mimetic identification with the debased comic object, the butt of the humor. In other words, the uncovering of the mimetic character of the comic process implies the erosion of a seemingly superior reference point. We may conclude that even conscious comic techniques are in no way an assurance of the supremacy of laugher over comic victim. Even the so-called comic of superiority (of Hobbes et al.) has a component of masochism: since both poles of the comic process—subject and object alike—are objects of identification for the divided ego, aggression against one pole implies aggression against the other. And if jokes and the comic may in fact be considered manifestations of the same desiring process, as I have argued, we may suppose that the kind of comic undertow emphasized by Mehlman is also at work in the joking process, even where (and perhaps even especially where) claims of superiority are made. But Mehlman's insights may be extended beyond the joking/comic processes to the notion of self since his reading of Freud's *Jokes* is based on the paradox of an identity always doubled and underwritten, in which the most secure "I" is overdetermined by the "thou" as "Other." Indeed, Mehlman's Lacanian reading of Freud casts Freud's theory as an allegory in the postmodern sense of the term, in which the joker is a figure for the desiring self, constituting itself (as ego) at its own expense.

Readings like those of Lyotard and Mehlman, and the reading of *Jokes* that I propose here, are postmodern in their tendency to read Freud by his own rules (looking for the importance of the under- and overstated) as well as in their emphasis on the joke's origin in compulsive, contagious desire. But we have seen that this compulsive repetition is the result of an effort to reverse a situation in which the listener, in a position of passive receptivity, is caught off-guard by the joke's technique. The urge to tell the joke is thus in a way a function of ideational mimetics, the device by which the listener follows the joke and so is made vulnerable to the intellectual pratfall at the moment of the punch line. This process, in turn, is related to our psychic capacity to follow the visual or verbal lead of the jokemaker. If we assume that ideational mimetics is a part of communicative process, we can see that even the purely visual comic (as when we laugh at a clown's antics) is a social affair in which the mimetic compulsion is bound up with the desire to understand.

This urge to imitate or to trace what we perceive is not responsive to conscious control; in fact, this phenomenon of lending in the joke is an automatic response that compels us to be caught up in the semiotic exchange. Thus, it seems finally unimportant whether the joking transgression violates a conscious or an unconscious inhibition (which is perhaps the only valid distinction that Freud makes between the joke and the comic) since this difference is still on the level of content. In either case, the process is the same since it may be understood as a transgressive move that makes use of any available content as a pretext to play its game of wish fulfillment (*accomplissement du désir*).

Mehlman's reading provides an apt demonstration of how the superimpositions of one of Freud's texts on another, "Freud on Freud," may serve as a point of departure for a postmodern understanding of textuality thorugh the work of Jacques Lacan, which will serve as the focus for the next chapter. For Freud's work on jokes, particularly when read though his theory on the compulsion to repeat, demonstrates why neither of the possible outcomes of the comic process—glorification or humiliation of self, mastery or sacrifice—may ever be considered final, since joking is revealed as symptom rather than cure for human desire. This is perhaps the postmodern punch line of Freud's comic text: the "dis-covery" that joking, like the fictive process itself, is a game of veiling and unveiling, an aesthetic striptease whose perverse "purpose" is a contagious pleasure. As such, the joke is perhaps an allegory for the textplay between reader and writer as well as for the intersubjective game of hide-and-seek played out in the familial oedipal scene and in larger social networks as well. Indeed, Freud's own work may be read as a sort of postmodern joke, an overdetermined *parole plurielle,* an example of that "other" textuality of excess and aftermath which perpetually and comically deconstructs itself, and in so doing, offers a paradigm of the postmodern self.

4. Lacan's Purloined Punch Line: Joke as Textual Paradigm

The letter of Lacan's law: Freud's postmodern allegory

In an essay entitled "The Object of Post-Criticism" (1983), Gregory Ulmer analyzes the deployment by postmodern writers of certain modern strategies, such as collage, montage, grammatology (Derrida's theory of writing), and allegory.[1] In Ulmer's view as in Lyotard's, postmodernism is an intensification and extension of modernism. Each of the strategies Ulmer discusses makes use of objects (hence, "The Object of Post-Criticism") to problematize the activity of representation and the notion of originality, making of reference a playful *sliding of signifiers* (Lacan's term) emphasizing meaning as a differential function of context rather than an expression of authority or legitimation. Therefore, postmodern allegory, as treated, for instance, in the later work of Paul de Man (especially *Allegories of Reading,* 1979) is profoundly different from traditional allegory in which a surface narrative simply represents a "higher" (usually moral) drama, with a simple one-to-one correspondence (Ahab versus the whale = Man versus Nature). But, as Ulmer points out, postmodern allegory enacts a process of what Derrida has termed *de-monstration* (Derrida as cited by Ulmer: "De-monstration proves without showing, without evidencing any conclusion, without entailing anything, without an available thesis. . . . It transforms, it transforms itself in its process rather than advancing a signifiable object of discourse" [93–94].[2] Ulmer concludes that "what the baroque or romantic allegorist conceived of as an emblem, the post-critic treats as a model" (99). The deconstructed allegorical object (Derrida's umbrella, fan, or postcard) thus demonstrates the process that it represents while always unfolding to suggest other associations and contexts (Ulmer: "Derrida becomes postmodern by putting mimicry to work in the interest of a new reference" [92]).

What Ulmer calls mimicry or de-monstration is a process of narrative representation (telling the story of the umbrella, the fan, the postcard) in which the dynamic of *écriture*—the play of difference as a kind of tracing or repetition—is reenacted through the exploration of the allegorical object, its function, and its etymological connotations: "The 'object' leads, criticism being a translation into the words of the inner logic of the object, thing, event, test itself" (98). Unlike the kind of authoritative interpretation that traditional allegory invites (a process that Derrida calls *allegoresis*), the postmodern allegory invites a kind of playful exchange and inventiveness, its narrative deploying the object as *polyseme,* the site of many meanings rather than one. Ulmer points out, finally, that all of Derrida's "objects" are borrowed from other writers (in an intertextuality that problematizes origin) to de-monstrate "the very structure of style as such" (99): "The umbrella counts for Derrida not as a 'symbol,' Freudian or otherwise, but as a structural machine which, in its capacity to open and close, de-monstrates the unrepresentable *gram*" (99). Unfolding a fan, sending off a postcard, opening an umbrella—these are more than explanations of Derridean *écriture;* they are instances of its process.

Significantly, Ulmer rounds off his discussion of postmodern allegory with a reference to psychoanalysis: "The 'example' in post-criticism functions in the manner of a 'fetish' object, thus linking allegory with psychoanalysis in paraliterature" (99). It is this link that I would like to de-monstrate in my turn, by reading Freud on jokes as an allegory of oedipal struggle. Of course the oedipal narrative is already an allegory of human subjectivity, allegorized in turn by Lacan as the story of the Symbolic in the *Seminar on The Purloined Letter.*[3] Indeed, the

Freudian allegory is a chain letter, picked up and recirculated by Lacan's "return to Freud."

The clue in full view

> Freud, the very name's a laugh . . . the most hilarious leap in the holy farce of history.
>
> Jacques Lacan, "A Love Letter," (*Feminine Sexuality,* 157)

Freud clearly loved nothing more than a good story, except perhaps a good laugh. From Dora to Moses, from Oedipus to the Jewish marriage broker, Freud's cast of characters play out the human drama in suspenseful narratives spiked with anecdote and warmed with wit. And as we have seen, some of Freud's most provocative insights concern the twin aesthetic mysteries dear to his heart: the writer's magic and the joker's art.

In his own "return to Freud," Lacan has followed the master story teller's example. For Lacan's own artful use of pun, allusion, and narrative technique creates a performative theoretical discourse (a *postmodern allegory* in Ulmer's sense of the term) that reenacts the plot of intersubjective desire even while it analyzes this plot. Lacan's work thus tends to speak to questions of narrative and textuality in an oblique manner, by example. In order to elaborate a Lacanian theory of narrative, one needs to decipher the clues in Lacan's own sometimes turgid and hermetic text.

In one of the best examples of Lacan's narrative craft—the much discussed *Seminar on The Purloined Letter* (hereafter *SPL*)—Lacan passes on a useful lesson learned from Poe's arch-sleuth, Dupin: the best clues are always at once marginal and obvious ("Perhaps a little *too* self-evident" [*SPL* 53]). One such marginal yet obvious clue to Lacan's *own* work, it seems to me, maybe found in the first volume of *Ecrits* (1966):

> For, however neglected by our interest—and for good reason—*Jokes and Their Relation to the Unconscious* remains the most unchallengeable of Freud's works because it is the most transparent, in which the effect of the Unconscious is revealed to us in its most subtle confines. (*Ecrits* I 148)

What are we to make of this puzzling statement of simultaneous homage and disparagement? Why does Lacan *marginalize* Freud's text ("however neglected by our interest—and for good reason") at the same time that he insists on its "transparency" and its centrality as "the most unchallengeable of Freud's works"? Perhaps like the purloined letter of Freud's detective tale, which has been hidden in plain sight, Freud's work may be a *somewhat too evident* clue to understanding Lacan's own version of the Freudian master-narrative. For as I have argued in chapter 3, if Freud's transparent text is "clearly" about what it promises to be—jokes and their relation to the unconscious—it is also about the transmission of sexual desire in a sociolinguistic circuit. In addition, it may be read as a model story, a paradigm tracing the possibilities of narrative itself. Indeed, such a reading of Freud's "transparent" essay on the joking process as an "evident" clue to the functioning of textual processes seems to suggest that Lacan's own punch line—the discovery that everything human is textual, caught in an intersubjective narrative web—has been purloined from Freud. Yet in returning this punch line to its initiator, we find that it has been transcribed in Lacan's hand, and that this rewriting will permit us to rethink the joking process so that it no longer appears as a guarantor of identity or cementer of the social bond, but rather as a symptom motivated by the same pre-text of desire that gives rise to the literary text.

In order to reread the Freudian narrative allegory/paradigm in Lacanian terms, with an eye to formulating a Lacanian theory of literary narrative, I want to trace the following chain of metonymic equivalences: subjectivity as intersubjectivity; intersubjectivity as play; play as narrative/text; text as "feminine" symptom; femininity as (a form of) subjectivity. This chain may be described as metonymic because in Lacan's view of intersubjectivity as a kind of text, each of these processes or phenomena is an overlapping link leading inevitably to the next. And this metonymic chain in turn describes a circular itinerary or plot where the final point—which visits the ques-

tion, perplexing to Freud and to Lacan alike, of a nature of femininity—returns to the point of departure, a questioning of the role of the subject not only in the creation of the literary text but in the forming of the larger human plot or text. For the question of feminine subjectivity—and of whether "she" as subject can speak or write—is a central one in Lacan's work and it is a question that must be addressed in reading this work as a postmodern allegory of textuality: that is, as a narrative, a theory of narrative, and a theory of human intersubjectivity and sexuality *as* narrative.

Subjectivity as Intersubjectivity

> Generally speaking, a tendentious joke calls for three people.
>
> Freud, *Jokes* (100)

A classic plot

As we have seen in our reading of *Jokes,* Freud's work tells the story of the origin of joking itself: the joker-protagonist overcomes a series of adverse circumstances and enjoys a happy ending of sorts ("Jokes make possible the satisfaction of an instinct—whether lustful or hostile—in the face of an obstacle which stands in its way" [101]). I want to return to Freud's scenario of the development of the tendentious joke in order to read it as a classic boy meets girl narrative (and a postmodern allegory as well), complicated by an equally classic love triangle.

Part I: Boy Meets Girl. "The one who makes the joke" (100) encounters a desirable "object," gets ideas, and makes them known in "wooing talk," which he hopes "will yield at once to sexual action" (98–99). The first in a series of detours from direct satisfaction of "a lustful instinct" is thus necessitated by the obstacle posed by social convention: wooing must precede action. If wooing proves unsuccessful—if the object resists because she is offended or inhibited—the frustrated wooer "turns positively hostile and cruel" and begins to express himself in "smut" or "sexually explicit speech" (98–100). A second detour from direct satisfaction is thus experienced, since the sexually exciting speech becomes "an aim in itself" ("sexual aggressiveness . . . pauses at the evocation of excitement and derives pleasure from the signs of it in the woman" [99]). Such a pleasure, as I have already argued, could be considered both aesthetic (since it is divorced from the biological need and diverted to a pleasure in signs) and perverse (since it implies derailment or detour from reproductive aim).

Part II: Boy Loses Girl. The plot thickens. As if the woman's inhibition did not pose problems enough for the wooer's design, enter a second male—a potential rival and decidedly importune third party ("The ideal case of resistance of this kind on the woman's part occurs if another man is present at the same time—a third person—for in that case an immediate surrender is as good as out of the question" [99]). Alas, even if "girl wants boy," the implicit rivalry between "boys"—a kind of shorthand for the whole corpus of societal laws and prohibitions governing sexuality—interrupts the natural course of events.

Part III: Joke Conquers All. But never fear, boy does get girl, by "exposing her in the obscene joke" and enjoying the spectacle of her embarrassment ("By making our enemy comic, we achieve in a roundabout way the enjoyment of overcoming [her]" [103].) Thus "boy" gets satisfaction, but only in the sense that one "gets" a joke, by effecting an imaginary exposure, humiliation or put-down which is clearly both voyeuristic and exhibitionist in character: the hapless woman has now been exposed before a listener who has "been bribed by the effortless satisfaction of his own libido" (100). The pleasure game is played out between poles one and three, joker and listener, who (boys will be boys) share a laugh at the expense of pole two (who is often so offended as to leave the room, Freud tells us, "feeling ashamed"). In this scenario, the locker room joys of male bonding have replaced the original goal of seduction, since the joker actually "calls on the originally interfering third party as his ally" (100).

Epilogue: Boy Gets Boy? Indeed, "boy" wins the attention

and complicity of his rival-turned-accomplice in his plot, and the complicit listener in turn receives a free entertainment, the "effortless satisfaction of his own libido." Pole three, the listener-voyeur, seems to enjoy the happiest ending of anyone in this narrative of obstructed desire.

But the freeloading listener does not escape unscathed. As we have seen, Freud points out the aggressive nature of the capture of the listener's attention by the device of ideational mimetics (192–93). If the listener gets pleasure from the joke process, it is only because he is taken in, caught unaware by the punch line. Boy must capture boy by an expert delivery, or the joking transaction will fail. Indeed, in a later elaboration on the technique of nonsense humor, Freud points out the pleasure the joker takes in "misleading and annoying his hearer" who "damps down his annoyance" by resolving "to tell the joke himself later on" (139n.) to the next victim in the joking chain. Thus, the joking triangle is always a quadrilateral of sorts, a social chain in which the imaginary capture of both the joke's object (pole two) and its listener (pole three) is perpetuated with a changing cast of players. Even though the joke seems to function as a tool for establishing community (between one and three) and for allowing the ego of the victorious joker to triumph over adversity by circumventing obstacles to satisfaction, the joking process nonetheless turns out to be as double-edged as its punch line. For the joke is a circuit in which no one's identity remains uncontaminated by exposure to the Other's desire. In the case of the joker himself, the joke betrays an incapacity to fulfill the original design, except in imagination (boy never really gets girl, after all), while in the case of the butt of the joke, the process signifies vulnerability to humiliation or exposure. As for the listener, the transaction entails being taken in by the joker's "bribe" and being used to arouse the joker's own pleasure; this listener, moreover, is subsequently compelled to pass this stigma of pleasure along to the next unsuspecting victim in the chain. As Freud insists, "a joke *must* be told to someone else . . .

something *remains over* which seeks, by communicating the idea, to bring the unknown process of constructing a joke to a conclusion" (143).

More love stories

Freud wrote *Jokes* early in his career (1905) but he returned to it again and again (in his own "return to Freud"), both by allusion to the original theory and by a perhaps unconscious repetition of the masterplot in a number of other avatars. Version number two is another shady story of love, aggressivity, and renunciation, even more "classic" than the first.

The subject of Freud's second love story is Oedipus; the desired object, his mother.[4] In the classic myth, of course, boy does indeed get girl, by simply eliminating the paternal rival. The bad joke is thus pulled on the subject by the Father/Fate, who reveals the punch line—"your girl is your mother"—too late to allow Oedipus to avert the tragic short-circuit, the incestuous bond. Significantly, Freud points out the importance of the dramatic device of surprise in this revelation.[5] We might say that the sudden revelation of the mystery, after the subject's prolonged and circuitous voyage toward a veiled truth, functions like a punch line of sorts, depending on something like the "bewilderment and illumination" that produces the impact of the joke. (It also might be considered an instance of "the rediscovery of something familiar"—all too familiar in the case of Jocasta and Oedipus—discussed in the fourth chapter of *Jokes*.) The shock of the revealed truth does, of course, obstruct the "wooing talk," undoing the incestuous bond that should never have been consummated in the first place, and reestablishing paternal legitimacy. Once the incest has been committed, however, it is too late to establish the comic bond (the understanding and complicity between male rivals, poles one and three of the joke), for the happy ending relies on a series of deflections and a play of "almosts."

Freud's own retelling of the Oedipus myth—the postulation of a normal outcome to the oedipal phase in human development—reinstates the happy ending of the joke paradigm:

the subject identifies with the former rival (the father), renounces the impossible love, and chooses a substitute object to ensure the long-circuiting of his desire. ("I want a girl, just *like* the girl, who married dear ole Dad.") Similarly, in the joke scenario, the illumination at joke's end is no longer the exposure of a tragic crime but the unveiling of some other forbidden (but less menacing) "truth." Freud repeatedly asserts that the joke has something forbidden to say; thus, an important function of the jokework is to disguise the joke's point until its timely revelation in the punch line, and even then to soften its punch, by wrapping it in "acceptable form" [*Jokes* 132]). The comic long-circuit is thus a drama of disguise and facade, requiring at least three levels of layering. First, it must veil its own point in order to surprise the listener at joke's end. Second, it must wrap the point in good taste in order not to offend the listener at the (always partial) unveiling. Finally, as the superimposition of the oedipal triangle on the joking process suggests, the joke cloaks the primal urges of love and aggressivity motivating all human creativity (does not Freud himself insist that all tendentious jokes are fundamentally hostile or obscene? [97]). Indeed, Freud's own comic retelling of the Oedipus myth is already a creative textual process, a weaving of motive and action in which the fundamental impulse toward the short-circuit of incest, the death-like quiescence of desire, always remains disguised, perhaps even to the master story teller himself.

Intersubjectivity as Play

To the reader acquainted with Freud's own account of the creation of narrative (in the 1908 essay "Creative Writers and Daydreaming"), all this talk of disguise and facade may seem uncannily familiar. For Freud's own poetics insists on the role of veiling [*Ankleidung*] in the creative process: the writer softens his or her own daydreams—themselves already veiled versions of the same sort of erotic impulses that motivate the joking process—by "changes and disguises" (153). In other words, in order to satisfy a wish, the writer must display an

"object" to a voyeur (the reader), but only after an appropriate veiling has taken place. Like the joker, who says something forbidden in an acceptable way, the writer stages a tasteful striptease, consummating the pleasure process by establishing a bond with the reader. The writing triangle, when superimposed upon the first two, emerges as yet another circuitous retelling of the masterplot of human desire in which the final union is one of social complicity rather than a short-circuit of illicit libido. The joking triangle may be overdetermined as shown in the following diagram:

2
desired female-butt of joke
Jocasta-Mother
Writer's "daydream" object-character

1	3
desiring subject-joker	intruder-accomplice-joke hearer
Oedipus-child	Laius-Father
writer-dreamer	reader

Play it again, Sigmund

It is interesting that both of Freud's major aesthetic treatises—the essay on writers and writing, and the work on jokes—insist on the relation of creative activity to child's play: first, as a source of pleasure entailing the rebellion against logic and propriety, and second, as the initial social process whereby the child gains mastery over reality, replaying unpleasant experience to his own liking. In addition, both essays insist on the importance of repetition in the creative process. Indeed, in *Beyond the Pleasure Principle* (1920),[6] a third work that holds clues to Freud's own poetics, child's play is described in two different scenes as a manifestation of the compulsion to repeat, and each of these scenes may be read as narratives concerning creative processes in general. In order to set the stage for Lacan's "play" of intersubjectivity, I would like to replay both of Freud's scenarios—one an intersubjective, the other an intrasubjective scene—as a kind of rehearsal for

Lacan's entry onto the scene of psychoanalysis.

Freud begins his investigation of the compulsion to repeat with two observations: first, that children take delight in an endlessly repeated story or game, and second, that this sort of repetition sometimes seems to run counter to the "pleasure principle" that equates pleasure with the maximum discharge of energy, especially since the mimetic play of children often reenacts a traumatic event and hence is similar in structure to a recurring nightmare or traumatic neurosis. Freud's essay is an attempt to explain "the remarkable cultural achievement" that allows the child to repeat a painful experience as a game (*BPP* 146).

Thus the prototypical child's play from which Freud suggests joking evolves may itself be considered as a social effect, as a "cultural achievement." If we look, for instance, at the paradigm of child's play in *BPP,* the celebrated *fort-da* game, we are confronted with a doubly social scenario: first, Freud's grandson's play is a creative activity in response to and in compensation for social restrictions (the mother has been taken away, presumably by the father); second, the play is carried out thanks to the dual axis of language (yes-no; here-there; *fort-da*) that marks the child's entry into the social and Symbolic order. Freud emphasizes that the social skill of play originates with the acquisition of language; similarly, in *Jokes,* he stresses the early linguistic origins of joking, which begins as jesting during the period in which a child is learning to handle his mother-tongue" (125). The social skills of play, of joking, and of speech are conascent and interrelated. Lacanians such as Jean-François Lyotard have stressed that the child's entry into language coincides with the birth of a certain non-need-oriented desire ("reality and desire are born together with the entry into language" [*Discours, figure* 125]), a desire of which language is the symptom:

> It is with the entry into language that the + and the − of pleasure [*jouissance*] can be cast upon the axis of reference opened by the designation and by the realization of the fact

> that the mother may be distanced as a visible object. This distance is depth, because what the child feels with the toy is that the object has two faces, one by which it gives itself up [*il se donne*], the other in which it holds itself back forever, and this depth constructed around the toy is the model of that objectivity to which the mother is conformed as well: reality is that which escapes (gets away) [*la réalité est ce qui nous échappe*]. (126)

In other words, what was experienced before the entry into language as a simple pleasurable oscillation is now articulated and experienced as desire, because of the lack upon which language is constructed ("because there is the *fort* and the *da*, the yes and the no, because the initial opposition of absence permits every speaking subject to postulate in and by discourse that which *is not*" [Lyotard 126]). According to this postmodern reading of Freud, then, the gap signaled by language—that "tension which forever separates the interior and the object" (128)—can never be closed. Paradoxically in Lyotard's reading of the play origins of language, as in Freud's reading of the play origins of joking, the compensatory role of these cultural achievements is emphasized: if desire may never be filled, it is also the source of all pleasure, subject to endless reactivation.

For instance, in the first of the two play scenes in Freud's essay, the *fort-da* game, the child compensates for the absence of the real object (the mother) by casting away and retrieving a substitute object, a toy spool at the end of a string, in a kind of yo-yo repetition that he controls absolutely. Lyotard focuses on the linguistic implications of this scene but it is possible to analyze the scene in oedipal terms as well. Like the writer, or the joker, the desiring child is able to come to terms with privation or frustration by means of a creative solution (play) that affords compensation for the satisfaction denied him by the interference of an importune third party (the father who takes the mother away and who thus initiates the child into the social bond, the Law to which all human beings are subject).

Freud observes that such play derives from the mimetic tendency in children who "repeat in their play everything which has made an impression on them in actual life" in response to their "dominant wish" to be "grown up and to be able to do what grown-up people do" (147). The reenactment thus represents what Freud calls a passage from passivity to "the activity of play." Now Freud describes this movement from passivity to activity in a second play scene (148), presenting a second version of the play situation. In this replay, a second child is involved; thus, the social significance of play in this instance is no longer merely implied (with other actors in the wings, as in the *fort-da* game) but explicit: the child repeats an unpleasant experience, a visit to the family doctor, by "playing doctor" with a playmate later on. But in the repeat performance of the traumatic experience, the usually younger or smaller playmate is forced to be the patient, the object of the experiment. The mechanism by which the child moves from a passive to an active role, mastering reality, is thus strikingly similar to that by which the joke's hearer gains vengeance on the teller by repeating the joke to the next "victim" in line (*Jokes* 109). Freud's own repetition of the "boy meets girl" scenario of jokes, then, replayed as "boy meets adversary/doctor," reveals that desire may be experienced not only as an impulse to possession of a libidinal object but also as an impulse to reality-mastery or domination. Frustration of either aspect of desire, the hostile or the erotic, seems to inflict a stigma of sorts, activating a compelling urge to pass the experience along, by sharing (or inflicting) the pleasure/pain. Freud emphasizes the painfulness of the source of play when he refers to the "demonic" nature of the compulsion to repeat.

The "trauma" of the punch line

Freud writes that perhaps the most demonic instance of repetition is found in the traumatic neurosis, in which "the dream life has this peculiarity: it continually takes the patient back to the situation of his disaster, from which he awakes in renewed terror" (*BPP* 145). This particular clinical model would seem to be the antithesis of the pleasurable repetition of the play situation, but in fact the same general explanation applies to both phenomena: both result from a shock for which the psyche is unprepared ("Fright is the name of the condition to which one is reduced if one encounters a danger without being prepared for it; it lays stress on the element of surprise" [144]). The traumatic dream is an attempt to gain control of this initial shock after the fact, for "what conditions fright is the failure of the mechanism to make the proper preparation . . . the dreams are attempts at restoring control by developing apprehension" (156).

Moreover, it is clear that the neurosis described has something in common with the joking process, namely, its insistence on the element of surprise, of being caught off guard. Freud defines the play mode so important to joke production as "an inclination to reduce mental cathexis" (*Jokes* 178); similarly, he suggests in *BPP* that a lowering of the psychic "threshold of tension" is responsible for the onslaught of the traumatic neurosis since it permits the breakthrough of excessive exterior stimuli for which the organism is unprepared. Could not the cheerful mood from which joking springs be seen as such a lowering of the psychic threshold, resulting in an increased vulnerability to the joke's punch line, a willingness of sorts to be caught off guard and to suffer the inflicted pleasure? Such a "wound" can be healed by retelling the joke to the next listener when one masters the situation of which one has originally been the passive dupe. Thus, in this exposure of the painful event upon which every comic victory is grounded we refind the other face of the comic of superiority: laughter is also a sign of passivity and desire. In fact, Freud suggests that in consenting to hear the joke, we cheerfully cooperate in our own downfall, "bribed by the yield of pleasure" (*Jokes* 155) into relaxing our guard. Like the child's playmate in the "play doctor" game, the third party in the joking triangle pays for participation in the fun by a compliant vulnerability to the tricks of the joker. Thus the compulsion to repeat seems to represent the point of convergence between pleasure and pain; it reveals the way in which any reality-mastery is undercut by the irrecoverable loss of which it is the symptom. (Cf. Lyotard: "Reality is that which gets away from us.")

Joking and play as detour

Continuing his discussion of the repetition compulsion, Freud points out a certain compromise between the urge to complete discharge of energy (pleasure) and the need to recharge the organism or to maintain a level of energy in order to protect it from the "excessive inflow of exterior stimuli." In a long digression of some import for his theory of joking as well, Freud speculates about the connection between the repetition compulsion and the workings of instinct in order to account for this oscillation between discharge and maintenance of energy. The key to this connection, Freud maintains, is in the fundamentally conservative nature of instinct defined as "a tendency in living organic matter impelling it towards the reinstatement of an earlier condition" (160). Surprisingly, it turns out that this "earlier condition" toward which all organic matter strives is the ultimate inertia of death: "We can only say 'The goal of all life is death,' and casting back, 'The inanimate was there before the animate'" (160). Freud believes that even the instincts of self-preservation only serve to "allow the organism to die in its own way," lengthening the path to death. This is Freud's own startling punch line: not only is death the final goal of life; it is also the ultimate discharge of energy, hence the ultimate "pleasure" ("the pleasure principle seems directly to subserve the death-instincts" [160]). According to Freud, the pleasurable push toward the void is hampered by the opposing preservative forces (the life-instincts that prolong the path to death). These obstacles to the ultimate pleasure necessitate a detour, a lengthened path to a deferred end: "There is as it were an oscillating rhythm in the life of organisms: the one group of instincts presses forward to reach the final goal of life as quickly as possible, the other flies back at a certain point on the way . . . to prolong the duration of the journey" (162).

Such a discussion of the oscillation set in motion by the interworkings of two sets of drives has a great deal in common with Bataille's concept of erotic faltering [*chavirement*], the urge to "sink without losing footing," inspired by the oscillation between the urge to death and the instinct to maintain life. In such a rhythm, we are also reminded of the pattern of the joking compromise, which reconciles the impulse to pleasure with the impulse to self-preservation, causing the organism to substitute a safe pleasure—the joking long-circuit sanctioned by society—for the impulse toward the dangerous or incestuous pleasure, a kind of antisocial short circuit. Elsewhere, and especially in the earlier essay "Two Principles in Mental Functioning" (1911), Freud has explained this notion of compromise as it applies to the creation of art, which he understands as a kind of long-circuit, the substitutive gratification of a rechanneled desire. He concludes *BPP* with the observation that it is precisely the "faltering rhythm" of human life that accounts for civilization's highest accomplishments (*BPP* 163):

> The restless striving towards further perfection is easily applicable as the result of the repression of instinct upon which that which is most valuable in human culture is built. The repressed instinct never ceases to strive after complete satisfaction which would consist in the repetition of a primary experience of satisfaction.

Thus the process of creation is by definition unfinished, destined to repeat its long-circuit in a ceaseless striving after a primal satisfaction, in a prolonged detour en route to the final satisfaction, the quiescence of death: "Out of the excess of the satisfaction demanded over that found is born the driving momentum which allows of no abiding in any situation presented to it, but in the poet's words, 'urges forward, ever unsubdued'" (163). In other words, the creative process, like Bataille's erotic act, is a function of maintained obstacle. As Freud puts it, "The path in the other direction, back to complete satisfaction, is a rule barred by the resistances that maintain the repressions, and thus there remains nothing for it but to proceed in the other still unobstructed direction, that of development, *without, however, any prospect of being able to bring the process to a conclusion or attain the goal*" (163, my emphasis). Since the goal of this creative urge is an *irrecoverable* or unattainable satisfaction (death, quiescence, incest), the creative process may be considered an aesthetic one, according to Freud's own understanding of the aesthetic as a substitute (or excessive) satisfaction, divorced from specific ends, needs, or biological goals (for Freud, of course, the ultimate biological goal, the goal of all life, is death). Societal achievement could be considered a vast intersubjective joke, motivated by the destructive undercurrent of the death-drive but always covering up this impulse with the veil/obstacle of aesthetic form and deriving pleasure from this disguise.

Enter Lacan, who hears this joke of human intersubjectivity from Freud; captivated in his turn, he resolves to retell it with his own inflection, playing on the Imaginary nature of all happy endings.

Intersubjective Play as Text

> This is precisely where the Oedipus complex may be said to mark the limits that our discipline assigns to subjectivity. . . . The primordial Law is revealed clearly enough as identical to the order of language.
>
> Lacan, *Ecrits* I (156)

In his translation and study of Lacan's "The Function of Language in Psychoanalysis,"[7] Anthony Wilden emphasizes two vectors of Lacan's Imaginary order (155–77) as that enthrallment with a fellow being first manifest in the mirror stage of human development: the vector of aggressivity or capture, aiming at the incorporation of the image of the other, and the vector of identification with the other as a fellow being, an alter ego (166–68). The Lacanian theorists Jean Laplanche and J.-B. Pontalis have pointed out (in *Le vocabulaire de la psychanalyse,* 1967) that Lacan also uses the term *Imaginary* to designate a type of understanding or logic essentially predisposed to delusion and in which resemblance and identification play a major role, enabling the subject to maintain certain illusions about self-identity or image. (Lacan, of course, concedes that some such "delusions" are necessary to mental health).

According to Freud's explanation of the joking process as a kind of defense mechanism against the obstacles to desire posed by reality, the joking reaction would seem to qualify as a pattern of Imaginary behavior that functions in support of the subject's self-image. For as we have seen, the mirage of the joker's identity as victor in the joke transaction is a Lacanian misrecognition of sorts, supported by mechanisms of mimetic capture and identification. Similarly, Freud's view of the writer's activity seems to suggest that the creation of a literary text is a related Imaginary transaction since it depends both on the writers' identification with an object (the hero of the narrative) and the reader's identification with the writer's desire, "misrecognized" as that of the novel's protagonist, thanks to the technique of veiling.

Of course, Lacan's insistence on the illusory nature of all Imaginary triumphs suggests that the transparency of Freud's masterplot masks a more complicated story. For it is equally possible to argue that the joking process functions in the Symbolic register, both because of its oedipal subplot, emphasizing the third term, and because of its reliance on the Symbolic order of language to effect a resolution of the oedipal rivalry.[8] One could argue that the Symbolic register, identified by Lacan with paternal Law, designates the domination of the pleasure principle by the reality principle:[9] the human subject's encounter with real obstacles, ensured by the very existence of the oedipal third term, initiates all creative response. This is the punch line of Freud's master anecdote, as retold by Lacan (and relaying, as the old joke says, "some good news and some bad news"): the Symbolic reign of Law both deprives and enables, frustrating the subject's desire and offering the possibility of creative recompense.

"The unconscious is structured like a language"

Lacan's purloined punch line, then, concerns the inevitability of the encounter of every human subject with the excessive circuit of desire and declares the primacy of the Symbolic order in this intersubjective system. Jeffrey Mehlman has defined Lacan's intersubjective linguistic unconscious as "a third domain, neither self nor other, but the system of communicative relations by which both are necessarily constituted and in which they are alienated."[10] In other words, if the "unconscious is structured like a language," to cite Lacan's celebrated formula, it is because the unconscious, as the locus of intersubjective involvement, is the very condition of language. And once again, we may look to Freud's "transparent" text of joking for an "evident" clue to understanding Lacan. For the main point of *Jokes* is that the jokework (condensation and displacement) is grounded in primary process. The paradigm of desiring intersubjectivity is written in the very language of the unconscious itself.

For Lacan, condensation and displacement are associated with metaphor and metonymy, the fundamental figural modes of language. Borrowing from Roman Jakobson, Lacan defines these functions as the two intersecting axes of language:metaphor corresponds to the vertical axis of selection (the paradigmatic axis in Jakobson's system) while metonymy corresponds to the horizontal axis of combination (Jakobson's syntagmatic axis).[11] Metaphor, moreover, as the substitution of one word for another, is associated in Lacan's system with the process of repression, which excludes the original terms from the spoken or conscious discourse; metonymy, as the linking of one word to another, is associated with the excessive chain of desire that acts like the motor of language, driving the signifying chain forward into meaningful combinations.[12] Thus, for Lacan, the metaphoric and metonymic structures are themselves metaphors for intersubjectivity: the trope of metaphor represents the function of repression which creates the split between the conscious and the unconscious; the trope of metonymy represents the social community of interrelated human subjects. Or it might be more precise to say that both figures function as synecdoches for the system of language to which they belong, for in Lacan's theory, metaphor and metonymy seem to function as parts representing the whole, moments in language that reenact the working of the whole system as a desiring circuit of interrelated subjects.

The art of procrastination

In a fascinating essay on *Beyond the Pleasure Principle* ("Freud's Masterplot," 1977)[13] Peter Brooks has described the interworkings of metaphor and metonymy as the motor of plot (again, in Brook's reading, these two tropes might be considered postmodern allegories of desire, which both represent and enact the desiring game of writing). Brooks argues that an oscillation between a kind of horizontal drive toward the ending of the story and a vertical blockage achieved by all the repetitions or doubling back in the text provides a kind of "grammar of plot, where repetition, taking us back again over the same ground, could have to do with the choice of ends" (286). In other words, the rhythm of narrative plot is a comic rhythm, a movement of starts and stops that defers the final Imaginary solution. When one views the narrative process through the transparent theory of the joking process—as a play of blockage (metaphor) and forward movement (metonymy)—one perceives that the work of fiction, like the living subject who creates it, is motivated by energies that must be bound or contained by metaphoric repetition so that the narrative (to borrow a phrase from *BPP*) may "die in its own way."

In his article "Desire and the Interpretation of Desire in *Hamlet*" (1977),[14] Lacan describes the circuitous plot of Shakespeare's tale in similar terms, emphasizing the role of the hero as a procrastinator, an idler who is forced to feign madness "in order to follow the winding paths that lead him to the completion of his act" (13). In this story of detours and deliberately missed opportunities, Hamlet's desire seems to be engendered by a privation: the absence of the slain father. Lacan points out that the plot is prolonged by a series of missed appointments (41–44) emblematic of the failure of the desiring subject to attain his goal or to possess the object of his desire. But what exactly is Hamlet's objective? If one reads the play in terms of Freud's master scenario (the oedipal-joking-writing triangular circuit), it becomes clear that the missing and desired object is not the dead father but the guilty mother (and her alter ego Ophelia, the sister-figure tainted by Hamlet's desire). The missed appointment to which Lacan refers, then, could be read as Hamlet's failure to consummate the incestuous union, that infantile short-circuit that is also the original temptation in the joking circuit. The forbidden incest, furthermore, may itself be read as a metaphoric stand-in, veiling the final satisfaction of death (return to the womb = return to the tomb). One might say that the missed appointment functions as a kind of comic obstacle, allowing the play to go on in a prolonged detour from its tragic conclusion.

Yet Hamlet's procrastination has its own double meaning; if it is an avoidance of the incestuous Imaginary outcome, the short-circuit of desire, it is at the same time an avoidance of compliance with the Symbolic Law. In other words, Hamlet's postponement is a hesitation between complicity with the maternal incest (Gertrude's marriage with her brother-in-law, which as guilty onlooker, the son enjoys vicariously) and compliance with the paternal demand for vengeance. Of course, just as in the case of Oedipus, it is already too late for Hamlet to establish a comic bond with the interfering third party; the father who could save him is dead, and Hamlet is in effect a co-conspirator in the crime of incest because of his silence. The choice for Hamlet, then, is not "to be or not to be," but how long to prolong being, whether to opt for the pleasure-death of incest or the punishment-death to which he is sentenced by the Father's Law, whether to go to death by the long or the short route. Hamlet's final act, of course, is a sacrifice to the Symbolic, a coming to terms with the Law. The play ends in that fatal duel scene wherein Hamlet "demands satisfaction" and finds it, in death. When the comic possibility is finally relinquished, so is the fiction itself: the play comes to its timely end after its dalliance with impossible comic detours. From Lacan's reading of *Hamlet,* we may perceive that the destiny of plot parallels and repeats that of the human subject, caught in a text of sexual and linguistic intersubjectivity. Narrative plot thus replays the human comedy itself: in a perverse gesture of deflection from goal, each of us plays a comic role of dalliance en route to the final scene of the play in which we are cast.

Text as (Feminine) Symptom

> For this sign is indeed that of the woman.
>
> Lacan, *Seminar on The Purloined Letter*

Narrative as pervasion

In Freud's *Three Essays on the Theory of Sexuality* (1905), a clear distinction is drawn between two types of sexual aberration. Writing that perversion is the negative of neurosis, Freud insists that any perversion—including the specific perversion of fetishism, which denies the observed "castration" of the desired female object—both displaces and satisfies sexual desire with an object substituted for the original unattainable one. In neurosis, on the other hand, the desire is not displaced but is repressed into the unconscious, leaving the neurotic symptom to signify what it has replaced. Transcoding Freud's theory into linguistic terms, Lacan has maintained that the neurotic symptom is metaphoric in nature because it replaces the original repressed sexual meaning with a nonsexual term. (Both hysteria—the result of repressed desire—and obsession—the result of unsatisfied, impossible desire—are thus metaphoric functions for Lacan.)[15] In the essay on *Hamlet,* moreover, Lacan differentiates between the metaphoric neurosis and the metonymic perversion in terms of the status of the subject in the symptomatic behavior: whereas the subject experiences a gratification of sorts in the perverse solution to desire, in the neurotic or hysteric solution the speaking subject is barred or silenced, repressed into the unconscious chain. (This is perhaps another way of framing Freud's assertion that the hysteric is not capable of recounting her own history without the intervention of the analyst.) We have seen that, in addition to defining perversion as the negative of neurosis, Freud considers perversion to be a derailment of sorts, a sidetracking by which desire is deflected from its original biological aim. Similarly, Lacan refers to metonymy as a "derailing of instinct," insisting on the fetishistic nature of the metonymic displacement, in which instinct is "eternally extended towards the desire of something else" (*Ecrits* I 277–78). In any case, Lacan's reading of Freud emphasizes that metaphor and metonymy are both symptoms of obstructed or diverted desire.

Postmodern readers such as Brooks and Mehlman have not failed to point out the implications in Freud's companion definitions of the perverse and aesthetic; indeed, by Freud's own logic, as I have argued in chapter 3, aesthetic activities may be associated with the perverse since such activities entail a derailment of instinct from "vital needs." Yet, a Lacanian reading of aesthetic processes as both perverse and excessive need not imply a divorce from real life—as does, for instance, the Kantian view of a "purposeless" aesthetic as the inspiration of "pure" disinterested art—since for Lacan the literary work must be understood as a function of the subject's involvement in a social web of Others.

Now insofar as metaphoric repression results from an encounter with the restraining and censoring agent of Law, it might be associated with the Symbolic register. Metonymy, on the other hand, might be linked with the Imaginary register, both because it seems to offer a satisfactory ending with a substitute object (happy endings are always suspect for Lacan) and because it is associated with a denial or misrecognition of the obstacles or privations to which the human subject is exposed (as in the denial of castration by the fetishist, for example). The interworking of these two registers—in the joking process as in the literary text—stands as evidence that the

Imaginary and the Symbolic modes are not successive stages of human development so much as coextensive principles of intersubjective experience.

Depending upon which register is perceived as the dominant one in aesthetics, as several postmodern theorists have argued,[16] the literary process may be viewed either as an Imaginary exercise of identification with a poet of superior vision (the artist as seer or Legislator of Mankind) or as an intersubjective (Symbolic) circuit that traps both author and reader in an ongoing "endgame," with no advantage granted to either of the players. In the second perspective, the Imaginary confidence in the literary process as a cure for desire is revealed as illusory, for the text is read as a symptom of the inexhaustibility of the desire that generates it.

The gender of symptom

> A man man enough to defy to the point of scorn a lady's fearsome ire undergoes the curse of the sign he had dispossessed her of.
>
> Lacan, *Seminar on The Purloined Letter*

If Lacan himself may be considered to have written a "transparent" text—containing an "evident" clue concerning the intersubjective nature of the textual process—it is doubtless the *Seminar on the Purloined Letter,* which comments on desire as a metonymic process, a transmissible symptom in a social chain. In the *SPL,* the desire of each of the players results not merely from privation, the absence of the purloined letter; it also results from contact with other desiring agents, and as such, functions as a social contagion of sorts. Even to enter the game is to function as an object oneself, in a curious kind of relay where the letter is passed from hand to hand. In a dazzling display of wit, Lacan describes this game as a play of a group of ostriches [*autricherie*], each of whom imagines himself secure, head in the sand, even as he is plucked bare from behind. This circuit of desire obeys the inexorable logic of farce, which we might sum up in the pithy (and somewhat untranslatable) *à trompeur, trompeur et demi.* For in this game of rogues and dupes, each Dupin is duped in turn; each rogue is assured of his comeuppance at the hands of a more clever scoundrel, "a rogue and a half."

The notion of the gender of the symptom of desire is central to Lacan's farcical "return to Freud." For Lacan as for Freud, femininity seems to be a stigma (of castration? or passivity?), a symptom signifying a vulnerability or privation that may be transmitted from player to player. Throughout Freud's work, the question of the relation between symptom and gender—a question underlying not only the "boy meets girl" formulation of the joking scenario, but also the classification of such disorders as paranoia as male and hysteria as female—is complicated by Freud's own hesitation between two views of sexuality. In some of his works, Freud seems to argue for a natural and gender-specific sexuality, as in his early formulation of symmetrical oedipal phases for boys and girls, with each sex attracted to the opposite sex. At other moments (especially in the *Three Essays*), he seems to assume a natural bisexuality whereby both sexes, as possessors of a "male" libido, are initially attracted to the maternal love object. In this view, femininity would be an acquired trait that the girl child assumes reluctantly, after the discovery of her anatomical "deficiency." In any case, Freud consistently associates the male gender with an active, armed state, and female gender with a passive, disarmed (and disarming) condition.

The notion of femininity as transmissible stigma and the corollary notion of the feminizing effect of entry into the desiring circuit are both crucial considerations for the expanding chain of discussions on Poe's celebrated story (Barbara Johnson on Derrida on Lacan on Poe).[17] The gender-related facts of the case appear "evident" (perhaps too evident?): the original victim in the circuit (the Queen) is archetypically helpless and female, and she is clearly violated by the theft of the incriminating letter. Like pole two in the joke circuit, her (guilty) sexuality is exposed to (and by) the Minister's male gaze. But once again, the evidence may be misleading; even this initial act of violation, apparently perpetrated by male on female, is marked by ambiguity of gender, owing to the phallic nature of the letter that the Queen-as-Ruler initially possesses. (Derrida, of course, has overlooked the question of the ambiguity of gender in Lacan's account, arguing that Lacan's entire reading is phallocentric; indeed, Derrida agrees with Marie Bonaparte that the purloined letter signifies the clitoris rather than the phallus, based on its anatomical position in the Minister's room.) In Lacan's reading, the "phallic" Queen seems to begin in the male position of power/possession and is only subsequently feminized as a result of the castrating act of the Minister. And as the plot thickens, so does the ambiguity: the male ravisher, now holding the phallic sign of power, has moved to an exposed position where he is vulnerable to attack by the next "duper," Dupin. This explains Lacan's characterization of the letter as a curse, a kind of "hot potato" destined to be passed on, and which inevitably causes its holder to get burned, as the next object of the next trick. In this curious game of tag, the player is never so feminine as when it is "his" turn to be "it," when she/he is *possessed* of the phallic object (and not when "she" is castrated or deprived of the phallus, as psychoanalytic convention would have it). Thus, the curious message of the purloined letter is that femininity seems to be a position or locus: anyone may be on the spot, the butt of the joke. (Indeed, we have seen that in the joking paradigm one is feminine if "she" has something the other wants—attention, love, maternal breast—and thus the feminine "object" is the holder of a certain ambiguous power over the desiring subject.) The ambiguity of the on-the-spot position of the letter's holder may be described as follows: one is stigmatized and objectified by the very power that defines her/him as agent. (The person who is "it" after all is galvanized to action by this stigma.) This is the paradoxical gist of farcical logic: *à trompeur, trompeur et demi.*

The logic of farce also seems to inform the Lacanian concept of desire as excess (the surplus of demand over need), since Lacan insists that the purloined letter is not only stolen but *prolonged* in its excessive journey. In Lacan's reading, the purloined letter is above all else a chain letter whose accruing returns are assured (*à trompeur, trompeur et demi*), and which thus provides a punch line of sorts to the archetypical non-sense joke: why does the chicken cross the road if not to come home to roost?

Literary trickery

Thus Lacan's retelling of Freud's masterplot clears up several points in the too transparent, too evident "boy meets girl" scenario. In Lacan's version, it becomes obvious that the supposedly distinct and gender-identified roles of the joking triangle are not only often interchangeable but are actually coincidental or superimposed: each player is active *and* passive, desiring *and* desired, giver *and* receiver, not only successively but simultaneously. Since one receives the punch line (like the purloined letter) only in order to give it away, the notions of active and passive lose their specificity as do the corollary notions of male and female gender.

Lacan's retelling of this masterplot also clearly reveals the fetishistic nature of the desiring circuit. In Lacan's narrative, each successive theft is concealed by the replacement of the missing object by something similar which veils its absence, a simulacrum of the original letter. The sleight of hand is all important: the ravisher must put something in the place of the stolen letter so that the victim will remain unaware of the trick, for a time at least. In this case, the feminine position (of dupe) is that of a fetishist whose attention is fixed on a substitute for the missing object of desire.[18] In this way, Poe's theft reproduces the technique of the joking exchange, which also depends on a sleight of hand, a displacement of the listener's attention until the unveiling of the punch line. Of course, in this entertainment the listener is a wiling victim, who, lured by the promise of pleasure without effort, a cheap thrill, voluntarily lends attention to the joker-trickster.

Similarly, the literary text pacifies its reader-receiver by a bribe of pleasure, enlisting the readers' cooperation in a pleasure circuit that would otherwise remain incomplete. But just as in the joking transaction, which depends on the art of the joker's technique or delivery to produce its effect, the textual transaction depends on the writer's art and thus places the artist on the spot: if the art fails, if we fail to enjoy the text (like a joke fallen flat), the writers' very identity as a poet-craftsperson is shattered. In fact, the artist's image is always constituted as part of an Imaginary bargain—Coleridge's "willing suspension of disbelief"—entailing the reader's acceptance of a code different from the code governing everyday communication. The completed pleasure circuit of the text relies on a tenuous agreement to grant the writer a certain power of enchantment and to accept what Freud calls the "bribe of forepleasure" that veils and softens the egotistical nature of the writer's fantasy. The textual exchange, like the joking exchange, is a power play for both reader and writer, but it paradoxically entails the vulnerability of both parties.

As an Imaginary satisfaction enabled by the Symbolic Law (the "truth" of the desire that the substitute satisfaction veils), the joking/literary transaction is in a sense the negative of the analytic transaction, which unveils the truth of desire. Of course, the analysis is yet another triangular drama, although the analyst plays two of the three roles (object *and* witness, like the woman in Bataille's erotic transgression). But in this particular triangle, the analyst must refuse the bribe of pleasure, adopting a posture of skepticism vis-à-vis the subject's discourse (the willing suspension of *belief*), in order to break the Imaginary bond between subject and object (the transference). If the analyst fails to refuse to get involved (and is thus implicated in the countertransference), the result of the therapy will be prejudiced, as is evinced, for instance, by Freud's celebrated failure with Dora.[19] (This, in turn, recalls Freud's assertion that if the hearer becomes emotionally involved with the butt of a joke, the sympathetic reaction will jeopardize the joke's humorous impact.)

What each of these instances of the desiring circuit finally underscores is that the Imaginary and the Symbolic are not distinct developmental phases in human life but are interacting registers of a continuing intersubjective drama. Indeed, the joking paradigm demonstrates how an interplay of recognition and misrecognition, bewilderment and illumination, passivity and activity establishes the essential plot or rhythm of all creative endeavor. This recognition of the interworking of the Imaginary and the Symbolic is accentuated in many postmodern texts, which—rather than insisting on writing as a triumph of activity, a masculine display of mastery—opt to emphasize the desire that motivates the textplay. This is perhaps the sense of the poststructuralist emphasis on *écriture féminine* and on *écriture* as *féminine*: the "stigma" of femininity as symptom becomes an apt metaphor for the writer's own situation in desire.

Femininity as Subjectivity: (But Can "She" Write?)

> And what does this experience, precisely, teach us about the phallus, if not that it makes a joke of phallicism?
>
> Moustafa Safouan, "Feminine Sexuality in Psychoanalytic Doctrine" (*Feminine Sexuality*, 134)

Our circular itinerary has visited several questions—the comic nature of intersubjectivity, intersubjectivity as text, text as play of metaphoric and metonymic symptom, symptom as femininity—and has arrived at a puzzling punch line. In Lacan's version of Freud's transparent master narrative, the closing line seems to read (comically) neither *Boy Gets Girl* nor even *Boy Gets Boy* but *Boy* Is *Girl*. For Lacan, the role of second—the objective locus in the master paradigm—is a role we all play in turn.

But if Lacan's lesson for the subject (pole one, the joker/writer)is that he too may be "female," it still remains unclear whether the obverse is also true: can "she" assume subjectivity? Can the shifter "I" shift genders?[20] Can "she" become the agent of desire, the active pole, the joker? What happens if "she" refuses to mediate the (male) comic bond? In terms of Freud's original scenario, what happens if "she," however offended by the male conspirators, refuses to leave the room, feeling ashamed? In other words, what does woman want?

The question first posed by Freud reverberates throughout Lacan's work and leads inevitably to a second query: What is Woman? Can "she" want anything at all? Indeed, in his later work, Lacan not only speculates about the femininity of metaphoric symptom (as veiling or masquerade) and of metonymic desire (as a perverse circuit that castrates its participants), but he also comes to posit Woman herself as symptom of the male system, at least insofar as Woman is idealized concept or myth ("Woman does not exist"). As Jacqueline Rose and Juliet Mitchell have pointed out in their introductory notes to Lacan's essay (*Feminine Sexuality,* 1982), there has been a lively debate as to whether Lacan's position maybe considered a feminist critique of the structures of patriarchy, refuting an Imaginary notion of Woman, or merely the latest patriarchal strategy for relegating femininity to the idealist and absolute category of Otherness, in which Woman is destined to function as predicate to the male subject.

While Lacan appears to espouse the Freudian notion of bisexuality, as opposed to the notion of pregiven gender, he nonetheless insists on defining femininity as a linguistically determined locus (Rose: "Woman is excluded by the nature of words, meaning that the definition poses her as exclusion. . . . Within the phallic definition, the woman is constituted as 'not all' insofar as the phallic function rests on an exception—the 'not'—which is assigned to her" [*FS* 49]). Thus, Lacan insists on assigning woman to the role of the excluded term, even while he stipulates that this exclusion is linguistically rather than biologically determined. Indeed, Lacan's exile of the feminine subject from language is reminiscent of Freud's theory of the feminine hysteric as a blocked speaker whose symptoms include lying (the misuse of language) and pantomime (the nonuse of language). Freud refers to the hysteric's discourse as "an unnavigable river whose stream is choked by masses of rock" and thus suggests that it is the analyst's function to steer a course through the shoals of "her" obstructed discourse.[21]

Thus Lacan is again following Freud's lead by insisting on woman's position as object, or even as absence, in the linguistic system. Even though he suggests that this position is not biologically inherent but is conferred by language ("woman is not inferior, she is subjugated" [*FS* 45]), Lacan nonetheless stresses the insoluble character of the feminine linguistic dilemma. (As Jacqueline Rose puts it, "All speaking beings must line themselves up on one side or other of this division of gender, but anyone can cross over and inscribe themselves on the opposite side from that to which they are anatomically destined" [*FS* 49]). One could argue that by placing the phallus at the center of the signifying system, Lacan has assured the predicative status of woman and has also effectively canceled the possibility of finding an answer to the question that persists throughout his later work ("what does woman want?"). As long as woman cannot speak, as long as she is excluded from the subjective roles in the desiring triangle (poles one and three, joker and future joker), she is limited to her role as "wanted woman," the object in the hunt for the feminine subject.

Other voices

Feminist theorists have not failed to point out the ideological problems inherent in Lacan's definition of femininity as acquired (or required) linguistic trait, persisting in their critique of Lacan's phallocentrism by pointing out the hidden agenda that informs the grounding of libido (or speech itself) in the male gender and the male anatomy. Luce Irigaray, for example, argues that the metaphorization of female sexuality (by which the clitoris is represented as an inferior penis) represses the feminine term in its specificity, designating it as a deficient copy of the male term.

Similarly, Gayatri Spivak has emphasized the ideological function of this repression of feminine sexuality, pointing out that the threatening aspect of this sexuality—the scandal that must be repressed—is the biological fact that woman's pleasure is excessive, insofar as it functions "perversely" in its independence from the reproductive process.[22] In the same volume of essays, Naomi Schor raises the related issue of the gender of theory. (For Freud, of course, the paranoid-theorist is a male; the female paranoid is an aberration.)[23] Schor points out that female theorizing seems to be grounded in the body, even in Freud's account, and that this is the source of its "feminine" specificity. This argument in turn is reminiscent of Julia Kristeva's characterization of feminine writing as a kind of *jouissance,* a pleasure grounded in the heterogeneity of a preoedipal semiotic mode.[24] But as Naomi Schor herself argues, any such emphasis on the grounding of theory in the female body is in fact "a risky enterprise" (215) since a valorization of the essential and biologically unique aspects of femininity may reinforce the assumption that anatomy is destiny.

Lacanian theory represents the antithesis of this essentialist view because it maintains that gender is a linguistic rather than a biological category. Furthermore, the notion of subjectivity itself is problematized by Lacan, with profound consequences for his theory of feminine sexuality. In her introduction to the essays in *Feminine Sexuality,* Jacqueline Rose sums up Lacan's rebuttal to feminist objections concerning the androcentrism of psychoanalytic theory (*FS* 29):

> He [argues] that failure to recognise the interdependency of these two concerns in Freud's work—the theory of subjectivity and femininity together—has led psychoanalysts into an ideologically loaded mistake, that is, an attempt to resolve the difficulties of Freud's account of femininity by aiming to resolve the difficulty of femininity itself. For by restoring the woman to her place and identity (which, they argue, Freud out of "prejudice" failed to see), they have missed Freud's corresponding stress on the division and precariousness of human subjectivity itself. . . . For Lacan the unconscious undermines the subject from any position of certainty and simultaneously reveals the fictional nature of the sexual category to which every human subject is nonetheless assigned.

In other words, Lacanian theory exposes the privilege of the (male) primary signifier as an Imaginary construct: the phallus is precisely what no one "himself" ever has. Yet the effect of this theory, as we have seen, is to lead woman back to her place (Rose: "[If woman] takes up her place according to the process described, then her sexuality will betray, necessarily, the impasses of its history" [*FS* 43]). Thus if she agrees to exist at all, in Lacan's system of signifiers, woman must take up her impossible place on the Other side of the divide.

There are of course many other feminist theorists—among them Kristeva, Schor, Spivak, Gallop, Jardine—who have taken a position somewhere between the extremes of an essentialist biological view of feminine sexuality and the linguistic view espoused by Lacan, which threatens to do away with woman altogether. These theorists generally posit an essential difference between male and female sexuality/subjectivity, and they tend to concur that this difference is grounded in the body rather than in a purely linguistic or symbolic determination. For Schor, however, a theory of feminine subjectivity must reevaluate the givens of linguistic theory. Schor proposes supplementing the Lacanian theory on metaphor and metonymy—which she sees as reflections of a masculinist perspective on sexuality and subjectivity—with a theory of synecdoche as a uniquely feminine trope. Gayatri Spivak and Alice Jardine (*Gynesis,* 1985) both insist that the search for an authentic feminine subjectivity must be grounded in the Real (Lacan's term for the third register of human experience), that is, in a critique of the assumptions and attitudes of patriarchy. Their work attempts to retain the radical thrust of Lacan's reevaluation of subjectivity without reentering that impasse by which woman becomes merely an empty locus, a place holder (the Other) or a sociolinguistic construct.

"Return to Freud"

It is somewhat ironic that Lacan's later work, which continually poses the question of the nature of femininity, seems to have lost sight of that important clue to the enigma hidden in Freud's "transparent" work on jokes. Before describing the "boy meets girl" scenario enacting the fundamental narrative of human desire, Freud makes a few seemingly marginal, and deceptively obvious, remarks about the nature of sexuality in general:

> A desire to see the organs peculiar to each sex exposed is one of the original components of our libido. . . . The libido for looking and touching is present in everyone in two forms, active and passive, male and female; and, according to the preponderance of the sexual character, one form or the other predominates. (*Jokes* 98)

This characterization of sexuality clearly manifests the bias that persists throughout Freud's work: the identification of active with male and passive with female. But Freud's own joking scenario reveals that the terms *active* and *passive* are ambiguous at best and are coextensive with all three loci of the joking triangle. In this "pre-text" to the joking discussion, Freud emphasizes the common nature of all human sexual experience, be it male or female: all sexuality is first manifest as an active voyeurism or its corollary exhibitionism. Freud suggests that the differences may be culturally determined, maintaining that the female's urge to exhibitionism is "buried under the imposing reactive function of sexual modesty" (98). The final sentence of this passage further reinforces the emphasis on cultural variables as determinants of female sexuality: "I need only hint at the elasticity and variability in the amount of exhibitionism which women are permitted to retain in accordance with differing convention and circumstances" (98). Convention permitting, women would seem as likely as men to engage in active exhibitionism, the primal expression of libido.

The essential point of Freud's allusion to the communality of human sexual experience seems to be that it is entirely possible to regard the masculine and the feminine as different sexualities without entering into the Lacanian impasse, using that perception of difference to authorize an exclusion of either gender from the creative role of subject. It would seem, ironically, that Freud's own most "transparent" formulation of the origins of human sexuality is ultimately more compatible with a feminist view—of the specificity but not the essentiality of femininity—than is that of Lacan. Freud at least seems to imply, perhaps unwittingly, that even if the female experience of subjectivity is not identical to the male experience, owing to sexual difference, there is nevertheless enough common ground on the subjective side of the linguistic divide to accommodate male and female subjects alike. This is perhaps the most important lesson to be gleaned from the "evident" clues in the joking paradigm (with the help of Freud's "Minister" Lacan): if man and woman do exist on opposite sides of a linguistic divide, neither side necessarily initiates the creative activity by which we may attempt to scale the wall.

Lacan has placed a telling epigraph at the head of the third section of "The Function of Language in Psychoanalysis," the same essay in which he alludes to Freud's work on jokes:

> Between man and love,
>   There is woman.
> Between man and woman,
>   There is a world.
> Between man and the world,
>   There is a Wall.
>
> Antoine Tudal, in *Paris in the Year 2000* (*Ecrits* I 170)

Like the aphorism that describes the farcical circuit of the joking paradigm as well as the intersubjective workings of the literary text (*à trompeur, trompeur et demi*), Lacan's cryptic epigraph contains some good news and some bad news concerning what the postmodernists might call the "undecidability" of gender. For if the Wall of desire as emblem of Law is an unavoidable part of our intersubjective experience, Lacan's "return to Freud" suggests the graffiti that will inevitably appear on the Wall may be read as a comic response to the Symbolic barrier, comic texts that play at "unworking" the phallocentric foundations of the Law. And as the work of feminist writers and theorists attest, "she" writes on the Wall as well.

Postscript: woman as post-Man

Lacan's *Seminar on The Purloined Letter* ends with the famous statement that a letter "always arrives at its destination," however long en route (*en souffrance*). Our roundabout route, rerouted via Lacan, has followed Freud's narrative allegory, also an allegory of narrative, to its destination (which is not to be confused with its end, since every letter solicits a response). And this destination is the *de-monstration* (in Derrida's sense of the term) of the Freudian joke as both fetish object and symptom, a roundabout response to the human Law that impedes the short-circuit of desire (in incest or narcissism or death). This circuit socializes us en route, enabling us to exchange stories, to talk to one another, to interact on the intersubjective scene. Moreover, in Lacan's purloined play the gender roles as cast in Freud's original scenario are no longer a matter of anatomy but of position; each of the letter's holders is feminized in turn, assuming in turn that place that is paradoxically the most vulnerable position and the position of greatest transmissible desire: in Lacan's comic text, woman is the allegorical post-man of desire.

Thus, it might be argued that long before the idea of postmodernism became common currency, Freud (and Lacan) were using "postmodern allegory" (in Ulmer's sense of the term) to mimic and demonstrate the workings of the human psyche as intersubjective scene. Indeed, the allegorical figure of the letter, which I have lifted from Lacan and which Lacan purloined from Poe and from Freud, was already a favorite fetish object in psychoanalysis, a "structural machine" whose circulation and reading de-monstrate the workings of the Symbolic as comic interchange. Like all postmodern allegories—which depend on citation, intertextuality, and a differential rather than authoritative frame of reference—Freud's stories refer rather than simply illustrate, and they demonstrate rather than simply legitimate: they participate in the play they activate.

But I have tried to suggest that Freud's master narrative is more than a postmodern allegory; it is also perhaps an allegory of postmodernism, or at least of a certain "postmodernism of resistance." Insofar as Freud's story of joke as fetish object occasioning a replay of the scene of deflected desire also works as an allegorization of the process of perversion itself, this story embodies and reenacts the major characteristics of the postmodern (discussed in chapter 2): (1) as problematization of the activity of reference (joking language undercuts that to which it refers; the joke depends on the equivocal nature of language as "sliding" signifier); (2) as ludic activity (a parodic process undercutting the seriousness of source, and the legitimacy of reference; and as process obeying the law of farce); (3) as polysemantic interchangeability, including the exchangeability of gender roles (each actor in the joking process is successively empowered and "castrated" or "violated" as part of the transaction); (4) as crisis of legitimation or origin (Who initiates the joking exchange? How may one determine the winner and loser in this bizarre power play where every dupe gets his/her due of dupery? Where does it end, since the joke must be retold?).

Reading Freud as an allegorist may then help de-monstrate the nature of a certain postmodern understanding of textuality. But more significantly, this allegorical transcoding of Freud, Lacan, Oedipus, Poe (and a cast of thousands) suggests how postmodernism may escape or exceed the tragic self-defeatism of thinkers such as Jean Baudrillard, who read postmodernism as the death of the social and an end to the possibility of meaningful intersubjective action. Through Freud and Lacan the postmodern social text may be read instead as a comic allegory of human desire initiating a process of circulation and exchange, whereby all space, even the interior space of the psyche, may be considered public space, a scene of agonistic intersubjective interaction. The agony rather than the ecstasy of communication, is a comic reading of the postmodern scene. This reading may help mobilize a certain psychoanalysis in the service of the postmodernism of resistance envisioned by Foster, Ulmer, Owens, Lyotard, the Lacanian feminists cited here, and others. For Lacan's intersubjective scene is the opposite of implosion since it entails a social understanding of the subject (after all even mass communication, however impersonal, is still a function of language, and hence remains intersubjective). In this light, the fetish does not signify paralyzation or denial, but functions as a model of all human exchange, enabled by desire and refusing the short circuit of "ecstatic," immediate "communication" (à la Baudrillard).

Joking pleasure, then, is not "the bliss of the averted gaze"—to use a phrase from Barthes's profoundly asocial *The Pleasure of the Text*—but is rather a celebration of text as interweaving, as circulated letter. With Freud as postman, posting the modern entails indicating the return address, assuring that the communication may be returned to sender, that all chickens coming home to roost are carrier pigeons. Better yet, Freud's message—rerouted by Lacan—allows us to participate in a chain letter with an ever-expanding circle of reference.

In the next section of this study, we turn from psychoanalysis to another kind of postmodern text, produced by what has been termed *poststructuralism,* which may be read as a related collection of comic strategies for delivering the message of desire, thereby disturbing and disseminating traditional notions of text.

PART THREE

Poststructuralism

Comic Text as Theory

5. Outwitting the Dialectic: Comic Negativity

Beating the System: Post-structuralist Error

> Let us wage war on totality.
>
> Jean-François Lyotard, *The Postmodern Condition*

The term *poststructuralism,* which has been widely associated with postmodernism, has come to refer to a collection of moves by a group too diverse to be considered a school or movement (Derrida, Foucault, Barthes, Lyotard, de Man, Kristeva, Deleuze—sometimes Lacan is mentioned in the same breath); but in spite of their heterogeneity, the poststructuralists seem to share a general preoccupation with negativity, both as philosophical and aesthetic issue. As Richard Macksey and Eugenio Donato have observed (in their introduction to *The Structuralist Controversy,* 1971), these proponents of "French thought" display "a cold and concerted destruction of the subject, a lively distaste for the notion of origin, a dismantling of unifying pseudo-syntheses of consciousness, a denunciation of all the mystifications of history performed in the name of progress, of consciousness, and of the future of reason" (Introduction x).

The poststructuralists do seem to have a negative attitude, concerned as they are with the de-monstration of the deconstruction of certainty, the de-centering of the transcendental subject of phenomenology, the de-flation of the logos, the de-ferral of satisfying solutions (and in Lacanian psychoanalysis, with the *dé-calage* between de-mand and de-sire, as well

as with Freud's own litany of negations: de-nial, de-negation, dis-avowal). Their practice conjures up a flurry of "D-words" (not the least of which are De-rrida and de-Man), which at times almost resound like a battle cry, heralding a kind of "D-Day" mounted against System (Lyotard: "Let us wage war on totality").

Not that poststructuralism represents anything like a united front against totality (such a concerted effort would, of course, be contrary to the spirit of these deconstructive moves); "French thought" introduces a great many strategies for beating the system. For Lyotard, as we have seen, it is a question of championing the postmodern sensibility and of tracing the tactics of an infinite number of language games against the dominance of traditional "metanarratives."[1] For Kristeva, the campaign is launched against another bastion of the Logos—the science of semiology—in the name of the dispersive force of "the semiotic," as the register of a radical poetic negativity associated both with feminine pleasure and with the maternal body.[2] For Foucault, the negative impulse is manifested in the critical analysis of social systems and institutions; his is a study of complicity, revealing how exterior or marginal phenomena—like madness, criminality, or sexuality—actually serve or reinforce the system that appears to repress them. In a related move, Paul de Man shows how the most illuminating of insights is not only shadowed by blindness (as suggested by his formula: "Every reading is a misreading"), but actually depends on error for its rhetorical impact.[3] And of course, Jacques Derrida has been concerned with dismantling centrisms of every sort (logocentrism, phallocentrism, ethnocentrism) in a network of brilliant moves de-monstrating that any totalizing system maybe deconstructed from the inside; indeed, Derrida has deconstructed the very opposition of "inside" and "outside."

This fascination with systemic error indicates that the poststructuralists are not simply naysayers, nor are they nihilists. They are perhaps more like knights errant, bent on jousting with the Dragon Error rather than on slaying it. Their fascination with error includes a fascination with chance as well, first as a mode of play (games of chance), and second as the very possibility of history as *histoire* (that is, as text created by human beings) rather than as telos or fate.

Perhaps it is this interest of poststructuralism in error, chance, and negativity that may account for the appeal psychoanalysis exerts upon French thought, since the Freudian allegory of human subjectivity emphasizes the role of lapse, error, and chance (as the "uncanny") in the drama of intersubjective relations as well as the role of the unconscious in deconstructing the aims of consciousness. Thus, it is not surprising that poststructuralism should take a cue from a certain psychoanalysis, lending attention not only to the error of traditional systems but to its own error as well; poststructuralism attempts to ferret out its own assumptions and to examine its own positions, less in the hope of overcoming error than as an effort at putting error into play as a deconstructive tactic. In a sportsmanlike move, the poststructuralists seem to decline the handicap of being too right, preferring a comic strategy of error as diversion or creative wandering (in the sense of the French word *errer*).

Given the influence of poststructuralism on our late twentieth-century scene, the stakes of this game of wits are high: what is the price of the valorization of error or the assumption of blindness as the corollary to insight? The political pitfalls of deconstruction have excited a great deal of controversy of late, and the question of whether a philosophy of error may take an ethical or even activist stance remains a subject of debate.[4] This problematic, which is perhaps endemic to the poststructuralist love affair with negativity, may be described as a double bind whereby the contestation of authority as repression may also undermine the notion of ethical or political responsibility: if all values are shadowed by "undecidability," how may we decide what is to be done?

The comic bind: avoiding the "Right"

> The double bind: when it is stretched to the limit, what threatens is cramp. . . . The game is thus paralyzed by the very undecidability that also opens its field.
>
> Jacques Derrida, "Où commence et où finit un corps enseignant"?

Before we may consider the politics of poststructuralism, we need to look at the nature of the double bind itself (and its relation to negativity), beginning with Derrida's own use of the term, which appropriately enough depends on the gaming deployment of an extended pun. Stephen Melville's treatment of the philosophical ramifications of Derrida's "positions" (*Philosophy Beside Itself,* 1986) characterizes the double bind as a game ("heads you win, tales I lose") and emphasizes the wordgames that Derrida plays with the term, which in French carries erotic connotations (*bande* as erection) as well as associations with wounding (*bandage*) and electronic technology (*bande* as tape; this last connotation, I might add, adds a Beckettian dimension to Derrida's wordgame, replaying the connotations of *La dernière bande de Krapp*). As Melville's discussion points out, Derrida is perhaps painfully aware of the dangers of taking any stance or adopting any "position"—including his own critique of the Logos—and of the paradoxical dilemma, on the one hand, of risking being too much in the right, by suppressing chance or difference (and hence presumably of being vulnerable to cooptation by the ideological Right), and, on the other hand, of being stymied in a kind of textual abyss, a paralysis of game and error, which can claim no "right" to act.[5] Melville cites Derrida (35):

> But if this double bind is ineluctable . . . *there must be,* somewhere, no last word. Without this it would arrest, paralyze, or petrify itself, immediately. . . . It must be that beyond the untiring contradiction of the double bind, an affirmative difference—innocent, intact, gay—succeeds in being absent without leave, escapes with a leap and laughingly signs that which it lets go, that which it makes and unmakes, *en double bande.*[6]

In this passage, Derrida makes a comic leap, adding another imagistic dimension to his *bande animée*—his comic band/bind/bond—escaped in a bound [*un saut*] that lands out of bounds, AWOL, permitting negativity to be absent without leave, to elude the consequences of an oppositional stance, and to sidestep (in a leap of nonfaith) the risk of cooptation by or subservience to dialectical systems of debate and resolution. But is this game of hopscotch a laughing matter? Or does being absent without leave imply a shirking of responsibility as well as a clever strategy for circumventing authority?

In a fascinating essay on Bataille's "Hegelianism" ("De l'économie restreinte à l'économie générale: un Hégélianisme sans réserve," 1967 [hereafter *EG*]),[7] Derrida has warned us not to take the question of reason or authority too lightly, particularly as concerns the authority of the Hegelian dialectic: "Misrecognized, taken lightly [*à la légère*], Hegelianism would only extend its historical domination, deploying its immense resources of envelopment" (369). Throughout his work, Derrida has continued to insist that not just any lighthearted leap may get us out of the dialectic, which is perhaps the craftiest of logocentric strategies, since it enforces its System by making use of opposition or negativity.

Similarly, in his essay on Mallarmé ("La double séance," 1972), Derrida writes of another (wildly comic) vault, the leap, "feet bound" [*pieds joints*], into the ideology of representation, ever associated in Derrida's work with the resources of Hegelian process: "In wanting to reverse mimetologism or in claiming to escape from it all at once, by simply jumping in feed first [*pieds joints*], one falls back immediately and certainly into its system" ("La double séance" [235]).[8] This colorful image of a leap feet first and feet bound into the abyss of positivity (an unwilling bound back into bounds by would-be combatants of the dialectic, AWOL from philosophy) results from Derrida's comic doubling of the notion of the poststructuralist bind in a network of associations, in French and in English, around the words *bondir* (to leap, to bound) and *bander* (to bind, to band, to record, to have an erection). Derrida's highly allusive wordgame playfully stages the paramount challenge to his own poststructuralist oppositional bent: how can one be negative without being swallowed alive by the Hegelian system, with its "immense resources of envelopment"? And Derrida's colorful image (of his own "band" of deconstructionists leaping feet first into the positivity they abhor) de-monstrates that if the stakes of the double bind are not trivial, they are nonetheless quite possibly comic. In any case, in this witty war on totality, Hegel is clearly the man to beat.

Matching wits: Hegel's hand

Hegel has the perfect scheme: the more seemingly absolute or nihilistic the negation, the more synthesizable it is, the more recoverable in the *Aufhebung*. It's an unbeatable system (thesis, antithesis, synthesis): negativity is neither repressed nor managed but is simply incorporated. No wonder, then, that throughout poststructuralist thought one encounters a pervasive fascination and frustration with this System to end all Systems; Derrida, Lyotard, Blanchot, Kristeva—and Bataille before them—have all matched wits with Hegelianism, taking on the "last professor of philosophy" (as Bataille calls him) in their own thought and in the work of others.[9] Nor are the poststructuralists the only ones to lock horns with the dialectic; a related spirit provides the impetus of much of the work of the Frankfurt school, and particularly the work of Adorno, whose "negative dialectics" attempt to recast Hegelian negativity in Marxist form.[10]

Yet if these various strategies for dealing with dialectical synthesis may be considered postmodern (because of their skepticism vis-à-vis logical system) in the poststructuralist camp at least the anti-Hegelian campaign may not be considered a simple case of "incredulity towards metanarrative" (to cite Lyotard's formula for postmodernism). Kristeva, for example, has argued that Hegel perhaps got it right, that his system already harbors that radical *négativité sans emploi* (a term used by Blanchot as well as Kristeva) that seems to be the aimless aim of so many of the poststructuralist maneuvers.[11] For Kristeva, Hegel's concept of "abstract negativity" (the most radical form of negativity since it entails a consciousness of death that finds no use or meaning in the dialectic system) may already be considered negativity without employ. She argues that we need to deploy—but not employ—the radical negativity residing within meaning (in poetry or in the "semiotic" register of language, for example), rather than trying to mount a futile opposition to Hegel. Her reproach to a certain kind of feminism has been couched in just these terms when she argues that some feminist discourse, by simply saying "no" to patriarchy in a categorical way, erects the mirror image of the system it opposes. Kristeva prefers to explore the negative possibilities within the system rather than refuting the system in its totality.

Derrida is not so optimistic about the negative yield of Hegelian system, but he too insists that the dialectic—as the most sophisticated manifestation of the Logos, incorporating negativity—is a force to be reckoned with, precisely because it is so infuriatingly complete. Indeed, as we have seen, in his essay on Bataille, Derrida chides those who would take the dialectic too lightly, suggesting that we take a page from Bataille's book and recognize just how clever Hegel is. But can this be Derrida? Defending *Hegel?* Insisting on the comprehensiveness of his philosophy? Are we to take Derrida's serious appraisal of the dialectic seriously? Yes and no.

Derrida's reproach to his readers for taking Hegel too lightly is not mere professorial grumbling, an upbraiding of students too lazy and nonrigorous to pay their philosophical dues. His is a philosophical position, an opening move in the match-up against Hegel, a warning of the strength of the adversary. (Derrida seems to be saying: "Let's not fool ourselves into thinking we can get rid of the old man so easily, by a simple act of opposition—we'll be swallowed alive.") As Derrida knows, Hegel is the master of the double bind ("heads I win, tales you lose"): dialectic transgression reinforces the law by opposing it. (This is just the sort of move about which Blanchot warns in *L'entretien infini:* "synthesize by negating, parole of reason" [*dépasser en niant, parole de raison*]). Moreover, in large measure, Derrida's notion of double bind is already anticipated in Bataille's theory of eroticism, which maintains that the experience of negativity—as "continuity" or the intuition of death afforded by the erotic act—is an effect of play-acting or cheating, *une naïve comédie.* In a different perspective, the double bind is also encountered in psychoanalysis (as the phenomenon of denegation or *Verneinung*), at least from the patient's point of view, since he or she, in saying "no" to any of the analyst's interpretations, risks reinforcing the validity of that interpretation. (Does not the dispute between feminism and orthodox psychoanalysis stem, in part, from Freud's refusal to let Dora say "no"?)

In the rest of this essay, I want to look more closely at the postmodern poststructuralist opposition to Absolute Knowledge, the search for a "negativity without employ," and to retrace several postmodern comic strategies (in Derrida, Lyotard, and Lacan) for saying "no" and meaning it. And if Freud has something to contribute to this postmodern war on Hegelianism, it is possibly to be found in the opening scene of his essay "Negation" [*Die Verneinung*] (1925), in which the patient is confronted with the double bind of psychoanalysis: when he emphatically declares that the lady in the dream is *not* his mother, Freud promptly deduces that the lady in question must indeed *be* his mother. This scene has farcical overtones, suggesting that even if the stakes of the dialectic game are not trivial, negativity may nonetheless lend a comic cast to the play.

Bedroom Farce: Hegel, Bataille, Derrida

Hegel did not know how right he was.

Bataille quoted by Derrida, *EG* (369)

L'enfant terrible of French philosophy (at least before Derrida came bounding onto the scene) was Georges Bataille, that enigmatic figure whose struggle with Hegelian negativity may be characterized as the passionate longing to experience something beyond the limits of rationality, of consciousness, of system. At various moments in his work, Bataille calls this something—this encounter with *"négativité sans emploi"*—by several names: sovereignty [*la souveraineté*], the interior experience [*l'expérience intérieure*], the sacred [*le sacré*], continuity [*la continuité*], the impossible [*l'impossible*]. All of these terms, however diverse their context, are related to the notion of risk or extravagant expenditure (an idea associated in turn with the tribal ceremony of potlatch treated in *La part maudite,* 1967) and at least suggest a confrontation with death as the ultimate expenditure of energy, the final incontrovertible loss of meaning, the irreversible transgression of consciousness and of individual boundaries. This philosophy (although this is clearly not the term that Bataille would have preferred) is sometimes Hegelian (because of the emphasis on transgression), sometimes Nietzschean (because of the emphasis on reckless expenditure) in its resonances. It is in any case often both seductive and disturbing ("I am," wrote Bataille, "of that number who provoke men to sacred horror.")[12] Politically left-wing, an advocate of revolution, Bataille has nonetheless not infrequently been accused of a flirtation with fascism, perhaps because of his fascination with violence as the transgressive means to an experience of sacred "continuity" (*L'expérience intérieure,* 1943). Indeed, Bataille's thought often emphasizes the sacred poetry of evil (particularly in *La littérature et le mal,* 1957) and of sacrifice, including human sacrifice (in *L'érotisme,* 1957).

The impossible limits of transgression

In *L'érotisme,* Bataille defines the erotic as the "affirmation of life even unto death" (*ER* 15) but insists that this vertiginous affirmation—in the erotic transgression—is not an abolition of law ("Transgression is not a return to nature: it lifts the prohibition without abolishing it" [*ER* 16]). And laughter plays a privileged role in Bataille's thought, both because of its association with a reckless expenditure of energy and because of the war it wages on reasonable thought. (Bataille writes of the "desire for laughter" as "that itch for pleasure, for saintliness, for death [which] has no further task to fulfill" and speaks of the power of laughter "to suspend knowledge."[13]) Yet, as is so often the case, Bataille's interest in what lies beyond expression leads him into terminology trouble: in this case, he is required to distinguish between two laughters, greater [*le rire majeur*] and lesser [*le rire mineur*]; greater laughter is also called whole laughter [*le rire entier*]. In the *Préface de Madame Edwarda* (1957; hereafter *PME*)[14] Bataille insists on the sacred quality of *le rire entier* only, which is not simply an expression of triumph or superiority but is also an effect of anguish. In fact, the difference between greater and lesser laughter seems to depend in large measure on the degree of lucidity of the laugher: while ordinary or lesser laughter is an uneasy mockery manifesting a fundamental hypocrisy in the face of an uncomfortable situation (entailing "a misrecognition of what is at stake" [*PME* 291]), whole or greater laughter requires a recognition of "the identity of being and of death, opening to the dazzling perspective of ultimate darkness" (292). So, in the case of whole laughter, the laugher no longer refuses to be implicated in the misfortunes of the comic victim, but is dragged down [*enlisé*] in an act of comic sacrificial abasement. (Although Bataille does not allude to Baudelaire's distinction between referential and absolute laughter, the similarities between his categories and Baudelaire's are striking indeed.)

In any case, Bataille is drawn to laughter—or at least to *le rire majeur*—as a symptom of that impossible negativity, that irrevocable transgression that would allow him to exceed dialectic reason in a playful (and at the same time unspeakably horrifying and poetic) "sovereign moment," the sacred continuity of *L'expérience intérieure.* Like so many important French thinkers, Bataille grapples with Hegelianism as the system that excludes chance, play, and error, subordinating all negativity to the work of reason. Bataille writes, "In the 'system' poetry, laughter, ecstasy are nothing. Hegel hastily gets rid of them:

he knows no other aim than knowledge" (*L'expérience intérieure* 142).[15] For Bataille, Hegel's greatest shortcoming is in being all too adequate, in shunning what the system must ignore ("To my eyes, [Hegel's] immense fatigue is linked to his horror of the blind spot" [*L'expérience interieure* 142]). It is in shortchanging negativity, and particularly the concept of abstract negativity (a confrontation with death as loss of meaning), that Hegel reveals his blind spot, misrecognizing the virulence of his own discovery of negativity, and failing to see "just how right he was" [*dans quelle mesure il avait raison*]. Thus Bataille opts not to confront Hegel, who has all the answers, including negativity, whether he knows it or not; for Bataille, the only possible "negative" response to Hegel and to Hegelianism, to Hegel as "*ism*", is laughter.

His own work opposes at least three laughing moments to Hegel. The first is an *ad hominem* attack (in *L'expérience intérieure*), in which the "professor's" life and work are belittled in a "brief comic recap" [*petite récapitulation comique*] that functions like program notes to a comedy, emphasizing the tame and happy ending to Hegel's professorial existence.[16] This first satirical treatment might be called an instance of that lesser laughter of superiority (Bataille's own *rire mineur*) or a referential comic instance (Baudelaire's *comique significatif*), which takes on the System merely by making fun of its manifestations in Hegel's own life. Bataille's second laughter [*le rire entier/majeur*] seems more serious in intent; rather, the greater laughter resounding throughout *Madame Edwarda* seems to be a manifestation of the inability of serious, reasonable thought to have the last word: it plays a deadly game aiming at the ruination of all meaning and the dissolution of individual limits in a kind of sacred, excessive sacrifice.

But a third kind of laughter makes its appearance in Bataille's thought, and this other laughter seems to undermine the greater laughter just as certainly as the lesser. I allude to that moment in *L'érotisme* when Bataille acknowledges that even the wildest of transgressions is always a "naive comedy," relying on play-acting and cheating at death; at the same time he ruefully points out the Hegelian nature of the erotic transgression: "no need to insist on the Hegelian nature of this move" [*inutile d'insister sur le caractère hégélien de cette opération*] [*L'expérience intérieure* 41n.]). It is this moment that becomes the focus of Derrida's essay on Bataille, and upon which I would like to focus as well, as the signal of a kind of postmodern moment in Bataille's thought, entailing an understanding of negativity as paradox or "impossibility" and even as a kind of affirmation. For as Bataille points out (in "Hegel, la mort et le sacrifice"), death is the only experience that can truly exceed meaning, but human beings cannot have this experience since they must be dead to "experience" it (a comic bind if ever there was one). Ritual sacrifice is no less comic a solution since it involves playing dead, letting someone else do the dying for you. Faced with the impossibility of experiencing the unexperienceable true negativity, Bataille haplessly exclaims, "But this is a comedy!" [*Mais c'est une comédie!*].[17]

Enter Derrida: a comedy of errors

Derrida rushes head-on into Bataille's imbroglio, adding to the complications of this negative scene, citing Bataille's rehearsal of Hegel's comic error, the underestimation of negativity. Thus, Derrida's play on and with Bataille's text unfurls under the banner of error ("Hegel did not know how right he was," reads Derrida's epigraph, a quotation from Bataille) and reproduces all the ins and outs, comic turns and misunderstandings, of Bataille's own erotic farce.

Derrida insists on reading Bataille against himself, taking issue with Bataille's concession of his own bind, supposedly inherent in the inescapable Hegelianism of the erotic transgression. Derrida, in fact, reproduces Bataille's move, echoing Bataille in a kind of poststructuralist *double entendre,* a doubled reading that is also, necessarily, a misreading of sorts. Indeed, Derrida opts to follow in Bataille's (negative) footsteps (*suivre ses "pas"?*) in his turn, by maintaining that "Bataille did not know how right *he* was" in his effort at finding a comic transgression that would indeed exceed Hegel's dialectic. Derrida thus takes Bataille's part . . . against Bataille, much as Bataille has taken Hegel's part, against Hegel.

Even before entering into this comic defense, Derrida deals with another (potential) error, this time on the part of the reader, concerning Bataille's project. Derrida fears that Bataille may be a misunderstood man; that is, he fears that Bataille may be mistaken for a champion of those bastions of the logocentric tradition: immediacy, presence, continuity, nostalgia. Thus Derrida insists that despite appearances, fostered by Bataille's own choice of terminology (the use of words such as continuity, sovereignty, and interior experience, for instance) Bataille is not a mystic (*EG* 401). Derrida warns that the reader would be in error in taking Bataille at his word, by taking any of these words at face value and out of their context, which somehow manages to deconstruct their usual connotations. Above all, Derrida cautions, it would be a mistake to take Bataille's many references to philosophy (Nietzschean as well as Hegelian) as a concession to any system.

Even if Bataille is not one to fall into the trap of taking the dialectic too lightly—and thus bounding feet first into its boundaries (writes Derrida)—neither is he one to take the dialectic deadly seriously—lock, stock, and barrel. But just what does Derrida think that Bataille refuses to take too seriously in the dialectic? Nothing other than Hegelian *negativity* (*EG* 380). For in Hegel's system, Bataille argues, negativity, however virulent, always remains a resource of reason, to be incorporated into the final inevitable end of Absolute Knowledge (*ER* 384). But is there a negativity that does not play the game of totalization? Bataille himself wonders if such an aimless aim is anything but "impossible." So, in this sense, paradoxically, Bataille's banner statement takes on a new cast; it is no longer a reference to Hegel's underestimation of the virulence of negativity. In this sense, Hegel perhaps "did not know how right he was" in claiming to get the better of negativity in the *Aufhebung;* for paradoxically, in negating negation, he has made the concept of negativity itself, essential though it is to dialectic reason, "impossible."

At this point, Derrida comes to the rescue: following Bataille's own example, he refuses to take Bataille at his word, the position expressed in *L'érotisme* that ruefully owns up to a certain Hegelianism in spite of itself (*EG* 404). Turing to Bataille's other writings (particularly the *Conférences sur le Non-Savoir*) in search of non-Hegelian negativity, Derrida claims to find a negativity deploying the "ne" of "neutrality" rather than of "negativity" (402), a "ne-utrality" signaling a negativity of no use to dialectic reason. For this negativity is a wasteful action and a waste product, the useless and extravagant expenditure of potlach, of leftover, of excess.

Playing doubles

The "ne-utrality" of Bataille's "negativity without use," Derrida explains, is a kind of comic mimicry that doubles Hegelian negativity insofar as it sacrifices it, spends it, refuses to use it as a resource of reason or logic, subordinate to the *Aufhebung:* "Sovereign transgression is a reduction of this reduction: not a reduction to sense, but a reduction of sense" (*ER* 393). Thus Bataille's transgression does not escape the dialectic by refuting it, but rather exceeds it and thus remains left over, continuing to haunt the dialectic in a comic mimicry that doubles over at the spectacle of Hegelian "mastery."

We might say then that Derrida's reading of Bataille sets up several doubles of the dialectic, step by step, by doubling Bataille's *pas* (in the double sense of tracing his tracks, his footsteps, and of doubling the negative of transgression, in the doubly negative "reduction of a reduction"). First, Derrida explains, Hegel's "mastery" doubles Hegel's own notion of "abstract negativity" (that is, by laughing at abstract negativity, Hegel's mastery subordinates negativity to meaning). Second, Bataille doubles Hegel's step, doubling "mastery" with "sovereignty" (that is, by laughing at mastery, Bataille's sovereignty undoes the meaning of Hegelian negativity as resource of reason). Similarly, Bataille's major writing [*écriture majeure*] doubles his minor writing [*écriture mineure*]; that is, his non-Hegelian view of transgression manages to laugh at the Hegelianism apparent in the deluded moments of his own minor writing. Similarly, Derrida suggests, Bataille's "greater" laughter laughs at the "lesser" laughter (of supposed superiority) and thus ruins any illusion of mastery afforded by the supposed triumph over the comic object. Concerning this mechanism of doubling—which we might call the negation of the negation or the transgression of a transgression, the double negative that yields a strangely affirmative "negativity without employ"—Derrida writes: "In doubling mastery, sovereignty does not escape from the dialectic . . . far from suppressing dialectic synthesis, [sovereignty] inscribes it and makes it function in the sacrifice of sense" (*ER* 382–83).

The point of all of this doubling—that is, Derrida's explanation of Bataille's thought as a doubling of Hegel's thought, and of Bataille's major writing as a doubling of his minor writing—is itself a kind of comic double cross of Bataille by Derrida, who insists on reading Bataille against himself (*"il nous faut ici interpréter Bataille contre Bataille"* [*ER* 404]). For Derrida seems intent on proving that Bataille was not, in spite of appearances and in spite of his own assertion to the contrary, Hegelian. Derrida's Bataille is thus a farcical hero, taking his place in the line of rogues and dupes (*"à trompeur, trompeur et demi"*); Bataille's comic flaw according to Derrida, reproduces Hegel's comic flaw according to Bataille—in each case, the "hero" in question "did not know how right he was"; his flaw is in not giving himself enough credit.

Thus when Derrida rehearses Bataille's reading of Hegel, he purloins Bataille's punch line and (just perhaps) repeats Bataille's error. Derrida's move of oneupsmanship reproduces and replaces that of Bataille, each reading over the shoulder of the other in a farcical chain where it is difficult, if not impossible, to *donner raison* (that is, to determine who is right in an act of granting reason) in what is, after all, a struggle against reason. (Even if we could *donner raison* to Derrida or to Bataille, would either of them want to take it, slipping into the position of the "right?") Indeed, Derrida's reading is haunted by a comic double bind, which is perhaps none other than the comic paradox of transgression as sketched by Bataille (and echoed by Freud, standing in the wings): rules are never stronger than when they are transgressed, negations (the lady in my dream is *not* my mother!) are never so doubtful as when they are strongly affirmed (Bataille is *not* Hegelian!).

If, for example, Bataille is right that Hegel is wrong for not seeing that he is right in being able to be wrong, and wrong in believing that he may always be right, then Derrida has to be at least partly wrong about Bataille's wrongness in describing himself as all too right, as Hegelian. (Who says poststructuralism is turgid?) Faced with this chain of comic complications, I can only echo Bataille's exclamation: "But this is a comedy!" Still if Derrida is not always reasonable, he is unfailingly witty; his essays often read like bedroom farce, depending upon chance encounters and masquerade, where Truth, like the cuckolded husband, is shadowed by a duplicitous double, Error, hiding in the closet.

At the risk of leaping *pieds joints* into this comedy of errors, I want to take Bataille's part and to suggest that he is perhaps "right" after all in conceding his Hegelianism; that is, the transgression described in *L'érotisme* must indeed fail to be entirely sovereign, for negativity may indeed never be absolute or *sans emploi.* Indeed, insofar as Bataille believes in sovereignty, he may be negated in what Lacan would consider an Imaginary construct, indulging in an illusion of sovereign meaninglessness that misrecognizes (in Lacan's sense of *méconnaissance*) impossibility as possibility. But in *L'érotisme* Bataille confronts that illusion, recognizing that of his various strategies of sovereignty—violence, sacrifice, tears, laughter—only laughter remains out of reach of the dialectic, a kind of leftover undermining the very concept of sovereignty.

But just what laughter resounds in *L'érotisme?* If the greater laughter [*le rire entier*] is conspicuously absent from this text, it may be because Bataille recognizes that this kind of absolute laughter falls prey to the illusions of eroticism, the "naive comedy." As we have seen in chapter 2, the very same illusions are played out in Baudelaire's absolute comic, producing a false absolute that is never so serviceable as when it simply refuses to serve. The upshot of *L'érotisme* is deceptively simple: the joker who wants to experience continuity has but two choices—to die or to cheat. And cheating is both the comic and the social choice, played out through our erotic objects, the Others who allows us to be satisfied with the illusion of sacrifice.

Bataille's erotic farce

> We satisfy ourselves with illusion. Possession will give us, without dying, the feeling of going to the end of our desire.
>
> Bataille, *ER* (267)

In other words, the distinction between masterful and self-sacrificing processes can be no more clearly drawn in Bataille's system than in Baudelaire's or in Freud's once one has acknowledged the mechanism of cheating underlying any satisfaction of desire. Or, as Freud's argument in *Beyond the Pleasure Principle* seems to suggest, the death-drive may be satisfied only comically, by avoiding death. It follows then that the only real difference between greater and lesser laughter, as is also the case for Baudelaire's referential and absolute laughter, and for Freud's innocent or tendentious jokes, resides in the joker's willingness to be implicated. It comes down to the question of masochism, and even so, the self-sacrifice is always doubled, underwritten by a comic guarantee, an assurance of the preservation of life in spite of the erotic sense of risk. This erotic interplay between the impulse of conservation and the impulse of expenditure (Bataille's "floundering" [*chavirement*]) is strikingly like what Freud sees (in *BPP*) as the rhythm of life generated by the interworking of two opposing sets of instincts (life and death, Eros and Thanatos); and it recalls the interworkings of the pleasure principle with the reality principle as well (discussed in the 1911 essay "Two Principles of Mental Functioning").

Indeed, both Freud and Bataille see the sexual nature of human beings as symptomatic of a psychic wound, suffered when the infant is separated from the original love object. Bataille writes in the third chapter of *L'érotisme* that in human life the violence of sexuality opens a wound [*ouvre une plaie*]; for Freud, of course, the original wound is inflicted by the loss of the mother and/or the threat of castration. (For Baudelaire as well, as we have seen, there is a primal wound masquerading as original sin, the fall from divine grace.) For Bataille as for Freud, the schism is only closed temporarily and provisionally; sexual pleasure subserves the death instinct and is thus subject to infinite repetition (*BPP* 167).

While all these observations refer to the individual's erotic experience, both Freud and Bataille concern themselves as well with the larger social and historical phenomena that reflect the interworkings of transgression and limit. When Bataille discusses the various forms of societal or "organized transgression" (marriage, war, religious sacrifice), he seems in fact to be adopting the orthodox Freudian view of cultural achievement as the result of the repression of libidinal impulse, in sublimation. Like Freud, Bataille emphasizes the seemingly paradoxical cooperation between human prohibition—which is there to be violated—and transgression, which he sees not as the negation of the prohibition but rather as its synthesis and completion. Bataille's own definition of transgression and of eroticism, then, seems paradoxically to domesticate the erotic sacrifice, granting an acceptable and even useful role to the erotic component of human experience (and thus even perhaps to some extent anticipating the "postmodern" arguments put forth by Foucault in *The History of Sexuality* [1976] about the complicity of sexuality with the systems that seem to regulate it).

Yet, as Derrida's essay suggests, a profound uneasiness with this concession to Hegelian system nonetheless makes itself felt throughout Bataille's work and even becomes manifest in the final chapters of *L'érotisme,* where Bataille seems to return to the insistence on the existence of something "other," beyond the reach of the "supreme interrogation" of philosophy. In this section, Bataille insists that this otherness can only be expressed as no expression at all, as silence. And philosophy, for Bataille, even though it claims to be "the sum of all possibilities," remains incapable of incorporating or explaining away this silence since philosophy takes place within language: "Philosophy does not get out of itself; it cannot get out of language. It uses language in such a way that silence never succeeds it" (*ER* 303). Language, then, marks a point of both possibility and of failure: "What would we be without language? It makes us what we are. Only it reveals, at its limit, the moment where it is no longer valid [*n'a plus cours*]. In the final analysis, the person who speaks reveals impotence" (*ER* 304).

In other words, if Bataille's work seems to express a frustration with the impotence and limitations of human expression, it also conversely seeks a way of getting out of the excessive possibility afforded by language: the discursive faculty expresses both too little and too much. But Bataille's emphasis is finally not on getting philosophy out of its comic predicament (the tendency to babble, to say too much and too little), thereby contributing one more achievement to the philosophical roster. He prefers to demonstrate that the impasse of philosophy is real and that this dilemma is two-faced, a double bind: on the one hand, we must remain within discourse (and hence within Hegelianism or philosophy) in order to be human; on the other hand, discourse is inadequate for expressing our experience of all that which is not possible. This paradox is suggested, for instance, in Bataille's definition of *"l'impossible"* as the sum of all possibilities, or, in his view of excess as that which always remains outside of limits, insusceptible to recuperation: "excess is that by which being is always already out of bounds [*hors de toutes limites*]"). It is perhaps *"inutile d'insister,"* in my turn, on the *Freudian* character of this desire, as the excess that both precedes and defines every human being's entry into social existence, the boundless desire that Lacan has called the desire "of the Other" (playing on the ambiguity of the doubled genitive).

I want to suggest that Bataille is right in his assertion that transgression, by its very nature, is always a discursive phenomenon and hence always "Hegelian" as he seems to understand the term (that is, as within language, meaningful); at the same time, Bataille may also be wrong in his insistence on something beyond discourse. Is silence really possible? If not, does Hegelian reason, system, and Absolute Knowledge get to have the last word? Or, is there another comic (im) possibility: Might not silence inhabit discourse, as part of discourse? Like Dorothy who cannot see Oz in her own back yard, has Bataille "misrecognized" the "impossible" silence (negativity without employ) that haunts his own discourse, the silence that perhaps dwells within language rather than exceeding it? ("There's no place like home. . . .")

In the face of the paradox of the impossibility of total possibility, Bataille does seem to conclude that only one sort of philosophizing is "possible"—comic philosophy: philosophy that laughs at philosophy, with the doubling implied by such a move. This laughter is then perhaps Bataille's most radical discovery: transgression/negativity taken a step further (another *pas*) in a kind of double negative. For at moments Bataille seems to have stumbled onto "something" almost in spite of himself: perhaps all transgression is inevitably Hegelian, but Hegel's system is itself inevitably "transgressed," inhabited and unworked from within, haunted by the impossibility of being too serious. Maybe Bataille did not know how right he was, after all; rather than positing the transgressive game as a kind of naive comedy equivalent to an act of existentialist bad faith, Bataille's work at least suggests at moments that the comic rhythm of discourse, the comic play of life with death, is the ground rule of social interaction itself, founding the community of Law.

But is this not precisely what Derrida is saying when he reads Bataille against himself, insisting that his thought reflects two tendencies (*l'écriture majeure* and *l'écriture mineure*): one which hears the impossible silence *inhabiting* discourse; the other which looks to the impossible as something mystical and *beyond* discourse? Is Derrida then right, after all, in saying that Bataille is wrong in calling his erotic transgression Hegelian? (And have I made a *faux pas* in taking issue with Derrida's reading?)

Yes and no. Derrida is perhaps, like Bataille, both right and wrong, and one might even say—referring to the familiar poststructuralist strategy put forth by de Man—that for Derrida, as for Bataille, a certain creative misreading, entailing moments of blindness, is necessary or corollary to the moments of insight. Derrida is, in my own (partial) view, right in insisting on Bataille's negativity as a kind of writing, an effect of discourse, rather than something beyond discourse. But Derrida goes wrong, or rather seems to reproduce Bataille's error, his blind spot, when he faults Bataille for owning up to the Hegelianism of his transgressive system. (For in Derrida's too forceful *Verneinung* of Bataille's Hegelianism—"he is not a Hegelian!"—he is perhaps repeating the misstep of those moments of misrecognition where Bataille insists on a "beyond," trying to take a mystical *faux pas* out of bounds).

Bataille's point, at least at some moments in his work, seems to be that the essence of Hegelianism is discourse rather than teleology, aiming at the production of meaning rather than the goal of Absolute Knowledge. Derrida sometimes appears to lose sight of this distinction, seeming to argue at moments (following in the *faux pas* of that other "misguided" Bataille) that discourse is always servile to Truth, because it is meaningful. Derrida may want to have it both ways: at one moment, he agrees with Bataille that negativity is always servile, a resource of discourse; at another moment, he argues that a certain negativity is precisely the type of move that is most interesting and radical in Bataille (the "major writing" inscribing negativity—as the opacity or slipperiness of language—into meaningful discourse) since this negativity plays tricks on Absolute Knowledge within the very system it serves. In other words, in the first instance Derrida seems to confuse meaning with Knowledge or Truth. But as Derrida himself is never tired of pointing out, meaning is always contextual and intentional, inhabited by the desire of the speaker (the *vouloir dire* of meaning as expressed in French). Serving meaning is not the same as serving up Truth or Absolute Knowledge.

In my turn, I want to suggest that Derrida does not (perhaps) always know how right *he* is, in suggesting that laughter exceeds the dialectic (*"le rire seul excède la dialectique"* [*EG* 376]), but only if the excess is understood as the motor of conversation, as the metonymic desire that moves dialogue as dialect and haunts discursive meaning. In other words, this excess or aftermath of the dialectic is not the *beyond* of meaning (madness or nonsense or death or absolute negativity); it is rather the comic possibility *within* the most serious of meanings, the capacity of language for double talk. In this case, laughter is not a reaction, a trump card *majeur* taking place above and beyond the dialectic (as in Derrida's portrayal of Bataille laughing at the dialectic in a sovereign burst of laughter that sacrifices Hegel's masterful subject). It is rather the play of excess inherent in the dialectic process itself, the extra leftover negativity *sans emploi.* Laughter is transgression as a differential working held up on its way to Absolute Knowledge in what Blanchot will call an "infinite conversation," but which could be called a social "text" or interaction.

So, in trying to take Bataille off the Hegelian hook, Derrida may have momentarily lost sight of his most radical insight: the capacity to inscribe the sovereign moment within the erotic comedy that he stages, and to put himself on stage as well (Bataille: "To be laughable and knowing myself to be so is to my taste").[18] Psychoanalysis has a name for such a renunciation of the sovereign position outside desire: it is the *countertransference,* the moment of the analyst's leap into the comedy of desire. At the moment of greatest insight, similarly, Bataille is not a sovereign joker, but a clown who plunges into the ring to perform with and for others and whose "negativity without employ" is the silence, the spacing, the comic possibility of language itself.

Tickled to Death: Derrida's Doubled Scene

I want to turn briefly now to Derrida's own erotic farce of negativity, this time related to the problem of mimesis in poetry (the subject of the essay on Mallarmé, "La double séance," 1972).[19] This double staging in a sense restages Bataille's erotic transgression, as Derrida redelivers a punch line "purloined" from Bataille (about the comic bind of transgressive negativity) in a brilliant network of cross reference and allusion, playfully reenacting the scene it describes.

Derrida's essay, which rehearses a transgressive and ceremonial theatrical scene, invites comparison with Bataille's work on eroticism and with Baudelaire's treatment of the absolute comic as well, for several reasons. First, Mallarmé's scenario depicts an erotic act, in Bataille's sense of the term; moreover, this erotic act bears a striking resemblance to the comic scene of Pierrot's self-sacrifice described in Baudelaire's essay on laughter. In Mallarmé's scene as recited by Derrida, Pierrot is again the protagonist, and once again, he comically "dies" in the course of the action. But in this case, it is a question of a mimed death: Pierrot tickles his wife Colombine to death in an imaginary remembered scene in which he mimes both roles. Thus death and orgasm are explicitly related in "La double séance", but because of the pleasurable and imaginary nature of this death, *la petite mort,* one could say that the "crime" takes place "without anything having finally happened" (*DS* 228), without, as Derrida insists, any stigma or "trace" of violence whatsoever. (In fact, in Derrida as in Freud, it is again a question of an absent lady, an imaginary victim, the object of desire who puts herself out of reach except in fantasy.)

Thus the questions of the erotic complicity of transgression with the limits of system and of life with death, as well as the question of the efficacy of final actions, are at the heart of Derrida's text just as they are in Bataille's. (Indeed, this is the very essay where Derrida gives his warning about jumping feet bound [*pieds joints*] into the philosophical ideology of representation that subordinates copy to "true" source.) For Derrida, Mallarmé's poetic task, which is also the task of any creative writer, consists in finding a type of poetic representation or mimesis that may not be subsumed by the logistic tradition and that will maintain the "differential structure" (*DS* 234) of mimesis by refusing to suppress the double in the name of the original, "the thing itself, the production of its presence, its truth, as idea, form or matter" (235). Unlike Bataille's transgressive festival, or Baudelaire's absolute comic—two notions that continue to be inspired at least in part by the nostalgia "of a lost continuity" (Bataille's words)—Mallarmé's double scene, his differential mimesis, marks a radical departure from the tradition hearkening back to a notion of full original presence.

Yet Derrida insists that this double scene by no means seeks to abolish imitation [*mimétisme*] but looks rather to deploy it in a text of proliferated cross references in which the very notion of true source is undercut in a "perpetual allusion, without breaking the mirror/ice [*sans briser la glace*]"). Mallarmé's mime, in one sense, imitates nothing since he follows no written text; still, his story and its characters are age-old conventions of the *commedia*. The improvised presentation is at once spontaneous and retold, like an oft-repeated joke: "a graft of the text as far as the eye can see [*á perte de vue*]" (231). Moreover, the mime is retelling an imagined scene; thus, he doubles his own gestures with those of Colombine in the staging of a non-event, that "crime" which never "takes place" outside the mind, a crime without a body, without a weapon, without a trace, "in a past-present whose present has never occupied the scene, has never been seen by anyone, nor has ever even been really committed" (228). So the order of chronology is completely overturned in this hall of mirrors. Furthermore, Pierrot's "crime" of murder by tickling is a playful one, a masturbatory fantasy that is doubly unreal: first, because it is remembered in a scenic *mise-en-abîme* or play within a play, and second, because it is committed on a substitute object, Colombine's "double" (Pierrot himself, miming the role of the absent Colombine, in a flashback memory). Nothing is real or present in this interplay of reflections; hence nothing is *illustrated* by the mimed scene, except for its "fragmented light" (236).

The nonauthoritative and playful nature of the oscillatory pattern of cross references is emphasized by Derrida's own choice of pun as focal point of the essay; the prismatic scene, he writes, is the representation of a "hymen" understood both as marriage and as a sign of virginity. In the first sense of the word, the scene portrays a fusion or total fulfillment of desire ("the identification of the two, their confusion" [237]) in a moment recalling the "continuity" of Bataille's erotic act. But the erotic nature of this scene also works to underscore a comic *inaccomplissement;* the scene in which Pierrot/Colombine drops dead from pleasurable exhaustion represents only a play death, doubly deferred, since it is the mimed imaginary death of the alter ego, which, in any case, is not death at all [*la petite mort*]. This scene therefore mimes a paradox: it is at once a fulfillment and a deferral of desire, a nonviolent violence, where passive action only acts by not acting, in the manner of an actor, *"sans briser la glace."*

This is a sexual union or *hymen* where, paradoxically, nothing takes place; it is a play within time and space, in which Colombine is both absent and present (like the offended lady in the joke and like the denied mother of Freud's patient's dream). Derrida calls this play in time "an oscillatory suspension between grotto walls" (240), thus literally a *"mise-en-abîme"* generated by the paradox in the pun (hymen as consummation and barrier to consummation), suggesting and mirroring the action on stage without breaking the fragile membrane of illusion. Language and theme are reflections of one another, mirroring and mutually reinforcing their overdetermined nature. In other words, the mimed comic scene that Derrida "purloins" from Mallarmé and doubles is based on illusion just as surely as is Bataille's erotic act ("We satisfy ourselves with illusion"), since the fulfillment of desire is a fiction, a substitutive and literally perverse (because masturbatory) gratification, like the joking process itself: "It breaks the hymen, but only fictively; it is the pure fictional place where only betweenness takes place [*où seul a lieu l'entre*]. . . . the threshold is never crossed. Pierrot remains before the gates, solitary captive of the threshold" (265).

Pierrot's comic paralysis, which keeps him from transgressing, from crossing over the threshold, is of course characteristic of the plight of many postmodern fictional characters, trapped in maintained possibility: from Proust's Marcel to Beckett's Hamm, the hapless protagonist remains suspended in an abyss between past and present, engaged in a compulsive reenactment of past experience in an infinite series of reiterative reflections, *sans briser la glace.*

Two more reflections. First, Derrida's essay, a postmodern allegory in Ulmer's sense of the term—since it formally reenacts the textual scene it describes—also furnishes a kind of allegory of Freudian ideational mimetics (discussed in chapter 3), the mechanism of comic lending that permits the audience to follow the joke or the exaggerated movements of the clown. For, as Jeffrey Mehlman has pointed out ("How to Read Freud on Jokes"), all comic comparisons are made thanks only to a residue of impressions, traces of formerly observed actions that serve as a standard for the presently observed action. The authoritative stance of the observer—who laughs at the inappropriate actions of the comic butt—must thus be put into question since the standard itself is only a result of imitations, one version in an infinite chain of possible standards. The putting into question of the source or original standard is one comic consequence of Derrida's doubling of Mallarmé's scene, in an allegorization of doubling or mime. The mimetic act of Derrida's "Double Session" is two-faced: it paradoxically both contests order and affirms it. But even this paradox, which is perhaps still dialectical, is exceeded, by virtue of the fact that the origin or point of reference of the mimed scene is lost:

while the model is clearly visible in the network of reflected references (as a traditional plotline of the *commedia*), no single representation can be designated original or "true." Pierrot's scene has become one link in a chain of nonverifiable versions, in which original is indistinguishable from copy.

A second postmodern speculation on Derrida's double session: this reading of Mallarmé's text, itself a doubling of a performance, provides a striking example of what Jean-François Lyotard seems to mean by the notion of a limited transgressive act, performed by aesthetic or poetic processes. Commenting on what he takes to be Freud's notion of the limited fulfillment of desire afforded by the literary process, Lyotard speaks of literary form itself as a barrier to complete belief, and hence to the relatively complete fulfillment of desire in dream ("Literary forms prohibit the fulfillment of desire because their manifest presence provides an obstacle to the compulsion to cross the page of the book; they maintain desire in a state of nonfulfillment" [*Discours, figure* 356]). Like Pierrot, projecting his partially fulfilled fantasies onto the "page" of the grotto walls (in *la petite mort* of erotic fantasy), the reader takes part in a comic (because partial) transgression, contained in literary discourse and literary form, falling short of a complete (and tragic) emptying that would be the ultimate and decidedly noncomic negativity, the final curtain of death.

I want now to deploy Lyotard's concept (of the limited nature of the fulfillment of desire by literature) as a kind of backdrop, in order to take a closer look at the postmodern strategy for outwitting the dialectic which consists in reading negativity as an effect of language. Once again, we call on the insights of psychoanalysis in order to catch a certain negativity redhanded in its comic crime of undoing the discourse within which it is inscribed, for Jean-François Lyotard's analysis of the play of negativity within discursive system suggests that bounding *pieds joints* into the discursive dialectic system may poke holes in it after all.

Lyotard's Comedy of Transgression: Negation in Discourse

In his psycholinguistic work (*Discours, figure,* 1974), Lyotard—like Bataille and Derrida—attempts to define a kind of transgression that would qualify as something radically other than discursive system. Lyotard maintains that the intrusions of desire onto the surface of discourse in fact represent formal transgressions (figures of speech) that may not be understood in terms of ordinary narrative discourse; in any case, Lyotard's linguistic theory introduces yet another postmodern strategy for getting around the Hegelian impasse.

Freudian strategy: three "no's" in language

In the chapter on negation in language ("Le non et la position de l'objet"), Lyotard begins by citing Freud's article on negation ("Negation," 1925), emphasizing the way in which *Verneinung* or *dénegation* ("the lady in the dream is *not* my mother") allows the patient to conjure up an absent or repressed object in speech and hence to satisfy desire in a substitutive fashion. In fact, in Lyotard's Lacanian reading of Freud, the human being's experience of both desire and reality are effects of language ("Reality and desire are born together with the entry into language. Then the loss may be a loss, the presence of a lack, and the object may be a reality, something that exists even when it is not present" [*DF* 125]). According to Lyotard, the "no" of discourse is no longer a simple rejection, the simple opposite of "yes." Rather, it is double and equivocal, positive and negative at once, since it simultaneously denies the existence of the designated object and reproduces it in its absence. Thus, the phenomenon of linguistic or syntactical negation can be understood as a sign of entry into human desire, expressed in the *fort-da,* present-absent, yes-no rhythm of the child's first verbal games. This first kind of negation or transgression (Lyotard seems to use the terms interchangeably) is tied as well to the faculty of judgment, the straightforward negation of the grammarian. The syntactical negation, writes Lyotard, occurs within the system [*au sein du systême*] and works to permit the juxtaposition and contrast of counterposed linguistic elements.

The second type of negation or transgression in language is called the "no of meaning or spacing" [*non de la signification ou de l'espacement*]. It can be thought of as the interval between words, or as a scansion or rhythmic hiatus, the spacing or articulation of language that allows intelligible meaning to emerge, acting as "the mute support of language" (120). Interestingly, Lyotard compares this "negation of spacing or meaning" to Hegelian negativity since the interworkings of word and nonword are meaningful only when synthesized in linguistic system.

The third type of negation in discourse results from what Lyotard calls the "opacity of the designated" [*l'épaisseur du désigné*] and bears witness that the task of designation is inexhaustible, since every designated face of an object suggests the existence of other invisible facets ("presence and absence are constituted together upon the edge of the object's entry into the world" [83]). This third negation—emphasizing the opacity of reality and the inexhaustible diversity that can never be adequately represented in language—suggests the inaccessibility of "reality" to the speaker, its resistance to comprehension in a single visual or verbal move, its refusal to be seen simultaneously from all angles. Thus, the third negation is an unbridgeable distance between the speaker and the object of speech, the mutual and permanent exclusion of speaker and object. This negation indicates that language is a symptom of impotence, a separation of the subject from his or her objects of desire, but paradoxically, it also implies a certain grasp of reality by the subject whereby the irretrievable object may be comprehended (in the field of vision/understanding) thanks to the irreducible separation between subject and object.

I want to suggest that each of these three negations in language—the "no" of syntax, the "no" of spacing, and the "no of designation—have important functions in the comic process as understood in Freudian theory, since joking is a linguistic phenomenon bound up in the confrontation between desire and reality. Like any linguistic expression, of course, joking is articulated thanks to the positive-negative opposition that grounds all verbal expression (the syntactical negation). But in the joking discourse, the importance of this negation is emphasized since opposition or contrast is always at the source of the joke's point. In other words, since the joke's effect relies on the interval between what is and what is not (or, as Kant says, between what is and what should be), we could say that joking puts the first linguistic negation of judgment to an aesthetic use, deriving pleasure from contrast. Hence this syntactical or judgmental negation, central to Freud's concept of denegation, is the negation that seems to figure most prominently in conventional referential comic productions, such as Hobbes's comic of superiority or Kant's comic of contrast.

Moreover, the "no" of denegation that Freud says both absents and possesses the repressed object (the "it is not my mother" that makes the forbidden lady available to thought) has a role to play in all joking formations, as a substitutive satisfaction of desire. (It is perhaps most obvious in the obscene joke that derives pleasure from exposing the hard-to-get lady who has refused the joker's advances.)

Unlike Lyotard's first syntactical negation, which operates within the grammatical system, the second negation of spacing is the founding precondition of language, the silence between words against which they may articulate their meaning. (Lacan has a great deal to say about this kind of void, the meaningful absence that is a place marker of sorts, like Frege's zero, allowing meaning to "take place.")[20] Lyotard compares this void to dialectic negativity, which in turn suggests a parallel between this "no of spacing" and Bataille's erotic transgression. In Bataille's terms, as we have seen, the transgressive gesture is a kind of sacred time, an extraordinary "festival" opposed to the ordinary domain of work or communicative meaning; it is thus a kind of temporal space, an intermittent consecrated moment that frames the ordinary, workaday time preceding and following it. But ironically, the moment of festival license—like the negation of spacing in language—bolsters and enables the rational discursive limits it opposes. In a similar way, as I have argued in chapter 2, the so-called absolute comic of Baudelaire and others acts as a support to the reasonable faculty it appears to contest. We could say, then, that ruinous or poetic comic productions (like Pierrot's mimed sacrifice)—seem to exploit something like Lyotard's second negativity of spacing or scansion.

Finally, Lyotard's third negation—the negation of designation—seems to be most characteristic of that third "other" type of comic expression, which I have associated with a postmodern notion of textuality. For this third negation, even while exposing the inadequacy of language vis-à-vis the reality it attempts to describe, nonetheless permits alternate or even conflicting meanings to be entertained as equally valid alternatives, by underscoring that no one meaning may ever have the final say. This is perhaps the kind of negation at play in the paradoxical punning of the poststructuralists, contributing to the open-ended and overdetermined nature of the postmodern text.

The parallel between three comic veins and Lyotard's three negations in language is in a sense merely a structural analogy; still, as the above examples suggest, it is possible to classify comic effects in terms of the emphasis placed on one or another of these negations. But a caveat is in order: such a categorization is not exclusive, since all three kinds of negation inhabit *all* language and thus are present to some degree in any comic transaction. The implications of this realization are far-reaching, since we must assume that any comic production may be read in any of the three ways, depending on which of the negations we as readers emphasize or notice. And the connection between linguistic negation and comic processes leads to another potentially far-reaching conclusion: no language may be considered entirely serious or intact since all linguistic "texts" are founded on the same negative or transgressive processes that motivate the joking intersubjective text. Hence the power to say something serious implies the power to joke about it as well, thanks to the negativity that inhabits language.

Figure as transgression of discourse

Lyotard's work does leave room for something extralinguistic, for in the discussion of the transgression of discourse by figure ("Le travail du rêve ne pense pas," *DF*), he makes it very clear that the kind of "transgression" performed by the dreamwork—condensation, regression, displacement—is distinct from the three kinds of linguistic negativity or transgression operating within language. If figural transgression is most evident in the dream, Lyotard maintains, it is because images are the only mode of oneiric representation (a dream is always a picture), due to the "regressive" (concrete, imagistic, scenic) nature of primary process itself. In Lyotard's reading, the dream is the ultimate fulfillment of desire since it is pure figural scene in which desire is given free play, fulfilling itself in the very forms it produces. In fact, the dream may not even be expressed in narrative discourse ("secondary elaboration" must rework the dream to make it comprehensible, as a narrative, to consciousness); therefore the dream transgression is not to be confused with the kind of negativity that grounds and inhabits language.

Lyotard even argues that the kind of figural transgression performed by dream is a violation of all three of the linguistic negations constituting the ground rules of language; as such, the dreamwork can be considered the negation of negation or the transgression of transgression, the ultimate affirmation, which effectively fulfills desire in its images. As Freud maintains in *The Interpretation of Dreams* (and in the essay on negation as well), "There is no 'no' in the unconscious"; the dream scene simply is; the plastic scene is always present in images; it cannot, by its very nature, represent what is not.

Lyotard does suggest that "figural transgression" is operative in waking discourse as well as in dream, although to a far lesser degree, because of conscious censorship. Figure manifests itself in discourse as figural language (punning, poetic figures of speech). Lyotard depicts these eruptions of desire in discourse as an exertion of force on the surface of rational discourse, producing tropes and irregularities, and providing a certain limited gratification of desire in the process. This suggests that this figural language, including the joke, may be read as an expression *between* primary and secondary process, *between* the fulfillment of desire in the dream and its repression in discourse, a perverse substitute gratification, a special transgression, an affirmative kind of unserviceable negativity, derailing the train of thought. As Freud puts it (in *Jokes*), the joke is a Janus, whose two faces simultaneously answer to two systems, the conscious and the unconscious, while double dealing with both.

But just how do joke and dream transgression differ? From where does this difference stem? And what does Lyotard mean when he calls the dream figure a "transgression of a transgression"? Lyotard says that the first linguistic negation—syntactical or judgmental negation—is simply absent from the dream, because the dream takes place in the unconscious space characterized by the absence of doubt (Freud maintains that "there is no 'no' in the unconscious": nothing is repressed; the dream scene is simply there). But in joking, as we have noted, there is a reliance on the faculty of judgment to make a comic contrast: whereas the dream *ignores* linguistic negation, the joke *depends* on it. Still, joking does to some degree transgress or problematize the judgmental function of this first negation, by exposing the double meanings that inhabit it, and by assuring that any judgment is always doubled by its "other" meanings ("it is not my mother" equals "it is my mother"). Thus, we could say that the transgressive process of joking is somewhere between the relatively complete gratification afforded by dream figures as transgressions—forbidden images that simply do away with the repressive/judgmental "no" upon which discourse is founded—and the relatively complete submission to reality required by the repressive ground rules of language, the judgmental faculty or negation that grounds language and enables it to mean what it says, because it may deny what it does *not* say. The first syntactical negation, denied by dream, maintained by discourse, is at once denied and maintained by the joke.

And the same kind of distinction may be made concerning Lyotard's other two linguistic negations. Lyotard maintains that both the second type of linguistic negation (the "no" of signification or spacing) and the third negation (the "no" of designation), may be understood in spatial terms: the negation of spacing is manifest in the space between words while the negation of designation is manifest in the irreducible distance between speaker and reality, and between the word and the thing it designates. Lyotard argues that both of these spatial negations are violated in the dream, which performs transgressions of both negations.

The negation of interval, for Lyotard, is transgressed by the dreamwork condensation, which "crushes and blends" the signifying unities, creating overdetermined images (244). We might point out that condensation is a favorite device of the jokework as well, but there is an important difference between joke and dream condensation. Freud tells us that the dream condensations work to render the dream-thought illegible, opaque: they disguise desire from censorship, and thus permit the sleep to continue. But in the joke, all condensations must be transparent, legible, or the joke will not work. ("Alcoholiday," to take Freud's examples of condensation in *Jokes* [22], is amusing only if both of the two components, "alcohol" and "holiday," are perceived.) In joke condensation, the linguistic negation of spacing is maintained even as it is violated, paradoxically, since both sources remain visible to the mind's eye. Once again, like the offended lady in the joke scenario, or the "negated" mother of *Die Verneinung*, each of the two components is at once presented and absented, denied and affirmed in the condensed word.

The third negation, the "no" of designation, is transgressed in the dream, according to Lyotard, by the tendency of primary process to transform the abstract into the concrete (to make ideas into pictures, in the manner of the rebus; in the dream, for example, someone who is troubled by a pesky problem, a "pain in the neck," may wear a neckbrace). Lyotard is borrowing Freud's idea of the concrete nature of regressive or infantile thought processes; this infantile and magical animism is a kind of privilege of the dream-world that not only transgresses but actually ignores the restrictions of reality. As Freud puts it (*Jokes* 203), the dream substitutes psychic reality for exterior reality, inspiring belief.

Another example of the transgression of the givens of reality by the third negation, according to Lyotard, may be seen in what Freud calls "the tendency to treat words as things" since, in reality words are not objects but transparent tools or pointers, designating things (275). We could say that their essence as transparent means to an end is in fundamental contrast with (what Lyotard terms) the opacity of the designated exterior world. The dream's play with words as objects, then, making concrete visual puns, transgresses the third linguistic negation of designation from which language derives its referential power. It may seem obvious to us that the joke has similar liberties and privileges, often ignoring the givens of reality and indulging in fanciful wordplay, concretizing words and making them the objects of delight. Indeed, Freud makes reference to this tendency to concretization in the joke (*Jokes* 119–20), stating that understanding a pun, for instance, requires the mental examination of words as objects in themselves, sometimes with different spellings but identical pronunciations. (This is precisely the technique of some contemporary poets, like Ponge or Queneau, who exploit the word as *ob-jeu* [Ponge's term] in a playful objectification of words on the page.) Yet, the joke, unlike the dream, must make a certain sense so as not to deteriorate into gibberish and to make its point, however disguised. In other words, the license to treat words as things is a kind of privilege of joking language, but these figures are never confused with reality as they are in the engrossing picture-puzzle scenario of the dream.

We might attribute all the distinctions between dream and joke transgressions to the social status of joke, compared with the profoundly asocial experience of dream, as well as to the different modes at work in waking and sleeping thought (primary and secondary process). While the dream is completely regressive—entailing a return to infantile modes of figuration leading to interior discharge of energy in hallucination—the joke is at once regressive (infantile, concrete, figurative) and outgoing, since its function is to be understood (but only of course in its own good time, after an initial deferral of understanding, a "bewilderment"). The joke makes use of "figure," as the transgression of linguistic negation, but this figural mode is put to a social use, rendered intelligible in a system of communication.

To summarize, Lyotard's discussion of negation as transgression deals explicitly with at least four levels or kinds of transgression: the three linguistic negations and the fourth "negation of negation," or "transgression of transgression," which is the abolition of all three discursive negations by the figural processes of the dreamwork. Into this scheme, we must insert a fifth (comic or poetic) transgression, which is "figural" but which plays with the negations in language rather than abolishing them; it is an in-between process whose technique is similar to that of the dream, but whose capacity of "fulfillment of desire" is much more limited because of the constraints of consciousness (secondary process) and the demand of social intelligibility. And this view of linguistic figural transgression as a function of deferred desire (a substitutive fulfillment) provides another way of thinking of Bataille's "naive comedy," since the erotic cheating to which Bataille refers—the stopping short of the final gratification in death—is in a way equivalent to the partial satisfaction of desire afforded in the transgression of discourse by the joking figure—the failure of the linguistic figure to satisfy desire completely (as the dream hallucination does), because of its social mission. When linguistic transgression is understood in this way, the cheating implied in the process is no longer just a sign of complicity with the dialectic (understood as a production of global meaning); it is also a sign of the inability of any such totalizing system to account for the excess of the figures that transgress it—its inability to hold itself intact and to mean any one thing unequivocally. The crossing of boundaries (transgression) is incessantly repeated in the production of meaning; thus, language, even when seeming to serve the dialectic of reason, endlessly exceeds it, rendering Absolute Knowledge impossible, laughable.

A word from our sponsor (Return to Freud)

But how Freudian is Lyotard's poststructuralist treatment of negativity? Where does Freud himself stand on the question of negativity, in discourse and in analysis? While the question is too complicated to be treated in detail here, at least partly because of Freud's own apparent confusion on the matter, it nevertheless has some intriguing implications for a postmodern reading of negativity. For there are at least four distinct types of negativity in Freud's writings: *Verneinung* (denegation), *Verleugnung* (disavowal), *Verwerfung* (rejection or foreclusion), *Verdrängung* (repression). The first of these, as we know, is linguistic negation ("it is not my mother"), and, Freud tells us, it is associated with the last type, with repression, since it is Verdränung that represses the threatening thought from consciousness and then exerts pressure on consciousness to negate it. We might say that denegation [*Verneinung*] is the discursive symptom of repression [*Verdränung*]. (In chapter 4, we have seen that repression is associated with the linguistic figure of metaphor, which replaces/represses one term by another.)

The second negation, disavowal [*Verleugnung*], is a term that Freud introduces when he speaks of perversion and its related phenomenon: fetishism.[21] In Freud's account, the "pervert" disavows the evidence of (female) castration, transferring and displacing desire away from the female genitals and onto substitute objects (in fetishism), or deferring and lingering on intermediate erotic activity (in perversion). (In chapter 4, I suggested that as a type of displacement, perversion could be associated with the Lacanian figure of metonymy, as that always unfinished desire displaced from one element to the next in the signifying chain.)

Finally, in his study of the Wolf Man, Freud posits foreclusion [*Verwerfung*] as an ultimate negation or repudiation, which expels castration from the unconscious, causing its return as hallucination in the Real. (Lacan elaborates on this idea in his writings on Hamlet, who is haunted by the "forecluded" ghost of his Father.) Lacan insists, after Freud, that foreclusion is the operative negation in psychosis, causing what Freud calls a loss of reality and what Lacan calls a loss of the Symbolic, a destruction of that social link allowing the subject to communicate and function in the Real.

I would like to venture a transcoding of Freud's negations into Lyotard's linguistic terms (although Lyotard himself does not make the attempt, perhaps with good reason). In any case, *Verneinung* or negation, sometimes rendered as "denegation," might be said to figure in all three of Lyotard's linguistic negations. Denegation is most obviously equivalent to Lyotard's syntactical negation, the straightforward "no" of the judgmental faculty, motivated by repression. But it is also at work in the second negation, the "no" of spacing, since it retrieves repressed material from the Beyond of the unconscious and makes it present in discourse, thus trans-gressing the barrier or boundary between the conscious and the unconscious (this is Lacan's metaphoric "bar" between signified and signifier, which also implies the "bar" that operates in metaphor, occulting one term).[22] Similarly, *Verneinung* bears witness to the primal desire that motivates language and is thus manifest in the third negation of designation, staking out the uncrossable space in which language is generated, between the self and its objects of desire. In this perspective, discourse would always be to some degree a neurotic function, based on repression of desire yet occurring in the irreducible interval hollowed out by desire, the space between the speaking subject and the Real.

At the other end of Freud's spectrum of negation, there is the psychotic mechanism of *Verwerfung*, which is paradoxically the most fulfilling of the negations since it entails a complete loss of reality rather than a subjugation to its rules, as well as a denial of castration and fulfillment of desire in hallucination. In this regard, the *Verwerfung* (foreclusion) most closely resembles Lyotard's figural dream mode in which there is a relatively complete loss of reality, accompanied by a gratification of desire in hallucination.

Between the negation that serves repression and thus operates in neurosis (*Verneinung*) and the negation that provides hallucinatory gratification in psychosis (*Verwerfung*), there is the other relatively "perverse" negation (*Verleugnung*) that Freud places closer to psychosis than neurosis (because it entails a denial of reality). Still, perversion is not a complete loss of reality but is rather a deflected gratification of desire in the face of the obstacles posed by reality. (Freud even says in the *Three Essays* that the pervert may be considered a happy person in a sense, fulfilled by an ingenious compromise between desire and reality.) This metonymic/perverse displacement of desire, then, seems closest to Lyotard's compromise linguistic/ "figural" transgression (poetry, joking), which replays reality or discourse to its liking, affording a substitute gratification of desire in the face of an obstacle.

With this erotic note, we have perhaps come full circle, back to our point of entry into this comic labyrinth: Bataille's notion of nonservile negativity, within discourse but not reducible to meaning. For the poststructuralist games with negativity suggest that Bataille's *impossible* should be read not as the beyond of language but as the impossibility that haunts language itself, the comic possibility. This (im)possibility is perhaps the Other of discourse, the "figural transgression" or "double scene" that undoes, doubles, reworks meaning from within, the absent presence that makes itself perversely felt in what Barthes has called the "fetish words" of Bataille's text, words such as sovereignty, eroticism, even laughter (Barthes: "Desire is not in the text by virtue of words which 'represent' or 'narrate' it but rather by words sufficiently cut off [*découpés*], sufficiently brilliant and triumphant, to make themselves love-objects, in the manner of fetishes").[23]

It is perhaps in this sense that we may understand the poststructuralist skirmish with dialectic negativity: as a perverse effort to cheat and lose by means of a prolonged comic detour, which doubles your pleasure in a dialectic game perhaps, but in a game with no *Aufhebung,* no winners and no losers, where all players are both winners and losers (Derrida: "*Qui s'y joue, s'y perd, s'y gagne*" [*DS* 265]) thanks to the comic work of overdetermination. This transgression as excess is expressed in what Derrida calls the *polysémie* of meaning, the punning process that Derrida, like Lyotard, understands as the intrusion of something alien, radically negative, onto rational discursive language (Derrida: "The white space is inscribed or noticed [*se remarque*] always as disappearance, an erasure, nonsense. Finitude then becomes infinitude, according to a non-Hegelian identity: by an interruption that suspends the equation of the mark with sense" [*DS* 285]). Derrida's polyseme could be said to expose and exploit the third linguistic negation in discourse as proposed by Lyotard—the negation of designation—which points out that the word and the designated object are never adequate to each other, that meaning is a *mise-en-abîme,* an always unfinished process of designation, leaving discourse open to intrusion by its Other, vulnerable to lapse, to error, to pun.

Similarly, in Derrida's reading Bataille's sovereign moment may be understood as the intrusion of silence into discourse—not as a literal moment of silence (though that, too) but rather as the admission of something "other" into discourse. (The allowing of something different or repressed to have its say can of course have political connotations as well, engaging a discourse that refuses to be stymied by the double bind of poststructuralist negativity.) In the case of Bataille's "negativity without employ," this rupture can be understood either as the entrance of something figural or nonsensical (Derrida: "an interruption or wound within discourse . . . that which can be opened to the absolute loss of sense" [*EG* 383], or the obsessive and unsilenceable quality of discourse itself ("One must speak; the inadequacy of all speech must, at least be said" [*EG* 376]).

Bataille writes, in *Méthode de méditation:* "One has to double language, by turning to ruses, to strategies, to likenesses . . . [finding] a reason to laugh."[24] The postmodern text, both literary and theoretical, provides just such a strategy for the interruption of serious discourse by highlighting and celebrating the inadequacy of language, a fault that the postmodern text seeks not to repair but to expose, by doubling language, by exploiting multiple meanings, and by constantly deploying the ruses and strategies afforded by primary process. Thus, Bataille's transgression is perhaps neither Hegelian nor non-Hegelian, but is rather post-Hegelian, a similacrum of Hegel, a mimetic strategy of doubling, putting into play a post-dialectic sensibility of aftermath as reason for laughter [*une raison de rire*], making use of a comic mask to conceal its subversive strategy of excess. And as Lyotard's Lacanian reading of desire in language suggests, the unconscious is perhaps a comic hero, the undoer of that repressive villain Hegelian Reason ("Curses! foiled again"), the source of that out-of-service negativity engaged by the postmodern text in its comic skirmish with dialectic totality. As Philippe Sollers has so colorfully put it, "The discoveries of psychoanalysis are the fragments of the explosion of the Hegelian system."[25]

But let us double Sollers's observation with a yet another double take. Perhaps the discoveries of psychoanalysis are not so much fallout of Hegelian system as they are the very tools that "unwork" that system, in what Maurice Blanchot will call "an infinite entertainment," purloining Freud's punch line, the discovery that the Other is the source of the laughter that inhabits, exceeds, and outwits the dialectic.

6. The Infinite Entertainment: Blanchot's "Unworked" Text

> How may the search for a plural word be affirmed, founded no longer on predominance and subordination but on dissymmetry, so that between two words, an infinite rapport may always be the very movement of meaning . . .
>
> Maurice Blanchot, *L'entretien infini* (9)

Like other poststructuralists, Maurice Blanchot takes issue with the tradition of Western philosophy, the prejudice in favor of unity or order, based on "the postulate as old as thought itself" (*EI* 10) that reality is continuous.[1] Blanchot argues that this ideal of seamless continuity—the search for one coherent system, one continuous truth accounting for all aspects of reality—has resulted in a corollary view of all discontinuous or articulated phenomena, including the differential signifying process of language, as faults or errors in understanding [*un signe de malheur de l'entendement*]:

> It's the great Parmedian sphere, it's Einstein's model of the universe. From which it would result that the very modalities of our knowledge, the structures of our sense and our psychic apparatus, the forms of our languages . . . require us to rend or to cut [*à déchire ou à dáecouper*] this beautiful seamless tunic. (*EI* 10)

Thus, Blanchot seems to imply that traditional philosophy tries to perform a kind of mending or patch-up, aiming to repair the flaws or gaps in understanding, reaffirming the seamless Truth of the Logos.

To this system, Blanchot counterposes a willfully playful double-talk (called at various moments *la parole plurielle/littéraire/fragmentaire*). Literary language provides the best example of this plural discourse, unworked by a desire that pokes holes in the fabric of the Logos. Like his postmodern fellow travelers, Blanchot seeks to undo the work of philosophy, but he more than any of the others relates this playful unworking to the "textwork" of literary expression.

Blanchot's concept of the plural word would seem to suggest that like Derrida and Lacan he has a radical view of language as text: language is a woven fabric that is not merely invaded or exceeded by *désir* but that is itself an effect of desire, harboring the process of its own "unworking," its own nondiscursivity or its own "dissemination." Of course, as we saw in chapter 2, Blanchot does concede that at least two relatively whole modes of speech do exist (the *paroles* of understanding and reason). Still, Blanchot's own radical formulation of human experience finally suggests that all language is subject to a comic rereading that would expose its plurality, the holes between warp and woof of even the most apparently "semeless" text. Nevertheless, the third type of speech that Blanchot elaborates—the *parole plurielle/littéraire*—is different from ordinary language; rather than seeking to cover up its duplicity or mend its "semes," it actually depends on them to wreak its dispersive effect. In other words, the language of the Logos (understanding) and of the dialectic (reason) must work at hiding or patching up its faults, its slips and derogations, if it is to "work," to be taken seriously; but literary or plural language must *play* in order to work, relying on a kind of "*sic*" humor to avoid the dead end of *le mot juste*. Blanchot's greatest contribution to the postmodern notion of text is perhaps this focus on the plural literary word and the notion of literariness itself; indeed, Blanchot's wordgames may be read as a kind of postmodern aesthetics.

The reign of light

Blanchot maintains that the traditional philosophical project, the search for truth, is characterized by a predisposition for things visible whereby knowledge is considered a process of "dis-covery" or "bringing to light." This enlightened tradition makes use of discontinuity of interval to achieve a unified overview ("To see is to make use of separation . . . to see is to have the experience of the continuous, and to celebrate the sun, The One" [*EI* 39]). It is interesting that Blanchot's view of philosophy anticipates to some degree the argument of contemporary French feminists such as Annie Le Clerc and Luce Irigaray, who have mounted a related critique of the ideology of domination and appropriation as an effect of an androcentric perspective characterized by the reign of the specular.[2] In any case, Blanchot's analysis concerns itself more with the literary than the sociopolitical effects of this reign of light; Blanchot argues that the philosophical prejudice in favor of the specular finds its literary counterpart in the ideal of classicism. Citing Foucault's formula—"classical language does not exist but rather functions" (*EI* 38)—Blanchot stresses the transparency of classical language, which strives to be identical to that which it designates, purging the unclear or ambiguous. In this "light," clarity is equivalent to transparency; Blanchot's argument thus has resonances of Heidegger's point, taken over by French existentialism, that the opacity and materiality of language—its existence as letters on a page or as a system of sounds—becomes evident only when "clear" communication breaks down.

Now, since for Blanchot (as for other postmoderns treated in chapter 5) the Hegelian dialectic represents the most subtle and sophisticated philosophical system—precisely because discontinuity or negativity is taken seriously in its process—the effort to cast a shadow on enlightened thought must entail an attempt at "unworking" the dialectic process. Indeed, Blanchot insists that any critique of the privilege of "continuity, unity, or reassembly of experience" (18) must first come to terms with the dialectic, accounting for its "validity as well as its limits" (18). Yet for Blanchot even more than for his fellow travelers, the ability to question the dialectic is itself a postmodern prerogative, a result of the culmination of the philosophical tradition; thus, Blanchot concurs with Hegel's view that modernity (as represented by dialectic reason) consummates the Logos, and crowns the whole Western tradition of logistic coherence. In order to "unwork" this finality, then, Blanchot turns away (in a move described as a *tournant*) from the idea of negativity—which only serves the movement of dialectic reason—and toward the notion of affirmation. A symptom of the inability of Absolute Knowledge to have the last word, this affirmation has Nietzschean overtones:

> Transgression, end of history, death of God are not entirely equivalent terms. But all do indicate the moment where the Logos comes to an end [*prend fin*], not by negating itself, but by affirming itself again and again, without novelty, by the obligation—the folly [*folie*]—of repetition. (405)

Yet, in spite of the obvious influence of Nietzsche in this insistence on endless affirmation, Blanchot rejects the temptation of nihilism as well as the Dionysian lure of madness, understood as silence, ecstasy, or absolute negativity. His affirmation, more in the realm of folly [*folie*] than insanity, stops short of the abyss of madness, the chilling excess of reason that posits final solutions; he never stops asking, "But what now?" Indeed, Blanchot is at pains to point out that nihilism is all too easily recuperated into a positivist tradition ("there is still too much positivity in nothingness" [592]), since the dialectic may recover such negativity in its final synthesis. As we have seen, a similar caveat underlies Derrida's critique of mimesis, which cautions that simply to deny mimetic hierarchy is to leap feet first back into the dialectic process. Blanchot's impulse of affirmation, then, should be distinguished from several moves that it resembles: it is neither the eternal rupture of forgetting of Nietzsche's (and de Man's) modernism (discussed in chapter 1) since it emphasizes and affirms history rather than repressing it, nor is it a celebration of a radicalized Hegelian negativity, in the manner of Kristeva or Bataille, since it insists on an aftermath that is not simply a transgression. Rather than trying to find a way of saying "no" and meaning it—as Bataille and others have done—Blanchot's affirmative postmodernism says "yes, but what now?"

In fact, in a curious sort of way, Blanchot's treatment of the dialectic dilemma seems to represent the opposite of Bataille's approach; when Bataille comes up against the limits of discourse, the impossibility of expressing the "sovereign moment" within the limits of language, he falls silent (or laughs). But Blanchot continues to speak, compulsively, about the very limits of the language he confronts: "How may we speak about this limit," he asks, "without allowing sense to 'unlimit' it?" (556). For Bataille the impossible is not expressible while for Blanchot it is all too expressible, and speech itself is its symptom.

Still, Blanchot and Bataille are perhaps after all merely emphasizing opposite sides of the same dilemma: they are both asking how excess can avoid subordination to system. Yet, while Bataille continues to be haunted by the specter of impossibility, and its binary opposite (possibility), Blanchot seeks to outwit these binary oppositions. For Blanchot, the "question of the whole" (27) can be put into question only by that "most profound of questions," the insatiable "what now?" bearing witnesses to "the excess of questioning over the power to question" (27). Since all answers are already contained in the dialectic, Blanchot concludes that this excessive question must be posed obliquely, in a long-circuit exploiting speech as detour [*la parole comme détour*]. Blanchot's own impossible question, then, *requires* a roundabout expression that "neither enlightens nor obscures" (557)—a *parole plurielle* eluding the reversibility of dialectic negativity. Thus, plural expression becomes a comic strategy for bypassing the ruses of dialectic logic even while avoiding the short-circuit of too-direct satisfaction. For Bataille, laughter is a symptom or response to impossibility, to the unworking of reason; for Blanchot, it is the process of unworking itself. Moreover, Blanchot insists that the plural word can only be a function of a plural relation [*rapport pluriel*] between self and other, a non-dialectic rapport exceeding the master-slave relation of the dialectic. This is perhaps the point at which a psychoanalytic perspective may intervene, proposing a third term not as synthesis but as obstacle, as emblem of desire; Blanchot's plural rapport may then be read as a relation with that exorbitant Other, the unconscious, beyond the totalizing reach of logic.[3]

Three modes of relation (or, the alien as Mr. Right)

Now In *L'entretien infini,* Blanchot outlines three possible modes of relation with a fellow being. The first is described as identification or reciprocal acknowledgment, the second as a fusion or incorporation, and the third as an estrangement. The first rapport entails the view of the other as an alter ego in a relation of equality and reciprocity, an other with whom one may reach an understanding ("when I seek to use him as a theme of knowledge or a subject of truth" [*EI* 38]). This first mode of relation belongs to the traditional order of light and visibility because it makes use of interval to create an identification with the other, who is included and appropriated in a "view" that "comprehends" him as like being (and denies or rationalizes his difference). This rapport is a function of clarity or transparency since the invisibility of the interval is necessary to this comprehensive vision ("Interval does not impede here; on the contrary, it permits the direct relation" [39]). The transparency of the connecting interval is both literal and figurative insofar as the phenomenon of vision, which orders and apprehends exterior reality, serves as a model for the act of understanding ("every view is an overview" [40]) as well as for the constructive activity of human work ("work, discourse [are] modes of action by which we transform nature into world" [40]).

This first rapport is consistent with Blanchot's first mode of cognition or expression (the *parole d'entendement* discussed in chapter 2 as the mode of Baudelaire's referential comic). It might then be considered to be the relation most characteristic of the conventional referential comic mode, either by virtue of its use of the other in the service of understanding or by virtue of its "gentlemanly" and civilized nature that permits two equals to share a good laugh together at the expense of the comic victim. We recall that like Blanchot's first rapport of identification, the referential comic emphasizes transparency by making use of (invisible) interval to appropriate and understand and by requiring that any momentary confusion be "cleared up" by an act of judgment in the move from bewilderment to illumination. (Of course, we have seen that the seemingly controlled and transparent referential comic actually masks elements of violence and vulnerability.)

All of this would seem to suggest that Blanchot's first *rapport d'identification* parallels his first mode of speech [*la parole d'entendement*] in its capacity for self-satisfied self-delusion. In psychoanalytic terms, we could say that this "identification," which takes the other as model and alter ego, nonetheless masks a certain competitive aggressivity aiming to capture and fascinate the alter ego by means of ideational mimetics.[4] In Lacanian terms, Blanchot's identification functions in the Imaginary register, both because it affords an illusion of solidity and "identity" (masking a fundamentally divided alienated ego, the Imaginary ego of the mirror stage) and because it masks the aggressivity subtending any Imaginary relation.

The second mode of relation that Blanchot describes aims at a different kind of rapport with the other, seeking a "spontaneous fusion" or "immediate unity" (96): "I may desire, by the ravishment of communication, to be united immediately with you in this very instant, to draw the other into myself in an effusion where neither will survive" (96). In this desire for a spontaneous merging, we recognize the same type of goal as in Baudelaire's absolute comic, motivated by the nostalgia for a lost unity; and, as we have seen, this urge for a kind of absolute loss of boundary between self and other is also consistent with the goal of dissolution of individual boundaries in

Bataille's erotic act. We have noted the problematic and even comedic nature of such impulses toward continuity or loss of self, and the "impossibility" that this urge (perhaps fundamentally a death-urge) represents. In psychoanalytic terms, we might say that Blanchot's second rapport, like Baudelaire's *comique absolu* and Bataille's erotic continuity, is still in the Imaginary register of misrecognition—seeking an always impossible/illusory oneness with the object of desire, an incestuous short-circuit that may only be circumvented with the aid of the third term, the intrusive Other who initiates the subject into the Symbolic order. Indeed, the desire of merger or fusion is a thinly masked desire of incorporation, associated (by Freud as well as by Lacan) with the function of identification.

Thus, Blanchot's first rapport overlooks separation by using it as a transparent field of appropriation; the second abolishes this distance in a violent act of ingestion. Both fail to acknowledge or maintain difference. But the third *rapport du neutre* is not a relation of identification or unity. Instead, it emphasizes the maintained exteriority of the Other:

> We can begin to sense what we have called the rapport of the third sort . . . that which founds the rapport, leaving it unfounded, is not the proximity of struggle, of service, of essences, of knowledge or recognition [*de connaissance ou de reconnaissance*] . . . it's the strangeness between us. (97)

Close encounters of the third kind

Thus Blanchot's "strangeness" [*étrangeté*] is not one of separation or distance but an "interruption escaping all measure," fundamentally alien to unitary, measurable increments. Blanchot thus insists that he is not seeking to do away with coherence but rather to indicate the limits of a comprehensive vision: "It is not from coherent thought that we are trying to free ourselves; nor are we trying, at one fell swoop, to rid ourselves of unity; but speaking, and speaking necessarily under the authority of comprehensive thought, [we try] to divine another form of speech and another sort of rapport with the Other, the presence of the Other, which would not send us back to ourselves, nor to the One" (95).

This interruption between self and Other is a function of betweenness; its identifying symptom is speech ("the void [that] cannot be confused with nothingness—this interval represented by the word 'between'—would be an infinite separation that is nonetheless a rapport, the compulsion of speech" [97]). The *"entretien infini"* that is the mode of the third rapport with the Other, then, is a postmodern symptom of sorts, ensuing only when "the proposition of a God has been absented" (97), when the possibilities of mediation are exhausted or inaccessible. But in psychoanalytic terms, this third rapport might be read as a version of the oedipal or Symbolic rapport, which requires that the subject confront the impossibility of simple appropriation of the other (as object of desire, Lacan's *petit objet a*), thereby renouncing an impossible satisfaction or bliss (*jouissance* as a kind of incest, death or absolute negativity). In the psychoanalytic scenario, an imploded *jouissance* (fusion with the desired object) must be prohibited (by the Law, the threat of castration), even as an untimely death must be deferred, in the name of life, growth, and human community. And just as the impossible dream of fusion with the object must be abandoned, so too must the *illusory* nature of a unified ego or simple identity be "recognized" as mere mirage, thanks to the encounter with one's unconscious desire (Lacan's "desire of the Other"). In the Freudian/Lacanian comedy, the deadly unity of two—a tragic possibility—is rendered impossible because of the interloping stranger (the third), who assures that close encounters will be close calls, but no more. The discovery of psychoanalysis might be something like what Blanchot calls the third rapport of neutrality [*troisième rapport du neutre*], the recognition that one is always divided from oneself and estranged from the object of desire in an oedipal or Symbolic rapport that is perhaps a "close encounter of the third kind," but where the Alien is the face in the mirror.

Oedipus as comedy

But this situation is by no means as scary as it seems; in fact, I want to suggest that Blanchot's third rapport is profoundly comic, both structurally and functionally, at least in the postmodern sense of the term. First, this rapport looks and performs like a postmodern joke; it is a plural phenomenon whereby the relation with the other has become an infinite relation, as in a hall of mirrors. To put it another way, all jokes are a function of separation or contrast and are thus by definition a function of plurality. But in classic or referential comic productions, the separation or contrast is made to serve the faculty of understanding, and thus light functions as a transparent means to an end, the clarity that makes the understanding possible. (Bewilderment yields to illumination.)

However, Blanchot sheds a new light on the notion of transparency itself, insisting that the apparent unity afforded by the simple act of seeing is only an illusion, a kind of trickery:

> Light erases its tracks: invisible, it renders visible; it guarantees the direct meeting [*la connaissance directe*], while it suppresses itself as presence. . . . Light is thus at least doubly tricky: because it tricks us about its nature and because it tricks us by presenting as immediate that which is not immediate. (244)

So, light is the master trickster perpetuating the illusion of unity with our objects of desire ("It only acts by being the hidden mediator, it plays tricks on us by a dialectic of illusion" [244]).

Thus Blanchot has two views of light: as servant of understanding and as master of trickery. The first emphasizes recovery in a field of unity, the second insists on maintained separation. And these two views of light—as servile dupe and as wily rogue—result in two definitions of pluralism. The first is still a philosophical pluralism, subordinate to the search for truth, which maintains that separation is the tool of examination and discovery ("*la vérité commence à deux*" [232]). But the second, Blanchot writes, is that "strange pluralism with neither plurality nor unity, which inhabits fragmentary speech [*la parole de fragment*] as the provocation of language itself" (232); it is the *parole plurielle* that is left over when all needs are sated; it continues to speak "when all has already been said" (232). This fragmentary pluralism finds a parallel in Lacanian theory, in the notion of language as metonymic desiring chain, whereby—according to Lacan's celebrated formula—"a subject is a subject for another signifier." Lacan insists on language as symptom of the inexhaustibility of desire; this endless desire is the motor of language, the drive that motivates "demand" (as reflected in the Lacanian formula: "desire is the excess of demand over need"). Moreover, since *désir* is an unfulfilled force that persists when biological needs have been gratified, we could say that the Lacanian notion of desire conforms to Freud's definition of the aesthetic. So, Blanchot's work provides another angle from which to consider the coincidence of Lacanian desire with the Freudian aesthetic; transmitted into Blanchot's terms, the excess demand constituting desire could be thought of as that persistent "excess of questioning over the power to question," the "what now?" that persists when the dialectic has answered all questions reasonably.

Ménage à trois (4): the comic fragment

For Blanchot as for Derrida, the excessive and desiring pluralism is nonsymmetrical, a play difference that resists appropriation by a unifying vision ("what is at stake . . . is dissymmetry as space"). This dissymmetry could be thought of as a sort of uncollapsable triangle in which the third point represents the "third rapport" or the maintained otherness of the Other, the exteriority that makes direct appropriation impossible. Rather than being a symmetrical and reversible "I-thou" dual relation, the shortest distance between two points, the *troisième rapport du neutre* is a relation haunted by thirdness, the incurable neutrality of the Other. This configuration can be compared to Freud's joking triangle, also defined by its thirdness, and by the inaccessibility of the object of desire, indifferent to our demand—an object who remains out of reach even when seemingly mastered in the joke. A similar paradigm insists, as we have seen, in the erotic triangle (priest-victim-spectator) defined by Bataille, as well as in the classical Freudian oedipal configuration. Each of these triangles is a long-circuit, the paradigm of deferred or deflected desire denied satisfaction because of the intrusiveness of the exterior Other. But in Lacan, this game of thirds is proliferated into fourths, in the four terms of the *Schéma L* (the subject, the ego, the object of desire, and the unconscious) whose intrication assures that every oedipal threesome opens outward to an Other term, and that every analytic transference is also a countertransference with an expanding chain of terms.[5]

In literature, Blanchot maintains, the plural dissymmetry of the *troisième rapport* is often manifested as fragmentary writing, as in the aphorisms of Antonin Artaud and René Char, writing that puts itself out of reach of a totalizing context. Yet the *parole fragmentaire* does not negate or contest wholeness; it simply exceeds it, has nothing to do with it: "It is an insufficient *parole,* but not because of incompleteness . . . [it] does not contradict the whole. The fragmentary does not precede the whole, but is said outside of the totality, and after it" (229).

Once again, Blanchot compares this plural/fragmentary speech to a persistent question: "Everything is now as though already accomplished. . . . What, then, remains to be done? [*Alors, qu'y a-t-il à faire?*]" (230). Psychoanalysis may speak to the nature of this question, to the meaning of the unremitting "what now?" For as early as 1905 (in the *Three Essays*) Freud alludes to the relentless excess underlying human drive as a function of sexuality, itself an excess that has been "laid on to" biological drive: a demand for an extra satisfaction beyond that of hunger.[6] The notion of excess never ceases to insist in Freud's theory, reappearing as the compulsion to repeat, as the life instinct, as the death-drive. For Freud, human being is propelled by voracious drives, and it is the unceasing quality of these drives that Lacan highlights when he formulates *désir* as the unreasonable *demande* that continues to be posed after needs have been sated and after all reasonable queries have received a reply. The *désir* of French psychoanalysis might serve as an apt example of what Blanchot means by *la parole fragmentaire* occurring "outside of totality, and after it."

Blanchot qualifies this extra-dialectical fragment (which occurs *after* "we have gotten out of history by history . . . [when] time has come to an end") as a Dionysian phenomenon (325). He is careful, however, to insist that this leftover speech may not be equated with fluidity, or continuity—nor with the ultimate resolution of death ("This fragmentation . . . is not the bold renunciation of unity nor unity which remains 'one' by pluralizing itself. Fragmentation is the god Dionysus himself, that which has no relation to a center, and which permits no originary reference" [325]). As I have argued, it is precisely this distinction between two concepts of Dionysian nonreason—understood on the one hand as fluidity or dissolution of boundaries (in the manner of Bataille's "impossible" moment of continuity) and on the other hand as an infinite fragmentation (in the manner of Blanchot's "plural word")—that also demarcates the essential distinction between the concept of the second absolute type of comic expression and the third desiring or aesthetic type of comic expression. (The absolute comic uses negativity to try to get out of the limits of language, but the postcomic remains an effect of discourse, even though it imposes intermittent silence on discursive language by insistently exceeding it and exposing its inadequacies in a comic *négativité sans emploi.*)

Blanchot's fragment is an aftermath, not an escape; his excessive questioning implies a proliferation of limits in the labyrinth of intersubjectivity (the "infinite conversation") rather than an abolition of limits in a final satisfaction of sovereign bliss. The fragmentary word is a compulsion rather than a *jouissance;* it is more akin to Freud's death-drive (as repetition) than to death itself (as ultimate discharge or pleasure). Blanchot's fragment is a punch line of sorts, insisting in the intersubjective chain as the something left over that induces the retelling of the joke. (The last word in a joke is always fragmentary, since its sovereignty as last word is undercut by its infinite iterability and the fact that it *must* be retold.) Thus, Blanchot's fragment is the antithesis of absolute or sovereign moments postulated by Baudelaire, Bataille, and others (although as we have seen, Baudelaire himself undercuts the concept of the absolute, just as Bataille's own notion of transgression as Hegelian comedy works to undercut the possibility of sovereignty. So, Baudelaire and Bataille are already "postmen" of the modern, comics whose own "delivery" undercuts their message).

Yet, the Imaginary specter of something like the absolute comic has persisted in our century, finding its full force in the notion of the *théâtre de la cruauté* of Antonin Artaud, or the *théâtre panique* of Fernando Arrabal, both of whom seek to provoke a vertiginous dissolution of the limits between actor and spectator (not unlike the reaction to Pierrot's grotesque self-sacrifice, described by Baudelaire). But these efforts have in turn given way to a theater of residue or aftermath, a comic "post-theater" of fragmentation that reflects a postmodern comic sensibility, providing a concrete image of excess by proliferating objects and characters beyond rational boundaries (Ionesco) or by extending the non-action into infinite repartee (Beckett).

Supply and demand: comic repetition

Blanchot emphasizes that such a fragmented, uncentered literature is a function of a certain desire, radically different from need: "Such a desire is not the sublimated form of need, nor the prelude to love. Need is a lack which is waiting to be filled; need is satisfied" (75). Significantly, the "prelude to love" to which Blanchot refers is strongly reminiscent of the "wooing talk" meant to act as a prelude to the satisfaction of sexual need in Freud's joke scenario (*Jokes* 100–02). For Blanchot opposes desire to the satisfaction of sexual need, just as Freud contrasts the joking process with purposeful wooing talk, reminding us that a joke, even when sexual in nature, is always a detour from biological purpose (*Jokes* 10). In fact as we have seen, it is in large part because the joking process is a deflection from goal that it fails to satisfy completely, and must give rise to repetition. The same is true of desire as Blanchot defines it: "This desire is desire of that which cannot be satisfied: it desires that which the desiring person does not need" (76). Like the desire motivating the repetition compulsion, Blanchot's "eternally maintained desire" remains ungratified and thus exceeds any single instance of transgression.

Desire is thus linked to error (as suggested by the French *errer:* to go astray, to wander): "Desire . . . is on the side of error, this infinite movement which always begins anew" (281). The defining characteristic of this erroneous desire is separation; like the desire of Tristan and Yseult, Blanchot writes, this desire is maintained in absence, by an unbridgeable estrangement that is also, paradoxically, a kind of rapport ("Whoever desires enters into the space where the distant is the essence of proximity, the place where what unites Tristan and Yseult is that which separates them" [281]). For Blanchot, the ultimate erotic relation is not a relation of fusion or unity but a relation of difference.

In his essay on Don Juan, Blanchot elaborates on the idea of erotic difference, pointing out that it is ungratified desire that motivates the urge to repeat even while assuring that the repeated element is never strictly identical to itself in two successive recurrences (as in Don Juan's renewed gesture of "similar but different" conquests). For Blanchot as for Freud, deflected desire is the motor of repetition, but it is also the motor of alteration, of change.[7] We have noted two such changing repetitions in the joking process: repetition of the primary game of desire, which puts on a new mask with each different joke, and repetition of the same joke with different poles of exchange each time (a new teller and a new listener). Furthermore, the joke's point can be thought of as a repetition insofar as it is a doubling of definitions, the means by which at least two different ideas are expressed in the same word or set of words.[8] Each of these repetitions reveals a difference underlying a recurrence of the same in each restaging.

And Freud's play scenario (especially as described by Lyotard) provides another way of understanding what Blanchot may mean by repetition with difference. When Lyotard describes Freud's *fort-da* scene, for instance, he presents the flinging away and the retrieval of the toy as an ever-changing ritual, concluding that the "most striking thing is not the law of reiteration, but the law of recurrence" (*DF* 353). Lyotard thus insists that the compulsion to repeat does not dictate an identical repetition but merely insures the repetition of different acts of play in response to the same underlying and ungratified desire (for union with the mother). Lyotard goes on to attribute the pulsating rhythm of the repeated game to the interaction of the life instinct with the death instinct, an interaction in which the death impulse represents the negative component of the play, the rejection or flinging away of the toys. It is this same impulse that accounts for the permutations in the game since it represents a sort of rejection of the status quo: "The death impulse is not that which makes [the toy] return, but that which makes it go away, and which assures that the formation is not maintained, cannot be maintained, identical to itself" (*DF* 354). The urge to rejection is the motor force that distances the desired object; the death instinct thus disrupts "unity" by producing an interval between the self and the desired object or end. As Freud himself seems to suggest, this game where the same is repeated differently, *beyond* pleasure, may be a prototype for the play of desire throughout human life.

Some Lacanians have suggested that this desiring repetition of difference may be read as the essence of literary/poetic repetition, especially if we refer to the conventional rhetorical definition of metaphor as the exploitation of sameness in difference, the masking of a familiar referent in a new image. Laplanche and Leclaire, for instance—in a formulation that owes much to Jakobson's notion of metaphor as function of the paradigmatic axis of language—have described metaphor as a figure that represses one (implicit) term and expresses one (explicit) term: the same idea is expressed by the new term, but differently, thanks to its substitution for the (repressed) original term.[9]

Blanchot's discussion of desire and repetition seems to be making a similar point about the literary process, at least as it is encountered in a certain kind of desiring text (he treats the work of Kafka, Hölderlin, Char, Gertrude Stein), a text that makes use of repetition with difference to prolong its aesthetic play. And while the works Blanchot treats are not all comic texts in the usual sense of the term, they may provide a way of thinking about the persistent ludic quality of postmodern writing in general.

An explicitly comic use of this type of repetition with permutation can be seen, for instance, in the writing of Raymond Queneau. In Queneau's very funny work, the repetition of words and formulae often seems to be engendered by an unfinished feeling; that is, his novels often seem to have more to say and to be playing out endless variants of the same material (the most obvious example is perhaps in the countless stylistic permutations of the *Exercices de style*). In other examples of postmodern writing, the excess that engenders repetition seems even more bizarre, precisely because it seems to occur when everything has already been finished (the novels of Marguerite Duras "begin" with their ending scene, repeated throughout the work; the plays of Beckett are about games played after some disaster has ended business as usual). Blanchot wonders about the curious nature of this kind of excess ("Strange surplus. What is this excess that leaves achievement unfinished?" [307]).

He later attempts to answer his own question by commenting on a celebrated example of literary excess: Stein's famous formula "a rose is a rose is a rose. . . ." Blanchot maintains that Stein's language serves a purpose of demystification by linking literary speech "to a neutral movement without beginning or end" (505), with neutral [*neutre*] understood as alien, rather than as simply uninvolved. He attributes the troubling effect of Stein's verse to the alternation of mystification and demystification (a movement recalling the comic technique of bewilderment and illumination): "The idea of rose resists very well here any development . . . it is even pure resistance: a rose is a rose. . . . But a rose is a rose is a rose comes in its turn to demystify the emphatic character of nomination and of the evocation of being" (505). Such a demystification serves to reveal the illusory character of the dream of full meaning, in which naming an object would be equivalent to capturing or determining its essence; these parodic repetitions are "unrooted and have fallen into the multitude of empty chatter [*bavardage*]" (505), providing a hint of the emptiness of all language, "speaking without beginning or end" (504).

But in addition, Stein's example serves to expose the difference underlying repetition, the identity that is undercut the moment the same is repeated, underscoring that the presence or authority of language is undermined by its iterability. Stein's demystification is thus related to the demystifying power of joking, which also exposes the unrooted character of language, the error whereby language fails to be identical to itself, connected to one meaning or essence. (To put it another way, Stein's language reveals difference in similarity while the joke reveals similarity in difference.) Moreover, an analogous game of hide-and-seek, bewilderment and illumination, is operative in the process of metaphor: a simple denotative correspondence between word and referent is obfuscated; poetic pleasure is produced when the reader is illuminated by the new, more poetic connection that the metaphor provides between the original referent and the new term.

It should be stressed, however, that all these kinds of repetitions with difference—which I propose as instances of Blanchot's parole *littéraire/fragmentaire/plurielle*—function not as dialectic negations or subversions of language, but as affirmations. Blanchot compares this "excess of repetitive affirmations" to a kind of compulsion or madness [*le jeu insensé d'écrire*], requiring the "putting into play of infinite interpretation and designation" (236). In his essay on Sade, Blanchot refers to this "madness" as an excess of sanity or reason, a logical outgrowth of the enlightened encyclopedic compulsion to account for everything, to write down every possible version of experience. Like a curiously rational insanity, Sade's own "senseless game of writing" as rewriting is an excessive affirmation, spurred on by an excess of reason (236). Interestingly, this also seems to be the upshot of Lacan's reading of Sade (*Kant avec Sade,* 1963), in which Sadian desire is described as an excess of linkage, the same kind of metonymic desire that Lacan considers the driving force of language, motivating the search of one word for another in the signifying chain. This linguistic desire of word for word is in turn a metaphor for intersubjective desire of one human being for another, linking subjects in a social network.

But whether writing is considered a kind of folly or an excess of rationality, Blanchot argues, it remains above all a symptom of the inexhaustible nature of human possibility ("Our existence is never anything but possible" [138]). Blanchot's kind of postmodern possibility is not so much a capacity as it is an ontological characteristic: it is "being plus the power to be" (59). Possibility is thus related to a certain open-ended future ("We never *are,* purely and simply; we are only in relation to the possibilities that we are"). Our human being, moreover, is linked with the ultimate possibility, namely, our capacity for a death that is always to come [*à venir*], in the future [*avenir*]: "This relation, which is always open to me until my end, adds up to another power. Dying, I can still die: this is the sign of our humanity [*notre signe d'homme*]" (60).

Paradoxically, this infinite impossibility is also the source of all human possible constructive effort: "From this excess of dying, humanity has built the world, has gone to work, has produced, has produced itself" (305). In such a definition we find an echo of Freud's theory of drive (*BPP*), which posits the instinctual push toward death or inertia as the excessive urge motivating all cultural achievement, the "development undertaken without any prospect of being able to bring the process to a conclusion or to attain the goal" (*BPP* 163). In Freud's account as in Blanchot's, human possibility is paradoxically overdetermined and undermined by impossibility.

Rumors

Now Blanchot considers the *parole plurielle/littéraire* to be the parodic expression of infinite, repeated possibility; its murmur [*rumeur*], reminiscent of Heideggerian "chatter," is incessant, irreverent, and playful, undercutting the pretensions of the author-ized text by always promising more (or less) than it delivers. In other words, the essentially indefinite quality of the (postmodern) literary text, its murmuring, or refusal to speak unequivocally, might be called a detour that exploits the fundamental playfulness of language, its ability to err from serious meaning. Blanchot writes that this chattering sort of multivalent literary language, whose meaning refuses to be pinned down (exploiting what Lacan has called the "sliding" quality of language), is encountered in the poetry of René Char, in which the slippery quality of the indefinite and anonymous narrating voice provides an example of "desire that remains desire" [*désir demeuré désir*]. In the desiring work of writers such as Char, Ionesco, Beckett, a kind of chatter is put to a poetic use, opening the text to layers of meaning and serving to demonstrate how the very least amount is taught or proved in that sort of public language whose manifest function is communication (i.e., the indefinite language of rumor, cliché, transmitted stories, even poetry). For these writers and others, the (postmodern) literary project consists in "unauthorizing" the text rather than in marking it indelibly with an idiosyncratic and original voice, for the poetic act undermines unequivocal statements.

It is interesting that Lyotard has defined poetic truth in precisely these terms; it is a useless and slippery truth, the antithesis of the philosophical tradition of the whole or True: "Its father is desire . . . this truth teaches nothing, is not edifying . . . it surges up alongside of the place where it is expected" (*DF* 282). Such a definition, then, is strikingly like Blanchot's characterization of the slippery half-truth of public murmuring or rumor (26); in both cases, the truth is unsilenceable and fractious (not unlike the forbidden point of a joke—or a case of the giggles—which is most insistent when an attempt to repress it is made).

"Ecriture": writing as poetic text

In Blanchot's work, as in the work of other French poststructuralists, the poetic desiring mode of expression is often simply called *écriture* or writing. But for these postmoderns *écriture* is not writing understood in the usual sense as a transcription of thought, a tool of communicative language that attempts to efface itself in the service of clarity. It is understood, rather, as something opaque, something that gets in the way of straightforward meaning. *Écriture* is the scene of the infinite entertainment, the encounter with otherness: "To write is to hold oneself—by means of interruption—in a relation with the Neutral [*le Neutre*] . . . without reference to the Same, without deference to the One" (384). Blanchot sees *écriture* as the mode of the interrupted third rapport with otherness, expressed in that plural speech that deploys difference and repetition ("Difference, play of time and space, is the silent game of relations, the multiple deployment that writing stages" [243]).

Writing, then, as postmodern process, is a working of difference coinciding with the putting of pen to paper—since the production of "trace" requires the differential workings of difference in chronological time and linear space—and yet exceeding that act. It is a postmodern allegory that describes and deploys the human response to desire; the Other whom Blanchot engages in conversation is a stand-in for desire, for the inevitability of detour, for the compulsion to live life even while being driven by death. The suspended quality of this "enter-tainment" highlights the negotiational quality of intersubjective desire, the compromise between life and death, between finishing and going on. Blanchot's work illustrates that this desiring compromise, which is perhaps the foremost theme of postmodern critical theory, is a poetic game whose rules may be cast in philosophical, psychoanalytic, or aesthetic terms. Consider for example, Lyotard's psychoanalytic formulation of desiring compromise [*DF* 359], which sounds a great deal like the volley of Blanchot's *entretien infini:* "Thus the instinctual order [*l'ordre pulsionnel*] when obstructed from its goals governs the fantasmatic by negotiating so to speak its staging [*sa mise en scène*] with the death-drive, each new formation being the effect of a compromise between fulfillment and nonfulfillment" (*DF* 359). Indeed, when Blanchot is transcoded through psychoanalysis—keeping an "infinite appointment" with the unconscious—the space of *écriture,* the page, seems to coincide with the intersubjective playing field between self and Other, the distance that engages and separates, revealing the duplicity of the Logos (dia-logue) as playful double-talk. But just how may we think of the ludic nature of this game of repartee, and what may a reading of Blanchot's aesthetic theory as *comic* theory tell us about the postmodern text?

Text as "infinite entertainment"

The central metaphor of Blanchot's work—the infinite conversation or entertainment—is itself generated out of pun; thus, it already represents a comic scene of sorts. For *"l'entretien infini"* is first a dialogue between interlocutors; the very give-and-take of their exchange lends a bantering, playful tone to the work. The *entretien* is also a suspension between—a *suspens mouvant*—in the sense that the very space upon which the verbal match is played is the irreducible interval between two players ("the otherness [*altérité*] by which he is not for me—it must be repeated—another 'I' nor another existence, nor a modality, nor a moment of universal existence, but the unknown in its infinite distance" [*EI* 108]). Thus, the encounter between speakers is an instance of Blanchot's third rapport where the fragmentary conversation is a kind of in-between speech [*parole d'entre-deux*]. (Here we find the echo of Derrida's punning in "La double séance," describing the "suspense" of Mallarmé's poetic act: *l'antre de Mallarmé* = *l'entre de Mallarmé* = *l'entre-deux Mallarmé.* The two speakers in Blanchot's text are like the two walls of the grotto [*antre*] in Derrida's text, demarcating the scene where thoughts are volleyed back and forth.) In this postmodern entertainment, it is not a question of reaching dialectic resolution by argument or negation; rather, doubling, iteration, or affirmation is the technique of the conversation ("This reflection is accomplished by the single fact that the word is divided and doubled; what is said once on one side is repeated on the other side and not only reaffirmed [because taken up again] but raised to a form of new affirmation where changing place, the spoken word enters [*entre*] into relation with its difference . . . suspended between two poles of attraction" [318]).

This volley—whereby speech crosses the abyss—creates an echo, a plural word suspended *en souffrance* in an always unfinished task; the abyss must be traversed again and again ("Distance is not abolished, but is maintained preserved and pure by that word which sustains difference" [318]). Thus Blanchot's *entretien* displays all the characteristics of comic interplay, originating in a double movement of "pursuit-rupture" (317) that recalls the compulsive repetitions of Freud's *fort-da* child's play.

In this passage, as in many of the theories of the comic mentioned in chapter 2, the image of two players serves as a metaphor for a kind of farcical sport in which the notions of victory and defeat are meaningless: "It cannot be a question of winning for the participants, that is to say, of arguing and proving in view of some knowable truth" (317). (This in turn recalls that literary game to which Derrida alludes in "La double séance," where winning is the same as losing [*qui s'y joue, s'y perd, s'y gagne*].) For in the postmodern face-off, the Other functions as referee, a stand-in for social necessity, an eternal witness to the rules that govern all human interplay. The presence of the Other across the abyss of desire, requiring that we face up to difference, is the ground rule of the human comedy.

In postmodern *écriture,* then, maintained desire is the name of the game. But several postmodern questions persist, and insist, around this gaming formulation of textuality. First, we may wonder, what is the difference between the *parole littéraire* and other instances of language? If all language is an effect of deflected desire, and if language is the paradigm of all human interaction—as *écriture*—what human activity is not literary or at least textual? (This is another way of questioning Derrida's oft-cited assertion that there is "nothing outside the text.") Second, are some literary texts more literary than others insofar as they conform to Blanchot's desiring paradigm, rather than to a classical ideal of closure? While not pretending to have the answers, I can add my two cents here, and perhaps "up the ante" of Blanchot's postmodern aesthetic.

In Blanchot's scheme, it seems to me, any literary text—as an example of the third rapport and of *la parole plurielle*—might be considered an instance of *écriture:* literature, all literature, defers desire and makes of this deferral an occasion for aesthetic creation. For Blanchot, literature exists to maintain a curiously hopeless hope [*espoir sans espoir*] rather than pretending to satisfy desire in an illusory triumph of logic:

> [For] in this "victory" there is a defeat, and in this truth . . . there is a lie. And in this (lying) hope, which turns us over to the "beyond" of illusion or to a logic without risk, there is perhaps the betrayal of a more profound hope that poetry must reach us to affirm. (47)

Herein lies what is perhaps the distinguishing character of literature for Blanchot, differentiating it from ordinary language. In all language, desire is the motor force and interval the scene. But only in literary language is the pretense to closure abandoned—the illusion of finality is relinquished in favor of a play of illusions—the pleasure of the text as labyrinth. Whereas ordinary speech and relations may function in the Imaginary order—pretending to abolish difference or to provide mastery of the Other—the *parole littéraire* is Symbolic (in Lacan's sense of the term), providing a pleasure based on the renunciation of the illusion of domination of the Other, or of complete identification with that Other.

The infinite entertainment provides the hope of maintained space, of the open parenthesis, where the end is always to come [*à venir*]. For Blanchot, literature is a spacewalk, a voyage in infinity turned labyrinth.

Literature as poetic "space"

The notion of literary space is a central one in Blanchot's thought (as evinced by the title of his 1955 work, *L'espace littéraire*). In fact, in *L'entretien infini* Blanchot refers to "the very idea of poetry as space . . . the space not of the words themselves, but of their rapport" (435). Thus poetic/literary language, for Blanchot, is a function of the interval between words themselves—and between words and that which they designate—allowing for a certain poetic play or oscillation of meaning. If we think of the function of metaphor, for example, as a revelation of similarity in difference, we may understand that poetic tension is a kind of spark resulting from the interval in meaning between the two unlike terms equated by metaphor. This kind of difference, of course, is already central to the surrealist concept of poetic image as the spark between two disparate entities brought together by chance encounter. But in Blanchot's postmodern formulation, the accent is on the interval between the two terms, not on the encounter or fusion ("[Poetic language] is a struggle against the essence of its division that nonetheless stems from this division, an arrangement that does not so much compose as juxtapose" [*EI* 453]).

This emphasis on interval is perhaps even more pronounced in the work of Lyotard, who writes that poetry delights in undoing the "inherited coherence of language" by "snatching" words from their ordinary transparent function of relation and communication ("Language is as though wrested [*arraché*] from itself: everything is without relation; one no longer passes easily from one word to another" [*DF* 282]). Indeed, for Lyotard, poetic desire is an interruption that fulfills itself just by its manifestation in figural form, the transgressive nature of the poetic trope: "This does not consist in exteriorizing in images the forms in which the desire of the poet or our own desire gets fulfilled once and for all, but in offering forms by which it is going to be reflected as a game, as primary process; the pleasure of the game reverses the game of pleasure" [*le plaisir du jeu renverse le jeu du plaisir*] (322).

A similar view of poetry as a function of interval or dispersion is also, of course, central to Derrida's work (especially *La dissémination,* 1972) and to the work of Julia Kristeva as well (*La révolution du langage poétique,* 1974). Like these fellow travelers, Lyotard disputes the tradition—culminating in Symbolism—of the poetic as an adequate or motivated language, somehow more whole or more satisfying than ordinary language, able to correspond more fully to reality. On the contrary, in the poststructuralist view, poetry is a sign of the distance of the speaker from the designated world. Its satisfaction derives not from a superior power of designation, of a closeness to an intact or "remunerated" language (Mallarmé's term), but in the playful process of dispersion itself, in the game of hide-and-seek with reality that it engages.

This view of the *parole littéraire* is a profoundly ludic vision, for we have seen the same type of play at work in the joking process as a function of a similar kind of formal reflection, the veiling that obscures clear meaning. In Blanchot's system, comic language itself might even qualify as a model of the poetic *parole plurielle* since it is a function of contrast or maintained interval exploiting multiple meanings, the *suspens mouvant* of connotative language. And in the joke as in the literary/poetic text, no real belief is elicited, partly because of its playfulness, the understanding that "this is only a joke" (or "this is only fiction") and that the whole process is a kind of made-up play, performed just for fun. Moreover, in the joke as in the literary text, some of the original desiring energy is always reflected back by form, by the jokework/textwork that veils the point, thus prolonging the volley and reserving the final gratification (the scoring of the "point") that would halt the *jeu du plaisir* (Lyotard's term). Lyotard's description of poetic reversal as a game conforming to a comic mission (the production of pleasure by deflection of desire) is very like Blanchot's notion of "the mad game of writing" as a process originating in desire and producing a bizarrely unsatisfying text, yet fulfilling a quotient of desire by the game of unworking itself, *le plaisir du jeu.*

Hearing double: the unworked text

> The literary word is left over [*reste la parole littéraire*].
>
> Blanchot, *EI* (505)

Blanchot's literary scene is one of paradox, of hopeless hope, where we perpetually learn to reaffirm a profoundly comic need to begin anew. Of course, Blanchot's own choice of texts for discussion seems to suggest that not all literary works manifest to the same degree the underpinnings of the game in which literature engages its players; he prefers aphoristic and hermetic writers such as Char, Kafka, Hölderlin, Artaud. He even heralds a book to come [*livre à venir*] that would make use of comic desire to lay bare its own shortcomings, its own absence:

> I would even say that every important literary work is all the more important if it puts into play more directly and purely the meaning of this turning-point [*tournant*] . . . a work that retains, as it always uncentered center, an unworking [*désoeuvrement*]: the absence of the book. (45)

For Blanchot, the important work is decidedly not self-important.

This type of work actually seeks to relinquish its presence and its authority; it is absent in its uncenteredness and its divorce from source: "*Écriture* traces but leaves no trace, not authorizing the return to source, by means of some vestige or sign; nothing more than itself as pure experience" (625). But this pure experience is not to be confused with nostalgia for unity or origin. One may think, for example, of Raymond Roussel's use of multiple parenthesis in *Nouvelles impressions de l'Afrique*, where the point of reference is obscured by the proliferation of references (parentheses). Roussel's effect is among other things a comic one, since the content of the parenthesis seems finally to be derived from nothing, the reference having been misplaced in the labyrinth. A similar technique is used by Ionesco in the famous Bobby Watson scene (*La cantatrice chauve*), in which the name is proliferated to the point of comic absurdity, causing us to lose track of all reference. Or we might think of Beckett's "absent" character Knott—whose name echoes as the "knotty" nonanswer to the curt nonquestoin of Beckett's title (*Watt?*). The maintained hope of Beckett's scene leaves it open-ended, prolonging the hope of maintaining the interval between self and Other, of "Knott" closing the parenthesis. (A central image in the novel is the portrait that hangs in Watt's room: a broken, interrupted circle, with a dot outside—what better image of the e-ccentric aesthetic that Blanchot "traces"?) Beckett's work is an apt example of what Blanchot means by "the absence of the book," an absence that erases the very notion of source along with the hope of resolution, leaving behind, "as a sign, the idea of difference or divergence as its first center" (594). In this sort of unworked text the closure of the circle has been replaced by the open curve of the parenthesis, in a proliferated reference (Blanchot: "The rapport between form and content has become infinite" [594]).

Reading any number of contemporary comic texts as examples of the unworked or absent text (one might cite the "forgetful" humor of Kundera, the mad proliferation of litanies and veiled identities in Genet, the mysterious mingling of dream and reality that overdetermines the work of writers such as Gabriel García Márquez and Isabel Allende) suggests that the postmodern text more often than not seems to be comic, not so much as a result of an aesthetic choice on the part of the writer but as a requirement of a certain gaming voice, a "post" modality. Such works deploy a cheating mechanism, a trickster's bag of tricks, to insure that they will neither win nor lose the game, that they will fail to "accomplish" what they set out to do. Thanks to their comic shortcoming, made possible by the veils of literary form obstructing and diverting our desire, their game fails at being an endgame and remains an ever reiterated double entendre.

In the final section of this study, we will look at Beckett's own unworked text—as a staging of the postmodern aesthetic—in order to ask some inconclusive questions about the future [*avenir*] of the *livre à venir:* Will there be a post postmodern text?

PART FOUR

Postmodern Aesthetics

The Comic as Postscript

7. Beckett's Aesthetic Play: The Comic Text *En Souffrance*

> But there is a suffering that completely loses time . . . that time may no longer redeem . . . it is without remedy.
>
> Maurice Blanchot, *L'entretien infini* (257)

> Nothing is funnier than suffering.
>
> Samuel Beckett, *Fin de partie* (33)

"The Unworked Text" En Route

The relationship between a certain comic of desire and the postmodern "unworked" text is perhaps nowhere as manifest as in the e-ccentric games of Samuel Beckett's wandering, out-of-work clowns. Hamm and Clov, Didi and Gogo, Murphy and Watt: all are stranded *en souffrance* (like mail diverted from its destination), engaged in a game that amounts to playful declaration of war on the feasible. Indeed, the striking coincidence between Beckett's comic aesthetic of suffering and Blanchot's comic aesthetic of writing emerges when one compares the comments of both writers on the nature and function of literature.

For both of these post-men, literature is always *en souffrance,* even as it circulates on its appointed rounds. For Blanchot as for Beckett, literature does not serve to gratify desire; it works rather to disappoint the expectations of the reader (Blanchot: "Literature is perhaps essentially made to disappoint [*pour décevoir*], being always in default in relation to itself [*en défaut par rapport à elle-même*]" [*EI* 594]). We have seen that for Blanchot language itself is always lacking, in default; but in literature, as Blanchot defines it, this lack actually becomes the end and focus, the absent center around which the text must err, rather than something to be gotten around. And this view of literature as *déception* (disappointment) seems to tally with Freud's view whereby literature only gratifies thanks to a process of veiling assuring that its process is deflected from goal, that its plot misses the appointment with an untimely end.[1]

Blanchot's perception of the literary process is even more radical than that of psychoanalysis; his literature of disappointment is characterized by a shortcoming that *tries* to fail at ending (Blanchot wonders: "Is there no relation or language that can escape from the power-play [*movement de la puissance*] by which the world never ceases fulfilling itself [*ne cesse de s'accomplir*]?" [*EI* 61]).

In strikingly similar terms, Beckett criticizes the tired art that has remained subservient to the ideal of feasibility or accomplishment:

> I speak of an art turning from [the plan of the feasible] in disgust, weary of its puny exploits, weary of pretending to be able, of being able, of doing a little better than the same old thing, of going a little further along a dreary road.[2]

To this excessively able literature he prefers:

> The expression that there is nothing to express, nothing with which to express, no power to express, no desire to express, together with the obligation to express. (*Three Dialogues* 17)

This formulation is strongly reminiscent of Smith and Kerrigan's definition of postmodernism (to which I have referred throughout this study) as the "embrace of the uncertainties of discourse" by a self-conscious, self-critical text. But Beckett's conception is a bit bleaker, a bit less upbeat; he writes that "to be an artist is to *fail*," and goes on to speak of the "new relation" that this failure necessitates:

> I know that all that is required now . . . is to make of this submission, this admission, this fidelity to failure, a new occasion, a new term of relation, and of the act—which, unable to act, obliged to act, [the artist] makes—an expressive act, even if only of itself, of its impossibility, of its obligation. (*TD* 21)

In Beckett's call to failure we recognize something akin to Blanchot's proposal of impossibility as the mode of the "unworked text" ("It is perhaps impossibility—a relation escaping power—[that] is the form of the rapport [of this text]" [*EI* 541]).[3] So striking is the correspondence between Beckett's literature of failure and Blanchot's literature of disappointment that the following passage from Blanchot almost seems to set the stage for Beckett's endgame:

> There is thus a region—an experience—where the essence of human being is the impossible, where, if one could penetrate, if only by a certain mode of speech [*fût-ce par une certaine parole*], he would discover that he escapes from possibility. . . . [A region] where speech would uncover itself as that which exposes the human limit, as that which is no longer a power, or not yet a power. A space where what we call "man" has as if in advance always already disappeared. (*EI* 273)

This region of impossibility is the domain of Blanchot's "game of writing," which he characterizes—in a formulation reflecting the postmodern crisis of representation and legitimation—as a "rupture with language understood as that which represents, as well as that which gives and receives meaning" (390). For Beckett as well, a new art of failure turns away from the project of adequate or exhaustive representation, the project of traditional aesthetics. ("The history of painting," Beckett asserts, "is the history of its attempts to escape from this sense of failure, by means of a more authentic, more ample, less exclusive relation between representer and represented" [*TD* 21].) Beckett considers the inadequacy of representation—the identifying trait of his literature of failure—to be a result of "the incoercible absence of relation, or, if you like, the presence of unavailable terms" (21). Such "unavailable" terms again recall the out-of-reach terms or players in Blanchot's desiring *troisième rapport du neutre,* a relation marked by the Other's absence, indifference, or irreducible separation. I have suggested that a similar unavailability or absence of the object of desire is one of the traits of Freud's joke process understood as a symptom of deflected desire, related to the compulsion to repeat. In all these instances, the absence or inaccessibility of the desired Other gives rise to a compulsive game of infinitely repeated expression, akin to Beckett's "obligation to express" (*TD* 17). Moreover, for Beckett as for Blanchot, writing is an antidote to power or closure, an interminable cure for the "malady of wanting to know what to do and the malady of wanting to be able to do it" (*TD* 17). And as Beckett's work attests, this postmodern scene is a comic scene, where "nothing is as funny as suffering."

"Erotic" play and comic "souffrance"

> Theater does the greatest wrong in making us believe in theater.
>
> Blanchot, *EI* (532)

As sadomasochistic games of witnessed suffering, the two Beckett plays to be discussed here could qualify as "erotic" sacrifices of sorts (Didi and Gogo even remark that they are "served up on a plateau," a word suggesting both stage and platter). Indeed, Georges Bataille has suggested that all literature is the heir of religious/erotic ritual ("Literature is in fact situated after religion, as the heir of religion. Sacrifice is a theatrical performance, a drama reduced to the final episode. The sacrifice is a novel, a story, illustrated in blood" [*L'erotisme* 97]). But Bataille clearly believes that even if the literary act is heir to sacrifice, it is nonetheless an attenuated and tame ritual that must stop short of actual physical risk: the author-priest merely exposes the character-victims to the scrutiny of the reader-witness in a relatively sanguine and civilized version of the triangular erotic sacrifice it mimics.

We recall that Freud, too, has emphasized the tame "sublimated" aspects of literature and other aesthetic phenomena, produced by veiled desire deflected from "serious purposes" or ends. In fact, Freud considers the main difference between fulfilling phenomena (in the sense of the French *accomplissement du désir*) such as ritual or dream, and aesthetic phenomena such as literature or the joking process, to be the lack of real belief inspired by the latter. ("Don't worry," we tell ourselves, "it's only make-believe/a game/a joke—nothing real is at stake here.") But in dream as in religion, we are believers, absorbed enough in our experience to be terrified, moved, or inspired by it. Freud maintains that religious experience, like dream, elicits a more or less total cathexis and hence effectively and directly gratifies desire; on the other hand, the very essence of art is the veiling that alters and deflects the desire motivating it. Thus, Bataille and Freud might concur that the literary gratification is a paradoxical one functioning thanks to the barrier of literary form: the veil of rhetorical technique as well as the material obstacles represented by page, stage, or canvas, are obstacles hindering complete absorption in the "performance." (As Lyotard puts it [*DF* 355], the presence of canvas or page reminds us that it's "only art" and "not real."[4])

Theater is perhaps that form of literature in which the erotic and paradoxical nature of this game is most clearly evident since it functions by a simultaneous identification with the absorbing action and a maintained distance from it, the spectator's armchair view of the "sacrifice." The obvious theatrical forms and trappings—scenery, props, costume, stylized intonation—paradoxically create the mood even while allowing the spectator to refrain from total belief; theatrical form thus fosters a certain mesmerized involvement even while it deflects total *accomplissement,* total investment or fulfillment. We can begin to see why a postmodern theater might encourage incredulity by emphasizing these forms as obstacles to enthrallment in order to highlight the playful status of theater, breaking out of the realistic rut of conventional theater. (Just so, that great comic modern, Alfred Jarry, insisted that a new theater must emphasize its artifices, the strings [*ficelles*] that make it work.) Such an emphasis would of course entail a corresponding deemphasis of the cathartic properties of theater (hence the disappearance of tragedy in the postmodern age?) insofar as these properties depend on complete absorption or identification on the part of the spectator. But the partial abandon characteristic of the spectator's response to this willfully falsified spectacle could still be considered an "erotic" abandon of sorts: the spectators lend themselves to the spectacle for the duration of the entertainment (the suspension of real life rules implied by Coleridge's "willing suspension of disbelief"). We recall that such a qualified lending is also characteristic of the joke process, which produces its effect through the phenomenon of ideational mimetics (the "comic lending" discussed in chapter 3).

Beckett makes ample use of this kind of comic lending device in the staged sacrifices of his postmodern scene; he serves up his comic victims to the voracious witness even while using the antics of his clowns to elicit a degree of identification on the part of this same spectator. Similarly, in the erotic sacrifice, the witness enjoys a vicarious experience of death or *continuity* (Bataille's term) at least in part because of an identification with the sacrificial victim. Still, Beckett's plays are indicative of a new direction in theater as well as an ancient sacrificial tradition, for they exemplify a postmodern preoccupation with the theatrical obstacles to cathartic fulfillment of desire. In other words, in these plays, the "pretend" aspects of theater are exaggerated at the expense of an illusionary realism that would facilitate belief or provoke the complete identification of catharis. The comic mode of Beckett's writing performs an all-important role by accentuating the gamelike obstacles in Beckett's scene, thus assuring that the theatrical act remains a detour, a gratification *en souffrance.*

Beckett's "discontinuous play"

In *L'entretien infini,* Blanchot proposes just such a turning from realistic theater, in which a certain facile "continuity of surface" engenders belief in the spectator.[5] Blanchot's essay contrasts conventional realistic theater with the "discontinuous" theater of Brecht, in which the spectator is encouraged to remain at a distance from the surface action of the play. This maintained distance, Blanchot suggests, creates a theater of maintained desire: because the spectators remain unsatisfied customers of sorts, unable to become absorbed by a vicarious theatrical experience, they are forced to remain attentive to the ideological and aesthetic implications of the witnessed action.

While Blanchot's essay centers on Brecht's work as exemplary of the theater of maintained desire, his concept of discontinuous play is equally germane to the work of Beckett. Beckett's curiously playful waiting game, after all, leaves an expectant (attending) spectator stranded in a no-man's land of unfulfilled expectation. Thus Beckett and Blanchot seem to chart a parallel course as artists and as aestheticians, each proposing and practicing a desiring literature in which failure or disappointment—the always incomplete transgressive act—functions as the generating mode of the text. (Or, in Bataille's terms, the "naive comedy" of erotic transgression, based on self-delusion that plays at "tragic" sacrifice, becomes a lucid comedy, caught in the act of acting.) For Blanchot as for Beckett, the truly literary expression makes of failure itself an expressive act, exposing the shortcoming at the center of *accomplissement* (achievement).

To be sure, Blanchot's criticism of believable theater is just one example of his objection to the all too adequate masterpiece that responds too fully to our expectations. To this immutable and perfected final product, he prefers the discontinuous, open-ended text, engaged in an ongoing conversation [*l'entretien infini*] that fails to deliver an unequivocal message. Furthermore, Blanchot suggests that the discontinuous work remains unsubordinated to utilitarian function or fulfillment of definite ends: writing is the antithesis of achievement, a therapy for the deadly adequacy of closure. In short, when Blanchot calls for a theater that would fail to elicit belief in its public, he is in Freud's terms, and in Beckett's, calling for a more aesthetic, less accomplished theater, a theater of deferred desire.

For Blanchot, as for Freud (and Bataille as well), the triangle is the privileged scene of desire; hence, discontinuous theater is characterized as a function of depth and triangularity, where the thirdness [*en tiers*] of the spectator is the key term:

> As soon as speech is divided to come and go on stage, the relation with the public changes; distance is deepened; those who are out there to hear no longer hear immediately, but act rather as respondents (witnesses), by means of their attention which carries and supports the process. Silence is henceforth a third term [*en tiers*]. (*EI* 529)

Discontinuous theater, unlike realistic theater, emphasizes the depth of the theatrical experience—wherein dialogue is witnessed by a third—rather than seeking to cover up this depth, ignoring the unnatural theatricality of the situation, for the sake of naturalness or credibility. The spectator has become the acknowledged witness to a performance rather than an invisible eavesdropper to a realistic situation. As such, the spectator lends a depth to the situation, in which dialogue is addressed "out there," beyond the footlights. Beckett's theater is just this sort of dimensional, discontinuous theater, in which the audience is estranged, one point in a three-dimensional space. Of all the plays, *En attendant Godot* (1952) provides the most striking instance of this aesthetic dimension, in which the humor of the clowns emerges as an important structuring device, a mode of maintenance of depth or separation, a diverting obstacle to belief.

Three's a Crowd: Godot as Odd Man Out

In *Godot*, an apparently reversible and dual *rapport de force* between players (Didi and Gogo) is always also a self-conscious three-way rapport [*en tiers*] where both the audience (the crowd) and the absent Godot function as "thirds" exterior to the Didi-Gogo exchange, but who are nonetheless alluded to in the text. These allusions to outsiders who exist beyond the confines of the stage add a depth to Beckett's text; in fact, here the three-dimensional structure of any theatrical scene is doubled, mirrored in *two* triangular configurations: (1) Didi-Gogo on stage and Godot behind the scene; (2) Didi-Gogo on stage and the audience beyond the footlights.

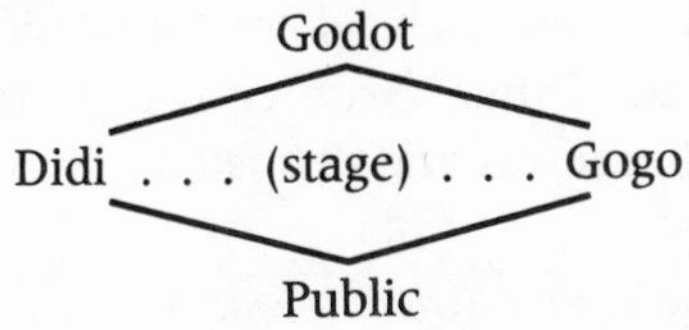

The clowns never relate to each other in a simple linear rapport since the doubled "third" is their reason for being there, the generating force of their rapport. The existence of the public explains the presence of two actors on stage; the existence of Godot accounts for the characters' presence and situation. In psychoanalytic terms, their Imaginary rapport is fated to be interrupted by a third whose importune presence cannot be ignored: the Symbolic Other obstructs their short-circuit (whereby the shortest distance between two points is a straight line) and initiates the diversionary long-circuit. In this drama, three is literally a crowd, a public demanding an entertainment.

In Lacanian terms, the doubled triangle could be read as the "Schema L" of analysis; the intersubjective order, for Lacan, is always composed of at least two triangles composed of four intertwined and overdetermined terms (self/ego—object of desire—Other [Freud's oedipal threesome]; self/subject—object of desire—Other). Lacan's "infinite conversation" among these terms (the Schema L) begins with the dual Imaginary relation—between a divide/doubled self (unconscious subject/ego) and the object of this self's desire; but this dual relation is then mediated and obstructed in the Symbolic Order by the Other/or unconscious. The Schema L deflects the straight line of Imaginary desire between doubled self and its object, diverting and transforming desire in a triangular Symbolic long-circuit, deepening and dual relation en tiers by adding an "Other" dimension:

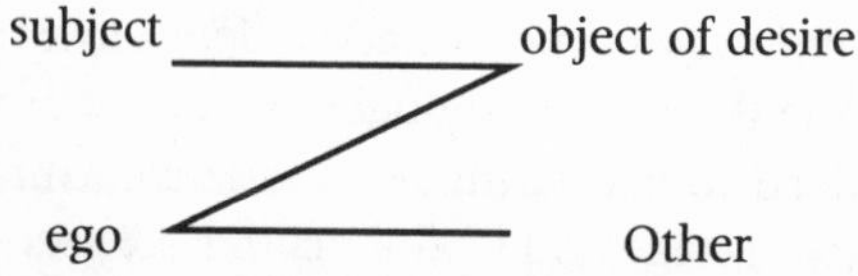

Lacan's structure is a primal scene of overdetermination; it is founded in labyrinthine pun where "the desire of the subject is the desire of the Other," with each pole implicated in the desire of the other terms and defined and limited by that desire.[6]

Beckett's scene in *En attendant Godot* may be read as an analogous overdetermined nexus of desire.[7] For in the playful checkmate that Godot stages—where the players are pawns who "play at failures" (*"jouent aux échecs"* = play checkers/ play at failures)—there is a convergence of excess and limitation; the characters are aware of their confinement in limitless time. The limit on the action of the play is the moment of Godot's arrival, since the players have agreed to amuse themselves "just up until he comes." The clowns are at once unlimited, since the end will not arrive, and severely limited, circumscribed by the borders of the stage ("We are closed in [*cernés*]," they declare ruefully) and by the playing time requiring that the performance end. Possibility and impossibility are thus identical on the Beckett stage. Leisure or freedom from responsibility (the *rien à faire* that opens the play) is synonymous with boredom, with "nothing to do," as well as with obligation, where nothing is something *"to be done"* [*à faire*], something that *must* be done. Furthermore, the empty project of the clowns is aesthetically motivated since that which must be done (nothing) is not pertinent to outcome; it has nothing to do with [*rien à faire avec*] satisfying solutions. Like Freud's joke transaction, which avoids hostile outcome, the play remains an aesthetic diversion from final solutions, such as the suicide that tempts the clowns from time to time.

Waiting for Godot, then, is the ultimate aesthetic activity, a game requiring that the players work (or play) at getting nothing done. Such a task does not come easily to Didi and Gogo, who still seek pastimes bound up in feasibility ("What do we do now?"/"We wait."/"Yes, but while waiting . . ." [25]). Their task is to stop looking for meaningful solutions or hopeful outcomes (with such biblical allusions to redemption as the parable of the thief saved by Christ on the cross) and instead open themselves to a playful suffering—a diversion *en souffrance*—which offers no final salvation. The play can be read as a sort of anti-messianic apprenticeship in powerless play, a learning to do nothing, not only *while* waiting for Godot but *by* waiting for Godot (as suggested by the double meaning of *en attendant* in French usage, implying both a pastime and a means to an end).[8] Waiting for Godot is learning to wait, without specific expectation, for an absentminded messiah who will not show, to attend to an absent customer (as "waiter") with an infinitely patient and playful desire.

Immobile moves

Now while Blanchot does not deal specifically with Beckett's work, his theories of literature (as advanced in *L'entretien infini*) seem uncannily descriptive of Beckett's postmodern scene of maintained desire. I suggest that reading Beckett with Blanchot, in an infinite dialogue between the two (with subtitles by Freud, the onlooking third), may show something about the postmodern and comic import of both texts. We might say that learning to play Beckett's waiting game requires a move from what Blanchot calls "ordinary and personal attention," oriented toward a specific goal, to "impersonal attention," where the center of attention is absent, a missing focal point around which "perspective, view, and order are [dis]oriented" (Blanchot, *EI* 176–77). While Blanchot's first personal attention functions as a means to an end, the "other" attention is as though *unworked,* unoccupied, not unlike Beckett's unemployed clowns. Whereas ordinary, goal-oriented waiting requires that time be emptied and suspended, Beckett's waiting-game is played in a timeless time related to Blanchot's "hopeless hope" [*espoir sans espoir*], the paradoxical disappointment that literary expression inspires even while it entertains us. Didi and Gogo must transform their busy attention, which seeks to fill time and to tell time, into a suspended entertainment, a holding between [*entre-tien*], which is playfully prolonged. Time is thus no longer an exhaustible quantity to be spent but is rather the scene of their suspended play (cf. Blanchot: "Time is though arrested, confused with its interval" [63]).

In the first act of *Godot,* it is the passerby Pozzo who seems most obsessed with the first ordinary temporality; he asks the ages of Didi and Gogo, and recoils at the suggestion that time has stopped, looking ceaselessly for diversion for himself and his acquaintances ("What can I do, that's what I ask myself, so that time seems less long for them?" [63]). In the second act, however, he has lost his sense of time, along with his vision ("Blind men have no notion of time" [147]). Because he is now blind, he has left behind the domain of "enlightened" comprehension, the search for a "dis-covered" truth, which assumes that the exterior world can be encased and sized up in measurable increments. Pozzo's loss of vision corresponds to his loss of personal, subjective expectation, his detachment from ordinary need; his blindness seems to be a symptom of his entry into something akin to what Blanchot calls the aesthetic realm of "pure waiting" where "suffering completely loses time" (*EI* 257).

These two experiences of time suggest two sorts of power. When Pozzo first appears, he is a powerful man, the master in a power-relation. This powerful mode of relation to the oppressed other is a dialectic mode, subject to reversal in time (and, in fact, Lucky later exercises a crushing power over Pozzo: "Now . . . *he* is killing *me* . . ." [55]). Like Pozzo and Lucky, Didi and Gogo might seem to be subject to a dialectic bond in which "he who can do the most can do the least" [*qui peut le plus peut le moins*] (26). In fact, Didi and Gogo seem at first, like Pozzo and Lucky at their first appearance, to be governed by a concept of time that corresponds to the first busy attention as well as to the belief in the power to do something "in time," even if the power structure itself is subject to reversal. For instance, they frequently refer to the possibility of suicide as if they had the power to end things; they also point out their infinite power to speak ("It's true, we are inexhaustible" [105]). Likewise, they refer repeatedly to their mimetic power as thespians (their *"pouvoir"*) to represent what they have seen ("We might be able [*on pourrait*] to play Pozzo and Lucky" [123]).

Didi and Gogo are thus in possession of real powers, but these infinite powers are excessive. These clowns stage a comic paradox: they are at once too powerful and not powerful enough. Their suspended existence is impossible to end now, in the present (shades of Heidegger); the rope always breaks; Didi and Gogo have entered into an ever-extended "stage presence." Similarly, their inexhaustible power of expression ("we can't shut up" [105]) coincides with their inability to fall silent (shades of Blanchot). Didi and Gogo often speak doubly, in puns, for the power to mean several things at once coincides with their inability to mean any one thing unequivocally. One of these puns, for instance, may be taken as a literal sign of potency: to Gogo's suggestion that they hang themselves, Didi replies that this would be "a way to finish [*bander:* which also means to 'get it up'] along with everything that follows. Where it falls, flowers grow" (25). Generative power is thus allied here with the ultimate limitation on power (death); potency becomes, in Beckett's system, not a power of accomplishment, but a way of falling short, missing the mark, erring in error ("I *can* go wrong [*je peux me tromper*]" [22]).

Didi and Gogo are not so much an example of a reversible power relation (Lacan's Imaginary register) as they are of a desiring Symbolic rapport, a paradox in Blanchot's sense of the term, where power and powerlessness coincide rather than alternating, where *"qui peut le plus peut le moins"* simultaneously. They are as bound to each other as are the master and slave, Pozzo and Lucky. Unable to escape the gravitational pull that keeps them together, the tie that binds ("I'm going away"/"You wouldn't go far"), they even play at dialectic dialogue of give-and-take ("That's it, let's contradict each other" [107]). Yet, it is never a question of working things out, of reaching a dialectic understanding. In Lacanian terms, Pozzo and Lucky are stuck in an Imaginary relation, as alter egos who rival and identify with each other; while Didi and Gogo have entered a Symbolic relation, mediated by the alien—the audience, or Godot—for whom they perform their "play" and to whom they address their communication, waylaid *en souffrance.* The mode of their rapport is not feasibility but maintained desire, and desire as rapport is named Godot.

Post-ing bond

> To speak is to bind oneself without binding to the unknown.
>
> Blanchot, *EI* (445).

> Bound to Godot? What an idea!
>
> *Godot* (32)

We have seen that Blanchot considers the desiring rapport to be a function of the unknown face of the Other, who is irremediably absent or exterior. (Indeed, Blanchot's strange desire—described as "desire of the self . . . in relation to that from which he remains separated, of which he has no need, and which is the unknown, the alien, the Other" [*EI* 76]—sounds uncannily like Lacan's formula for the subject's desire as intersubjective "desire of the Other," an alien desire overdetermined by the double meaning of the genitive [of the Other]: we desire the Other, and also what the Other desires.) That which binds Didi and Gogo is precisely this sort of non-oriented "other" desire, couched in terms of a non-binding obligation to Godot leaving them "free on bond" ("Bound to Godot? What an idea!"). Godot is a symptom of their mutually maintained otherness, their mutual exteriority, since he is the third in their relationship, an exterior party who is at once the reason for the continuation of their relationship (they are there to wait for Godot) and an obstacle to its consummation in double suicide (they may yet be saved by Godot's intercession). As this onlooking obstacle, Godot is party to the kind of infinite entertainment or conversation to which Blanchot refers (recalling the notion of the Lacanian unconscious as an alien conversation, coming from outside as "the discourse of the Other"). Hence, the longing of Didi and Gogo for a final union in death—they refuse to commit suicide unless both can do so—or for any united escape is frustrated by the obstacle the Other poses: their expectation of Godot, which is also their responsibility to each "other" (there is only enough rope for one to die, and they are a package deal, bound in a non-binding obligation). Godot, then, is the Other in all nonspecificity: no face, no occupation, the missing center in an endlessly interrupted orbit, the object of an intensely unoriented desire (like the e-ccentric center of the broken circle in the painting that hands on Watt's wall, in that other Beckettian fable of desire for naught [for "Knott"]. Indeed, the painting itself is the missing focal point for *Watt* [for what?]). Godot is the absent presence, the non-binding "Knott" who, as the unknown, inspires error, causing the errant clowns erroneously to identify first Pozzo and then the child messenger as Godot. As inspirer of error, as promised end of the pointless play, Godot is the activator of a game analogous to the kind of immobile flight to which Blanchot refers: "a flight which is, at any rate [*au reste*], a stationary flight . . . the engendering of a space without refuge" (29–30). This leftover flight [*au reste*] is a "rest" without rest.

Godot is, then, less a character than a mode of the play; as the third—the Symbolic Other, the oedipal Father, the unconscious, the audience—he conditions space, his exteriority adding a witnessed dimension to the play as well as movement, which he stymies, and time, which he suspends. He is the date who never calls, the postman who never cometh, the postmark of an excessive existence that seems to go on [*au reste*] after all questions have been asked and answered adequately, an excessive vitality (the inexhaustible post-age of our "post" Age) that causes the clowns to wander and to wonder "what do we do now that we're happy?" (101). The answer to this persistent query is of course that Didi and Gogo have nothing to do [*rien à faire*]; engaged in an immobile orbit around nought (Knott?), they are plagued by a forgetfulness that seems to allow them to shirk responsibility, to miss the point in an extended detour. The eccentric orbit around a missing focal point is the shape of what Blanchot calls the "third rapport with the neutral" and what Lacan calls "the desire of the Other."

But Godot is more than the oedipal Other who lays down the rules of the game; Godot is perhaps also himself an instance of Blanchot's third *parole* [*la parole littéraire*], a fiction or constantly reinvented story that serves to keep the characters together—"bound" for nowhere by a common project—as well as to separate them since the *parole* in which he is invented (the discourse of the Other) is always between them, like Blanchot's *parole d'entre-deux* (*EI* 97, 237). The unsilenceable chatter of the clowns is a playful link to the unattainable Other, a vaudeville patter that "entertains" the listener (cf. Blanchot: "To speak is to bind oneself without bonds to the unknown" [445]). This banter is compulsive: Didi and Gogo are incapable of falling silent; indeed, their role as eternally "waiters" or "supplicants" ("Our role? That of the plaintiff [*suppliant*]" [29] requires that they speak, that they unceasingly make their case. Stood up by Godot, they become stand-up comics. Moreover, their compulsive fictions are a means of suspense, diversionary tactics to keep their activity off-track and to assure that the "end" is out of reach of the "entertained" spectator as well ("If we all speak at once, we'll never get out of it" [49]).

The "post" delivery: joke technique

In this infinite deflection from goal, the jokework—as a kind of post speech, or *parole plurielle*—plays a crucial role, aiding in the apprenticeship in the desiring relation. First, the work as a whole can be likened to a vast joke of sorts if one compares its form to the tripolar joking configuration as described by Freud in *Jokes* (an exposure of a victim by the joke-maker before a complicit onlooker who also acts as obstacle to direct satisfaction of hostile or lustful impulses, since "his" presence precludes the joker from fulfilling his fantasies toward the victim). Joking is by definition a desire deflected from its original end, and hence a sign of unfinished business that will give rise to the joke's retelling to a new listener. The aesthetic transaction is then a contagion of sorts, a kind of pollinating agent inflicting a stigma that enjoins the Other to enter into a renewed social transaction in a perpetuated signifying chain.

Beckett's discontinuous play (discontinuous because indirect and roundabout even while it is ongoing) suggests an analogy with this game of "hot potato," especially when one reads the character Godot as a stigma, a symptom of desire, an absent presence like the Lacanian unconscious itself, an Other that permeates the work and functions as a mode of relation between the clowns. When Godot is spoken about, or waited for, he is like the unattained object of the joke (the offended lady of Freud's scenario who absents herself from her suitors), the object of unfulfilled courtship (dating for Godot? mating for Blanchot?) whose inaccessibility motivates the joking exchange. But Godot may also be considered analogous to the third pole in the joke transaction, the joke's audience, insofar as he represents an obstacle to ending and to the union of the two complicit parties.

It is in this sense that Godot and the invisible spectator beyond the footlights occupy analogous positions in their situation of thirdness or exteriority (like the unconscious Other who intercepts and reroutes the desire of the Lacanian subject, or the Freudian oedipal Father who disrupts the dual Imaginary relation, forcing the infantile desire to take the long-circuit through human interaction in the Symbolic). I have suggested that Godot and the public are like symmetrical apexes of two reflected triangles, of which Didi and Gogo are in each case the base (as sketched on page 205 above). If the play scene is thought of as doubled in this way, then Didi and Gogo are literally enter-tained between two configurations in three dimensions, suspended in the space between Godot, on the one hand, and the audience, on the other (back stage and in front of the stage).

If this doubled triangle is overdetermined yet again by Freud's joke triangle, both Godot and audience may be considered superegos of sorts, the internalized oedipal Father in Freud's system, the conscience who witnesses and judges. Godot in his godlike omniscience and the public in its role of spectator and critic are each voyeurs looking down from afar at the offering of the comic victims exposed for their sport (the laughing faces to whom Gogo refers when he peers into the darkened house). Didi remarks on their situation as comedic offerings, dished up on stage: "We're served up on a platter [*nous sommes servis sur un plateau*]" (125). In this configuration—as in Bataille's erotic sacrifice—Didi and Gogo are victims, clowns who tell their own joke at their own expense, both subject and object in the joke exchange, priest and victim in the erotic play. Yet, in this entertainment as in a joke or in the oedipal drama the third position is not inviolate, out of play; the spectator/Godot is involved, implicated in a kind of countertransference because of "his" own voyeuristic desire. For the audience is caught up, suspended in the entertainment, like the hearer of the joke, by virtue of a kind of identification or *ideational mimetics,* Freud's term for the mechanism by which the joke's hearer follows along. The spectators are thus, by virtue of their attention that "attends to" an empty non-event, given over to something like that second "aesthetic" attention to which Blanchot refers, drawn into a desiring suspense or play, by the "willing suspension" of their critical faculties, and the loan of their own desire. As Freud came to know, the position of third, of outsider, of analyst or judge (Lacan's *sujet supposé savoir*) is a risky position, every transference entailing a countertransference, calling on the analyst to make a move.

But there is more than a mere structural similarity between Freud's comic scenario and Beckett's comic scene; the psychoanalytic understanding of joke technique also furnishes a working analogy with the postmodern technique of discontinuous play. For a kind of comic repetition with difference is at work in *Godot* as in the joke: the shoes left behind in the first act turn out to be different shoes when they are refound in the same spot; the barren tree has sprouted leaves in the second act; Didi remarks that "you don't get off in the same pus twice" (102). These modifications are wrought during the (temporary) interval of nightfall, which, like the temporary relief of the joke's punch line, is a surprise ending giving rise to a new repetition. (And nightfall arrives suddenly—a sort of scenic punch line—catching the players off-guard and thus giving rise to a different repetition of the same scene in act two.) In spite of all these repetitions, in fact, there is no stability in Beckett's play; because of the recurrence of the "sameness with difference" (comparable to Freud's joke technique of "repetition with modification"), every returning element in the play seems to be temporary or passing, a link in a chain (even Pozzo and Lucky are just passing through [*de passage*] 130). As in Lacan's signifying chain, these visual elements and devices of plot are linked in a desiring reference, enjoining repetition in a command performance.

This joke-like structure—in which the various poles of exchange, like the clowns themselves, seem to be just passing through—seems to give rise to a kind of slippage (again, one is reminded of Lacan's notion of words as sliding signifiers); this lack of fixity is as important to the play's continuation as is its open-endedness. If there is any fixed point that anchors all this slippage in the play, it is perhaps Godot himself; as a kind of Paternal Metaphor or representative of the ultimate Name of the Father (God) he might be compared to one of those "points of anchorage" [*points de capiton:* "upholstery tacks"] that limit the sliding of meaning in Lacan's signifying chain. (For Lacan, we recall, the Paternal Metaphor or the *nom du père* is the ultimate "tack" that permits meaning, providing some limited mooring for the sliding of signifiers.) But the absent, dead, metaphorized father (Lacan's Paternal Metaphor, a concept purloined from Freud's *Totem and Taboo*) offers even less anchorage in Beckett's scene than in Lacan's, for Godot cannot be pinned down; his function is to keep things going, rather than orienting them toward a meaningful goal, or ending the slippage of passing time. In fact, Godot seems closer to Freud's tribal father than to Lacan's Paternal Metaphor, for in *Totem and Taboo* (1912) Freud provides the model for a powerless/voided patriarch, who may confer meaning—as the law against incest—only when he is absent, after he has been slain by the victorious sons of the clan. (Indeed, Freud's Father is the antithesis of inviolable authority since he himself is sacrificed and consumed in the ritual act of totemic cannibalism, becoming himself a victim of desiring ritual in the primal transgression against authority, later reenacted as the slaying and eating of the tribal totem. This primal Father, like Godot, is a slippery character indeed, who slides right down as he is ingested by his offspring.)

All of this slippage, promoted by Godot the Father who declines to lay down the law, is exploited for more than its comic effect; it is a means of prolonging the play. Just as a joke's repetition is ensured by the change of poles with each retelling, in Godot the intrusion of an exterior element—any new link in the chain—acts not to clarify or anchor the indefinite messages that the clowns receive but to keep things going, with added levels of ambiguity (as when the messenger arrives with news of Godot just when Didi and Gogo have decided it is not worth waiting any longer, or when Pozzo's arrival provides an entertaining new subject of bantering conversation and stage business just when the bored and impatient spectator might be tempted to leave the theater). In other words, in Beckett's postmodern comic performance, obstacles/intruders have a paradoxical function: they hold up the progress of the action toward ending at the same time that they generate a continuation of the game. In *Godot,* even hiatus in the dialogue can work to keep it going, as when Didi interrupts Pozzo's story with a request that he continue (69).

Another type of slippage in the play results from the multiplicity of conflicting versions, the shifting perspectives of the absent-minded characters; the "truth" about Godot—that he will always keep us waiting—is like a giant banana peel lying in wait to trip us up as the indefinite punch line at play's "end." Beckett's truth is always a slippery commodity, clouded over by layers of successive stories; like a joke's overdetermined double talk, the truth of *Godot* is a plural truth veiled in layers of possible versions (he will come/he won't come; he said he'd come/he didn't promise; he's real/he's imaginary; he loves us/he loves us not . . .). Words are all too slick in Beckett's human comedy, where it seems impossible to stick to one's word, to demonstrate that one's language is unequivocal. Godot is the very emblem of the slippery Other who cannot be held to his word ("he didn't say for sure [*il n'a pas dit ferme*]" [21]); it is precisely this failure (of the Symbolic Father, the Paternal Metaphor) to make his word good—to show up and prove his existence and solidify the foundation of his Law—that assures that the play will go on, and that no one interpretation of the play will stick. Of course, in Lacan's system, the Symbolic Father is the Dead Father (of *Totem and Taboo*) who cannot keep any appointment, except as buried or double meaning, as metaphor. Like Beckett's un-God Godot (God = 0), Lacan's Symbolic Father does not possess the Phallus, as the power of meaning, the ultimate signifier—so much as he possesses the Law of universal "castration" read as separation, renunciation, frustration of desire. (Indeed, for a certain feminist psychoanalysis the Symbolic Father is the emblem of the illusionary status of the phallus, and the erroneous eccentricity—lack of center—at the center of phallogocentricism.)

Straitjacket humor

The characters repeatedly emphasize the staged aspects of their play by commenting on their situation as performing actors (Didi: "Someone out there [*un autre*] is watching me, saying, he's asleep and he doesn't know he's asleep" [157]). This self-conscious theatricality—certainly a characteristic of much contemporary theater—is nonetheless closely allied with that which is unique in Beckett's comic vision, and which reveals the postmodern affinities of that vision. We recall Freud's assertion that in the normal joking situation a transgression is performed by the joke-maker and shared by the hearer, allowing something forbidden to be expressed, thanks to the lowering of inhibition by the jokework. Thus, joker and audience must share the same norms and the same inhibitions in order for the joke transgression to work. At the joke's beginning the joker and hearer are at the same level of inhibition; the joking transgression pierces through to a realm exterior for both of them (the realm of forbidden fruit); that is, the joke constitutes and effects a move beyond (a transgression of) their shared "normal" inhibitions. The joke is literally an extraordinary play with words, since it says something outside the boundaries of ordinary expression.

In Beckett's theater, this is no longer quite the case. The clown-like automatism of the characters makes them seem, in a sense, subhuman. (In the terms of Henri Bergson's famous analysis [*Le rire,* 1900], they could be said to be operating at a less flexible, less adapted level than the normal spectator.) The limits of the stage to which Beckett's clowns are confined constrict them to a universe that is smaller than life (the *petit monde* to which Beckett refers in *Murphy*), a circus arena more restricted than the real world of the spectator and interior to the larger world of which the audience is a part. In other words, joker and audience are no longer at the same level of inhibition—as in an ordinary joking situation—nor are they governed by the same limits, as in an unstaged joke. By continually exposing his player's situation as a rigidly constrained one (in such stage directions as "Estragon gets up and follows him up to the edge of the stage [*jusqu'à la limite de la scène*]"), Beckett plays with a restrictive humor of disappointment, consistent with Blanchot's "literature of disappointment." Beckett's comic aesthetic depends on inadequacy and diminished possibility rather than on the illusion of super adequacy or the promise of "sublime" boundless experience, beyond limits.[9] Or rather, Beckett's comic mode might be called a postmodern use of the sublime intuition of limitlessness, where humor paradoxically inflicts limits at the same time it affords an endless transgression of limits. In the postmodern comic, the liberty afforded by the joke transgression is itself undecidable, since the joke simultaneously transgresses and proliferates limits.[10]

In this brand of impoverished humor, joking form itself is "unworked." For unlike the situation of the classic Freudian joke, the audience and the clown in Beckett's joke no longer share the same limitations. Therefore, an action or statement constituting a transgression for the "straitjacketed" Beckett character subject to the boundaries of the stage would not necessarily violate or exceed the standards of the spectators, who inhabit a wider psychical and physical space.[11] The clowns' urge to transgress their staged situation is first indicated by Gogo's question to Didi as he surveys the limited theatrical space: "Is this one [this universe, this stage] enough for you [*celui-là te suffit*]?" (23). This question and others hint that the clowns are tempted to exceed their one-ring circus, the givens of their performance, the imposed limits of the actor's *petit monde;* at several points they complain of being tired by the glare of the endless day (the footlights) and long for the restful night (the unconscious? Death? The larger realm of the spectator in the "beyond" of the darkened theater?). Thus, a transgression for one of Beckett's ringed clowns often merely constitutes a reaching out to what is only an ordinary level of experience or flexibility for the audience. In *Godot,* the extravagance of a tree with one leaf—the decor for the second act in the English version—is wildly funny, even though it represents a normal or even subnormal situation as far as the spectator is concerned. "I'm leaving" becomes the stock "transgressive" refrain, and in Gogo's mouth, this very possible action (witness his name) comes to seem like a wild fantasy. Nightfall is a similar normal phenomenon that violates Beckett's subnormal universe, and it is exploited for its comic effect when it falls like a ton of bricks, instantaneously, at the end of the long first act, just when we have lost all expectation that intermission—let alone Godot—will ever come.

On the level of verbal humor, the same mechanism is encountered. Perhaps the funniest line in the play is a perfectly normal unaltered proverb: "How time flies when we're having fun." This ordinary proverb seems transgressive or out of line, even though unchanged, because the ordinary statement it makes represents a striking transgression of the restrictions under which Didi and Gogo operate. (In their world, time often seems not to pass at all, let alone quickly.) In this joke, as well, Beckett pokes fun at the tedious nature of his play, using the spectator's own impatient expectations—the longing for some conventional plot or action—to comic effect.

Still it is curious that the audience laughs at this kind of statement (especially in light of Freud's economic theory of the generation of laughter, whereby we laugh off the excess energy engendered by the excessive transgressive act to which we lend our attention—the jokework having liberated some energy normally required for keeping up our defenses against "forbidden" thoughts). The laughter of Beckett's public indicates a reaction to his jokes, even though the gags often actually represent a limitation for the spectator, requiring a reductive rather than an expansive move, an entry into Beckett's *petit monde,* the padded cells of his hyperlucid cerebrum. Beckett's postmodern spectator is curiously bound by the rules of his comic penal system: in Beckett's post-world the comic transgression is paradoxical since it is more restricted than is the pretransgressive state of the spectator outside the theater. Thus, Beckett's humor is reductive, a move from the norm backwards, effected by the imposition of additional limitations. Witness, for instance, the constriction of Didi's comic observation following the reunion with Gogo: "Now . . . (*joyous*) there you are again . . . (*neutral*) here we are again . . . (*sad*) here I am again" (99). Or consider the comic effect of Didi's expansive offer to carry Gogo, followed by the imposition of a condition: "I'll carry you (*pause*) . . . if it comes to that [*le cas échéant*]" (52). The *trans*gression in the humor is an *in*gression for the audience—the comic extravagance reaches out only as far as their own normal inhibited state.

The audience is able to laugh at Beckett's comic of disappointment because they have followed the play, invested in its action; like the clowns themselves, the spectators are "in suspense" in the nonaction. Through the theatrical pact—the lending of attention that implies an acceptance of the rules of the play—the audience is caught in the straitjacket of Beckett's bizarre humor.

Here the spectator's willing attention is not equivalent to the conventional "willing suspension of disbelief" inducing the audience's vicarious participation in realistic theater. The spectator to Beckett's play plays a part in the comic transaction (the empty shoes at the front of the stage might even be considered an invitation to the spectators to "put themselves in the clowns' [oversized] shoes"). Indeed, the spectator's suspended attention is an example of the "comic lending" essential to the functioning of all humor: we are in fact able to laugh at the clown's antics only *because* we have put ourselves in his shoes, through the device of ideational mimetics. But in the case of Beckett's discontinuous theater, this participation is perhaps less an Imaginary identification than it is Symbolic lending of attention while in "attendance (*en attendant Godot*), a transaction in which the distance between joker and audience is painstakingly maintained.

Humor is crucial to the maintenance of distance between the two clowns and the spectators—the exterior third of this discontinuous theater; laughter resonates in the unbridgeable chasm that separates the laughing faces beyond the footlights from the spotlighted clowns. Suspended between real life and the play, Beckett's audience lends itself to the clowns' predicament just enough to be entertained in maintained desire, implicated in the playful disappointment of the missed appointment. But we are not here in the realm of the referential distance of disdainful superiority, as in a classic comedy. Even while maintaining their distance from the clowns, the postmodern paying customers pay attention and pay their dues, thus in a sense occupying a position similar to the paying patient in analysis, who pays for the analyst's time. And like the patient patient, postmodern spectators laugh because they are disappointed, stood up by *Dr. Godot* at the appointed hour (still waiting at play's end for proof of the doctor's approval or affection), dispossessed of their normal context and ordinary privileges during their paid session. In Beckett's post-world, the customer is always left waiting while the idle waiters "attend to" the absent Godot. Insofar as Godot *is* the audience, each spectator is stood up by an alter ego who may remain unrecognized, in a Lacanian *méconnaissance* where one's own desire is disowned as the desire of the Other. This kind of misrecognition is "disappointed" because it misses the point: that Godot (the analyst, our own double) is required not to show in order to move our Imaginary expectation into the realm of the Symbolic open-ended exchange, the "interminable cure."

Beckett's technique is interesting in light of Blanchot's theory that discontinuous theater or unworked literature is made to disappoint. Of course, many traditional theorists of the comic (most notably Kant, in the *Critique of Aesthetic Judgment*) have explained laughter in similar terms—as the result of a disappointment. But Beckett has been one of the first to take this disappointment to a postmodern—and rigorously logical—lack of conclusion, in which laughter is experienced as a constriction rather than a release, and comic lending or identification is also an alienation. This type of humor, where power and powerlessness coincide, is possible only because the dual dialectic relation has been hollowed out, deepened *en tiers,* rendered discontinuous in an apprenticeship of infinite diversion, where the postman-Doctor (Godot) never quite makes his appointed rounds, in a play always performed "*en attendant.*"

The Party's (Almost) Over: What Kind of Game Is Not Ending?

> Here the two partners don't play one against the other, playing rather one for the other, in a game that separates them . . . without any gain other than the possibility of playing.
>
> Blanchot, *L'entretien infini* (321)

In *Fin de partie* [*Endgame*][12] we encounter a particularly apt instance of the unworked text, understood as something like Blanchot's "game played without any gain other than the possibility of playing," suspended in "a present which never ends" (*EI* 64); indeed, the half-light of *Fin de partie* exemplifies the in-between quality of the scene of desire as Blanchot describes it, characterized by "nuances, degrees, the clair-obscur, undecidedly mediocrity" (*EI* 141). The nonevents of Beckett's endgame transpire in just such an "undecided" region ("I prefer the middle," Clov even declares at one point [67]); Hamm and Clov seem caught in a finality where all is ended ("Finished, it's finished . . .") and yet a future remains ("It's going to finish, it's maybe going to finish . . ." [15]). They are stranded in temporality, between the already and the not yet; death itself remains visible but out of reach, across the threshold, which will not be trans-gressed in a final erotic climax ("outside of here, it's death").

The play describes what happens when enough has happened, and yet when it is still possible and necessary to speak, where the moment of ending, however desired ("it's high time that it finish") is always future. The play thus almost seems like a fulfillment of Gogo's prophecy in *Godot,* that the "final moment will be long." This detour is attributable to that Beckettian potency which dwindles but never dies; even Nagg and Nell, Hamm's ancient and crippled parents, still have a lively interest in "fooling around" [*la bagatelle*]. In this domain of residual potency and exasperating possibility, it becomes necessary to speak in the conditional tense, the mode of held-out promise (Hamm dreams about freedom from the wheelchair:

"I would maybe make love. I would go into the woods. I would see . . . the sky, the earth. I would run" [33]).

For in this world of remnants, where human lives are scrappy leftovers stored, like Nagg and Nell, in garbage cans, where all has been realized and nothing finished (after the final war?), the spoken word lives on, a mark of the excessive vitality of the survivors. Like Blanchot's "ultimate question," formulated after dialectic reasoning is finished ("when the whole has been socially or institutionally realized" [*EI* 27]), Beckett's endgame makes the questioner feel something like what Blanchot calls "the excess of questioning over the power to question" (*EI* 27). Again, this formulation recalls Lacan's characterization of desire as the excess of demand (hence language) over need: desire—for Beckett as for Blanchot as for Lacan—is leftover language. In this game, all the old questions have been asked and answered, yet are revisited nostalgically ("Ah yes, the old questions, the old answers . . .") and somehow life goes on. This is the gaming moment where possibility and impossibility coincide, where chattering language (as Blanchot puts it) "escapes from the movement of power by which the world ceaselessly accomplishes itself" (*EI* 81).

What sort of game never gets finished? What sort of language escapes closure? In Beckett's game, the players literally do what they can, that is, nothing; or rather, by the rules of this game, nothing is something. The double meaning of the line "My turn to play/act [*à moi de jouer*]"—like the *rien à faire* that opens *Godot*—is Beckettian double-talk, which paradoxically calls on the players to "act" and marks the limitations of their acts. In Beckett's post-comic, as in Freud's innocent comic, the aimless aesthetic play of the actors seems to be the only aim. But just how innocent is this postmodern no-man's land of purposeless action? Is Beckett's scene innocent of social implications? Just how innocent is Blanchot's hopeless hope and timeless time? What is the social/political valence of postmodern undecidability, in which "nothing is as funny as suffering"?

Chance encounter: the roll (role) of the dice

My turn—to play . . .

Beckett (16)

There can be no doubt that Beckett's players suffer, in a parody of Cartesian reason ("He cries, thus he is" [94]). They long to be done with their game, yet it drags on, in a progressively impoverished state. It is never a question of running out of life or its symptom (words); like a fraction divided ad infinitum, the possible reductions in Beckett's closed system are endless.

Yet, in spite of their irremediable nature of their suffering, Beckett's players suffer with a bitter gaiety; in this game, nothing is funnier than suffering. Beckettian suffering is a farcical form of play, in which—*à trompeur, trompeur et demi*—each long-suffering character must take a turn on the spot ("*à moi de jouer*"). In this long-cut, daily suffering is a diversion from death (like the letter *en souffrance,* diverted from its end), a lifegame where all diversion is a less than deadly bore. Indeed, suffering is likened to a dramatic art, where "acts" are "performed," or rather rehearsed, in endless soliloquy so that the diversion may be savored ("I say to myself sometimes, 'Clov, you have to manage to suffer better than that'" [108]).

Indeed, play suffering is the founding condition of Beckett's game, an art with its own aesthetic. It is a game played in pairs who are infinitely linked and infinitely separated, absent from each other and from themselves (Hamm: "I've never really been here; absent, always . . ." [98]). The banter between teammates is like the throw of the dice (Blanchot makes a similar analogy between games of chance and the dialogue: "Speech is, in this case, the dice that are cast and recast" [*EI* 98]); repartee is a gaming device that both activates the play and determines the course of the game. The verbal exchange is a sign of the separation of the players, since it takes place on the stage/field/game board between the stymied players, pawns who play at endless checkmate. Like all games, this one contains an element of chance; Hamm and Clov are brought together by an arbitrary destiny governing Cov's chance arrival at Hamm's door. This primal surprise encounter, recounted in several versions of Hamm's mythic tale, represents an intrusion of the exterior world on his closed world. If Hamm ceaselessly retells this story of chance encounter, it is because this surprise—like the joking punch line that contaminates its hearer, implicating him or her in the game—compels Hamm time and again to enter the intersubjective game, to become an actor in his turn ("my turn to play" = "my move"). The story of Clov's intrusion, retold in ever-changing versions, serves as the opening move of Hamm's renewed game, the pre-text of his own aesthetic activity (the retelling of his own tale as history [*histoire*]) as well as the pretext for the perpetual sparring between players.

Thus, while chance and game are important preoccupations of modern literature in general (and particularly of literature inspired by surrealism, which builds its whole aesthetics out of chance encounter and surprise), Beckett's chance is a particularly postmodern phenomenon, reflecting concerns similar to those expressed by thinkers such as Derrida (in the 1982 article "Mes chances"),[13] Lacan (in his treatment of the role of chance and game in the *Seminar on the Purloined Letter*), and Lyotard (in *Au juste* [1979], translated as *Just Gaming,* a discussion of language theory as a set of moves in which chance plays an important role). While these various moves are too complex to be treated here, it is perhaps fair to say that a postmodern view of chance deconstructs the distinction between absolute determinism (history as causality) and absolute randomness or chaos (history as accident). Chance is rather seen as a game effect: chance moves history along rather than simply disrupting the chain of cause and effect. Chance operates within the rules of a preestablished game (social history) but it alters the course of the game whose rules it obeys.

This view is consistent with the role of chance in Beckett's endgame: the element of chance (Clov coming to Hamm rather than someone else) is a roll of the dice (a role of the dice?) that activates this particular game of the ongoing intersubjective match, helping to determine the course of Hamm's particular case history [*histoire*]. Chance also enables change, even in repetition (introducing or facilitating the intrusion of difference into repetitions of the same). In the postmodern reading, chance is allied with error as wandering; Beckett's clowns themselves are errant leftovers who seem to have outlived history and reason, vagabonds who meet up by chance, in the "error" of their wanderings [*errances*]. Chance is another term for that which cannot be accounted for, the uncertainty that ungrounds the modern belief in achievement, "posting" the modern in skepticism. For Derrida, chance marks the difference between teleology and history: it is the locus of possibility, and of difference.

All of this seems to suggest that the antidote to the closure of tragic "fate" is comic "chance" understood as the process that admits difference; indeed, the comic mode is based on contrast and surprise, and thrives on the permeability of closed systems to uninvited intrusions (like a Freudian slip, like Clov on Hamm's doorstep, like the unwelcome intruder whose arrival initiates the joke exchange). Long before the "post" era, of course, the surrealists already emphasized the role of chance in engendering laughter as well as the spark of poetic imagery; their concept of *l'humour noir* owes much to Freud's theory of the comic as an effect that is found by chance, much like the surrealist *objet trouvé.*[14] For Freud was the first to point out that the intrusion of unwelcome unconscious material on unsuspecting conscious thought, when given a chance, can derail the most serious statement (in a Freudian slip-up), turning the most authoritative statement into an overdetermined joke.

Thus chance, as understood by moderns and postmoderns alike, has a role to play in aesthetics—spacing, activating, overdetermining language by trope. But chance, in the postmodern sense, has a curious historical mission as well. Chance assures that history may always have a surprise ending beyond the preordained answers of fate or determinism, that history may be made up as we go along, as histoire. Paradoxically, an affirmation of undecidability as a certain margin of error in determinist causality is that which permits human beings to shape history and introduce change. It is also chance (as in the chance opportunity of the lapse that opens language to unsuspected meanings) that accounts for the opened-up nature of the aesthetic in Derrida's game of "dissemination," a language game that exploits any chance to deconstruct linguistic and logical systems. Thus, postmodern chance is not hazard nor alibi (can one disown a Freudian slip as a mere accident?); it is rather a chance in the sense of an opportunity. This postmodern chance, in fact, is a certain grim hope. In Beckett's system, chance unends the game; when Hamm tosses the whistle out to the audience at play's end, who knows where it will fall? Chance determines who gets the chance to play next, but we will all have our turn to determine the next link in the chain, to play the next set and to set the next play.

Like all games, Hamm and Clov's exchange is driven by an urge to get on with it, to accomplish, even to end—not unlike Freud's inexorable death-drive, which pushes all creative activity along, "ever unsubdued." Like the creative impulse that veils the death instinct—the urge of all organic life to revert to a state of quiescence—Clov's creativity manifests itself in a persistent urge to settle things ("I love order. It's my dream. A world where everything would be silent and immobile and everything would be in its final place, under its final dust" [78]). But Beckett's play shows that Clov's totalitarian fantasies of order—which border on the chilling vision of final solutions—are as unrealizable as are the always unsubdued creative urges propelled by the death instinct: the dream of ending is as inexhaustible as drive itself.

So in Beckett's diversion, where neither player may win for losing, the alternating power dynamic between Hamm and Clov is an indication of the final powerlessness of both players, the failure of a totalizing sadistic impulse of mastery. Clov functions like the distanced and retrieved toy in Freud's *fort-da* game; he is a plaything summoned and expelled at Hamm's infantile demand, in a series of clownlike comings and goings. This infantile game of appearance and disappearance is also played by Nagg and Nell, who alternately pop up and disappear into their trash cans like lifesize jacks-in-the-box. All three slapstick puppets (Clov, Nagg, and Nell) seem to be subject to the Hamm actor's control, since it is his histrionics and tantrums that determine when they will speak and when they will "put a lid on it" [*boucle-le*]. Thus Hamm, like a spoiled child, is a director-ventriloquist who calls the shots, runs the show, and assigns the roles, often demanding more than his share ("my turn to play").

But since no one wins in this farcical play [*à trompeur, trompeur et demi*], these objects of Hamm's power-play exert power over him as well, taking turns in the game of reciprocal comeuppance. Indeed, Clov controls Hamm's very existence, since he metes out the ration of supplies, and he also exercises the power of pardon, for which he forces Hamm to beg (27). As for Nagg and Nell, they are the locus of a certain power over Hamm because it is they, as the "parents" in the original familial drama, who seem to be the source of Hamm's unassuageable desire. Like the absent parent who is the object of the *fort-da* game—and for whom the toy substitutes—Nagg and Nell are the objects who first refused Hamm's excessive demands for affection ("We used to let you cry. Then we moved you far away, so that we could sleep" [77]). In Lacanian terms, these negligent parents leave some "demands" unfulfilled—as all parents must do, especially when all "needs" seem to have been satisfied—refusing to give in to excessive leftover desire. But even as an adult Hamm is still in a sense addressing his demand to Nagg and Nell, forcing them to be the audience for his compulsively retold tale (in a kind of reverse transference, these listening parents stand in for the analyst, the attentive ear—for the Beckettian "Hamm" is never free from the compulsion to play for an audience).

Wrong address

A hilarious crowd, things are cheering up again [*une foule en délire, ça redevient gai*].

Fin de partie (49)

Above all, the endgame is a spectator sport: the audience is constantly acknowledged, either implicitly—by the use of theatrical terminology like "to make an exit" [*gagner la sortie*] or "to speak in an aside" [*faire un aparté*]—or explicitly—as when Clov turns his telescope on the audience and reports that he sees a "delirious crowd" rolling in the aisles. The audience literally thickens the plot of the play by adding an exterior presence, a crowd of Others who may influence the course of the game. And as in *Godot,* the public also thickens the theatrical space, deepening it into a dimension beyond the confines of the stage. (The same observation could be made concerning the child spotted outside near the end of the English version of *Endgame.* Has Godot finally arrived, in an intertextual allusion?) In any case, Clov's discovery of the exterior outsider is couched in comic terms ("a happy crowd; things are cheering up"). Indeed, the intrusion of the third party—the assessment of the outsider as a "good audience" delirious with laughter—may be compared to the arrival of the interloping third in the joking transaction, the onlooker whose presence transforms a goal-oriented process of biological courtship into the occasion for a little locker-room humor.

In Beckett as in Freud, the addition of an outsider transforms a game of doubles into a social occasion, a *partie* in which language is itself the "dice" determining the stakes and the course of each move. Beckett's game thus stages something akin to Blanchot's concept of *la parole plurielle* as a type of language voicing a non-serious seriousness [*sérieux sans sérieux*], a layered message in which meaning plays a game of hide-and-seek, throwing the message into a diverted path (like a misaddressed letter). Beckett's grim comic voice (a seriousness without seriousness) like Blanchot's plural speech, proliferates possible meanings and thus overdetermines and clouds the too-clear prosaic pretensions of "true" or didactic discourse, in which polemic actually only masquerades as truth. Comic wordplay leaves the message *en souffrance*, assuring that "we are not in the process of meaning something" (as Hamm and Clov repeatedly worry).

Fin de partie is thus in a sense the least serious of Beckett's plays, insofar as it constantly points out its own insignificance: Beckett's eternal suspense of meaning causes words to lose their mooring in true or original reference. (In Beckett's game of slide, there is not even anything like Lacan's upholstery tacks [*points de capiton*] to pin down meaning; language is at best a "slip cover" that acts to cover up its own indeterminancy.) Nor is there anything like a determinate historical contingency in Beckett's game, since words are suspended outside of time ("Yesterday? What does that mean?" [109]). And Beckett's clowns look not for solutions but for tricks or gags [*trucs*] (35) that may serve to prolong the comic suspense of meaning ("I'll give you just enough to keep you from dying," says Clov to Hamm, with characteristic expansiveness [20]). In Beckett's pastime, the "settled" state for which Clov longs [*coite*] and the "seminal" state of coitus [*coïte*] are comically confused; joking ambiguity thus turns the impulse to tragic fatal settlements into one of generation and renewed possibility.

Perhaps the central joke of *Fin de partie* is that Hamm, like Beckett himself, is a poet of sorts in whom creative accomplishment coincides with failure. Hamm is also a blind man (like many a visionary, including Oedipus when *his* game is up); thus his visual faculty has been replaced by the faculty of hearing, the ability to listen to interior voices, the plural chatter that dictates the many versions of his story. And like all of Beckett's fictions, Hamm's story recounts a founding myth of unallayed desire (Clov's arrival): it retells an historic event that has been transformed into myth, "unworked" and clouded over by poetic forgetfulness. (This is Freud's definition of myth, as elaborated in *Moses and Monotheism* [1933]: myth is a historical event worked over by desire, cloaked in symbol, which must be deciphered like a dream.) Like all of Beckett's fictions Hamm's story diverts its listeners from purpose, as when Clov complains, for instance, that he is unable to finish off the rat because Hamm's story has left him "distracted" [*dérangé*].

Indeed, Hamm himself is deranged, a crazed poet of sorts engaged in what Blanchot calls "the mad game of writing," a sport that attempts to exhaust the excesses of language by endless bouts or rehearsals. As Blanchot points out—in a postmodern formulation of the term *parodic*—the very repetition of a situation may serve to make it comic: "And thus, repeating repetition ad infinitum, [writing] renders it parodic somehow" (*EI* 238). *Fin de partie* is a dizzying game of blind man's bluff, in which the spectator (like Hamm himself) is left in the dark concerning the "ends" of this game, shaded from the deadening glare of unequivocal interpretation.

In Beckett's later works, comic language becomes more and more rarified, reduced to an almost inaudible murmur from beyond the grave (the ultimate understatement). But no matter how subtle the joke, Beckett's literature of disappointment continues to fail to take itself seriously in order to function as an "unworked text" which—like Watt's painting of the broken circle—"undoes" the very notion of closure (cf. Blanchot: "The unworked text opens the circle, marks its point of singularity—the point where the non-circularity of the circle would be defined—where closure coincides with rupture" [415]). The unworked text thus represents a revolution of sorts, but the revolution may be won only at the point at which it is conceded; the circle starts only where it is ruptured; the play recommences in response to unsatiated desire. Beckett's unworked work disappoints creatively thanks to the ludicrous motto of his play: "The end is in the beginning, and nonetheless, we go on . . ."

The final scene of *Fin de partie* describes just such a paradox, a break that will engender a *renvoi* to the beginning. Posed on the edge of the abyss (the darkened theater, the rupture in theatrical space where the Other awaits permission to leave),

Hamm makes the ludicrous promise to be silent, to finish speaking, even as he speaks ("Let's not talk about it any more . . . let's not talk" [112]). He immediately ruptures this promised silence by (literally and comically) airing his dirty linen in public: "Old linen! [*vieux linge*] (Pause). You—you I'll keep" (112). This reassumption of the opening pose (handkerchief over head) and the staging of the final gag (that he speaks after his promise to fall silent) signal the replay of the bout: the whistle is cast away, like the expelled toy in the *fort-da* game, but only (presumably) to be retrieved for the next bout. Indeed, the ultimate joke of this endgame is that the final whistle fails to end the game. The rules of the "mad game of writing" (Blanchot) call for the literature of disappointment to fail to keep its word (*tenir parole*), failing to fulfill the implied promise of the play's title (that the game will end). Instead, Beckett's writing is a staging of what Blanchot calls the *parole plurielle* "suspended in the chance between reason and madness [*dans l'aléa entre raison et déraison*]" (*EI* 607).

What kind of game is not ending? A postmodern textual game that overworks language, putting it out of work—in a series of comic moves transforming the work of desire into the play of the text.

But a niggling question remains. Beckett's aesthetic, however grimly delightful, poses a real challenge for the elaboration of a postmodern aesthetic of resistance rather than reaction, which would not rule out ends and purposes. Is the Beckettian clown a reactionary, a postmodern aesthete? Is the postmodern aesthetic of purposelessness finally a Kantian aesthetic of artistic purity, validating and enforcing a divorce between reality and art? Is the postmodern aesthetic just a new aestheticism, a veiled avatar of the modernist elitist aesthetic of art for art's sake? Does unworked textuality preclude social reference and concerns, leaving its protagonist post-man stranded in exile? Some postmoderns might have it so, but I don't think we need count Beckett (nor Derrida nor Blanchot for that matter) among them. (In fact, Derrida's recent activism around the issue of apartheid might serve as evidence that a postmodernism of resistance is indeed possible, rather than a postmodernism of reactionary aestheticism.) In any case, Beckett's discontinuous play at least suggests that Clov may leave Hamm (the play's "end" doesn't tell us) to arrive on another doorstep, opening another chapter of communication, making another delivery, like the next teller in the joking chain. Does the fact that "something is taking its course" (as Clov tells us) mean that the message "will always arrive at its destination" (as Lacan insists) even if it is diverted along the way?

Open questions—certainly one interpretation might read Beckett's game as a charter for endless rumination (let's put the kerchief on and go to sleep). And yet when Hamm, at the end of the game, tosses the whistle into the darkened abyss, into the audience—he calls us on stage, puts us under the spotlight and on the spot. It's our move [*à nous de jouer*] . . .

8. Postaesthetics: After the Endgame

> What shall we do, now that we're happy?
> We wait.
> Sure, but while we're waiting?
>
> Beckett, *En attendant Godot*

> It's obvious we can't stay here . . . after so many tears and so many tricks, what are we to do?
>
> Ignazio Silone, *Fontamara*

Planning the next move

Gratuity, impasse, play, perpetuation—these are the qualities of the postmodern endgame. And the comic modality of this unworked text, as we have seen in Beckett's work, may be apprehended on at least four levels: as a technique of the writing itself; as a theme or source of subject matter (an emphasis on clowning or play); as a metaphor/paradigm for the literary process in its entirety (a "postmodern allegory" of writing); and finally, as a performing metaphor for the working of the human psyche, in an ongoing social exchange (Lacan's intersubjectivity; Blanchot's "infinite conversation"). At this final level, the comic process may be read as *écriture*, that is, as an allegory of human desire, a transactional scene that not only reenacts the genesis of play in the child—thereby manifesting the rhythm of compulsive repetition that Freud suggests is characteristic of all social interaction—but also restages the primal oedipal drama whereby the child becomes a social being.

With the move to this final extratextual level of interpretation, the literary process completes its rounds and comes home, for if there is a punch line to the postmodern comic text, it is perhaps that the concept of the interminable cure or the inexhaustibility of human desire is as applicable to our own everyday experience (including our experience of reading literature) as it is to the therapeutic situation in psychoanalysis. And the endgame teaches us not to expect an ending, least of all a happy or definitive one.

Given the impossibility of winning or even ending the game, just what kind of conclusion or assessment of the unworked text is possible? Has the encounter with Beckett's clowns left us stranded in a comic impasse, like Didi and Gogo, unable to draw critical conclusions? Given "the excess of questioning over the power to question" (Blanchot), perhaps the only possible response to the challenge of the unworked text is the framing of the next set of questions, a shaping of that persistent query ("what do we do now?") that haunts so much of contemporary writing. Even if we have learned to relinquish the habit of looking for conclusive solutions in the process of reading and interpretation, we cannot help wondering, along with Didi and Gogo, where we go from here, after the final whistle of the endgame. Indeed, the "final" gesture of Beckett's game seems to call us into the play, as the third party who completes the theatrical triangle and who will perpetuate the play. Beckett's unworked text is an infinite encounter that blows the whistle on the comfortable armchair spectator: after the endgame, the ball is in our court.

Instead of concluding, then, I want to suggest two axes of inquiry—two directions among many possible directions for further exploration—that seem to follow from a reading of the postmodern text as a "comic" or "aesthetic" effect of desire. Both are questions about the aesthetic itself, which entail readdressing some of the premises of this study, but from a slightly different angle: first, are the comic and the aesthetic modes simply equivalent in the postmodern text? Second, to what degree is the postmodern comic aesthetic a gratuitous one, manifesting a "purposiveness without purpose" (Kant's definition of the aesthetic) estranged from ordinary life or real aims?

But before trying to draw any conclusion about the relation of the aesthetic and the comic in general, and the postmodern aesthetic and the postmodern comic in particular, it is perhaps worthwhile to take yet another detour, pausing briefly to consider a more concrete question: what is the relation between "the comic" and "the poetic," conceptually and technically? For poetry is often deemed to be the most literary of literary genres, perhaps because it is the furthest from ordinary communicative and realistic speech, the most dependent on linguistic trope. (As Lyotard puts it in *Discours, figure,* poetry is the Other of ordinary discourse, haunted and inhabited by primary process as "figure.") In considering the fundamentally comic modality of a certain desiring literary text, it may be useful to raise the question of how and why the jokework and the poetic textwork—as the ultimate in aesthetic desiring expression—coincide.

The second question is even broader in scope: having argued for the gratuity and aimlessness of the literary transaction, how may we relate the postmodern aesthetic to reality? This is a restatement of a familiar postmodern bind: how do we live our lives after we have assimilated the lessons of the comic apprenticeship (Beckett); after we have learned that the cure is unending (Freud); when we know that our clearest statements are "plural" (Freud; Blanchot); after we find that history itself is subject to farcical repetitions (Marx)? If literature seems to function as an effect, or even as a celebration, of aimlessness and error, what aims may we have as readers and teachers? Must an open-endedness, a refusal to end, imply amnesia, ahistoricism, a refusal of ends? Or may the interminable cure be read, in the analytic sense, as a "repeating, remembering, and working through" that solicits historical memory and a commitment to a certain progress through ongoing effort ("steady work")?[1]

Both axes of questioning imply an examination of the transgressive nature of aesthetic processes: can the violation of limits fundamental to the comic process serve to reshape the rules of the game, or are aesthetic transgressions doomed to reinforce the order they contest? What, in other words, is the nature of aesthetic excess—is it merely a kind of pleasurable extra, an *Anlehnung* (Freud) "laid on to" biological function like icing on the cake? Or does all truly human experience qualify as aesthetic excess, a profoundly social process beyond biological need (whereby that which is creative and human goes beyond the simple needs of survival)? Does desire *im*plicate us *in* or *ex*tricate us *from* responsibility to "Others"? Any conclusion about the comic nature of the postmodern condition must address these kinds of questions about the stakes of the aesthetic play between writer and reader, after the endgame.

The Comic Nature of the Aesthetic: Jokework as Poetic Trope

> The creative spark of metaphor does not surge forth from the juxtaposition of two images . . . its is produced between two signifiers when one has been substituted for the other . . . one word for another—such is the formula for metaphor. We see that metaphor is placed at the precise point where sense is produced in nonsense; that is to say at that passage whose meaning was discovered by Freud, and which, crossed in the opposite sense [*franchi à rebours*] produces that comic word [*ce mot*] which in French is the joke [*le mot*] par excellence.
>
> Jacques Lacan, "L'Instance de la lettre dans l'inconscient," *Ecrits* I (264)

We have seen how the comic language of unconscious desire (primary process) makes itself felt in literary language through the devices of condensation, displacement, regression; I have even suggested that *Jokes and Their Relation to the Unconscious* may be recast as a paradigm of the textual process itself. Throughout this study, I have referred to the reading of the unconscious itself as a kind of text by Lacanians who understand unconscious processes in linguistic terms (Laplanche and Leclaire, for instance, see repression as a metaphoric process). As the quotation above attests, all these takes on the relation between joke, the unconscious, and textual trope are Lacanian in inspiration and suggest a concrete and functional way of thinking of "jokes and their relation to the aesthetic/poetic." For Lacan purloins Freud's insight that jokes are related to the unconscious, and adds his own punch line—"the unconscious is structured like a language"—having also purloined the definition of language as trope from the structuralists along the way. (For Jakobson, for example, the paradigmatic axis of substitution is metaphoric; the syntagmatic axis of combination is metonymic: language is thus essentially "trope" in a sense.) It follows from this double pick-up that a Lacanian reading might consider jokes to be profoundly and fundamentally related to aesthetic/literary technique, especially since the unconscious is itself a joker of sorts, a master trickster.

For instance, it is significant that when Lacan defines metaphor, which he considers the poetic trope par excellence (in the tradition of structural linguists such as Jakobson), he equates the metaphoric substitution of "one word for another" with the doubling of speech in pun ("*'le mot' par excellence*"). Lacan contends that in poetry as in joking language, a single referent is overdetermined by hidden meanings. Even though the original prosaic meaning may have been replaced by the new signifier (the poetic image or metaphor), the ordinary or prosaic meaning nonetheless remains present because of its connection to the original syntactic statement, the signifying chain of the original sentence ("the occulted signifier remaining present in its metonymic connection to the rest of the chain" [*Ecrits* 265]). In the metaphoric image, "a thousand candles appeared in the night sky," for instance, the term *star,* occulted by the metaphor *candle,* remains "present" even in its absence because of the meaning of the rest of the phrase.

Similarly, in a pun, both terms are present in one referent: indeed, if the joke goes in the opposite direction from metaphor as Lacan suggests ("le *passage . . . franchi à rebours*"), it is only perhaps because the joke effect depends on the retrieval of the lost meaning, rather than its repression. (For a pun to work, both meanings must be clearly in view in the mind's eye; while for a metaphor to be effective, unhackneyed, the ordinary meaning must not be too evident.)

Lacan seems to be making the point that something like what Freud calls the "finding of similarity in difference" or the "rediscovery of something familiar," a technique of the joke, is also characteristic of the poetic process; but whereas poetry seeks to downplay the connection between the two terms, joking seeks to expose it. Still, both processes depend on the veiled or absent presence of the repressed term, which becomes even more significant *because* it is veiled (not unlike the unavailable prudish lady in Freud's joke scenario). When Lacan insists on the plural or overdetermined quality of poetic speech, comparing it with joking language, he evokes a kind of figural intrusion of underground meanings that emerge into the train of thought: ordinary thought is always shadowed or doubled by what is not said, by the "repressed" terms underlying every spoken chain. Poetic meaning is produced when an ordinary term is veiled and another slipped comically into its place, when something familiar is veiled in mystery (as in many a classic comic imbroglio, where the disguised mystery lover turns out to be the protagonist's own spouse). In other words, comic meaning is produced when the veiled mystery lady turns out to be "the word next door," when something unfamiliar is revealed as familiar, in a linguistic game of peekaboo. In both cases, language does a tantalizing fan dance, giving us a peak at the fascinating figure of the unconscious.

This kind of technical equation between the poetic and the comic has been enlarged and allegorized in the work of poststructuralist writers like Derrida, Blanchot, and Lyotard, who see poetic language as more than just poetry: in Blanchot, poetic overdetermined language (*la parole plurielle*) becomes synonymous (a synecdoche?) with literary expression in general as that comic *parole* fundamentally opposed to the deadly serious discourse of reason or philosophy. Similarly, Lyotard refers to poetry as the Other of prose, a (potentially comic) lapse or trip-up in the discourse of knowledge (*"le leurre au savoir"* [*DF* 323]). And Derrida refers to the poetic as the rupture of sense ("an eruption uncovering the limit of discourse" [*L'ecriture et la différence* 383]), an opening up to a kind of comic capability represented by "that part of every discourse which is capable of opening itself to an absolute loss of meaning, to a backdrop of the sacred and the nonsensical, the playful and the unknowing" (383). Similarly, Lyotard sees poetry as "the order of discourse that keeps itself open to its Other, encouraging disruption" (*DF* 324). Still, in poetry or art, unlike dream, formal order must be maintained in the interests of communicability; hence, poetic form acts, to a degree, as an obstacle restricting gratification afforded by poetic figure; in fact, Lyotard writes that artistic form such as meter or rhyme actually works to "maintain desire in nonfulfillment" (356) simply because "these forms cannot be ignored" and their presence is a barrier to the kind of total absorption or belief elicited by the dream-scene. Indeed, while Lyotard argues (*DF* 323ff.) that poetry is a prime example of the workings of desire in language, his discussion of poetic transgression seems equally applicable to the joke transgression, a transgression which is substitutive (hence metaphoric) in nature.

According to all these postmodern views, comic language might also qualify as a poetic phenomenon. Like the dream and like poetry, it deploys the figures of primary process to fulfill desire; but like poetry and unlike dream it must outwit conscious censorship, even while remaining intelligible to consciousness. In other words, comic language, like poetic language, depends on the disguise of form to realize its pleasure-mission, getting around the rules of discourse; and paradoxically, joke-form itself may also serve as an obstacle to straightforward, short-circuited gratification (such as that provided by dream hallucination or infantile gibberish, which, however pleasurable, would be unintelligible to the Other to whom the joke is addressed). Joking, then, like poetic language, is paradoxically both a fulfillment of desire and maintenance of desire in an intersubjective circuit. And in a postmodern perspective, this comic capacity for paradox, and for partial fulfillment, is the aesthetic faculty par excellence.

Poetry as fetish

Another way of thinking of the limited nature of the poetic/comic transgression is suggested by Freud's view of joking as a compromise between two competing urges: the urge to fulfill desire immediately, and the need to respect societal obstacles. Interestingly, Lyotard makes use of an analogous concept in his discussion of scansion in poetry, which he attributes to a kind of compromise between two competing drives, in accordance with Freud's theory of repetition in *Beyond the Pleasure Principle.* For Lyotard, the gratification afforded by art may be considered a substitute for the most final and absolute "gratification" of death (the aim of the death-drive, which motivates the repetition compulsion): "The death-drive does not lead the psychic apparatus to its destruction . . . but to the substitutive formation of this satisfaction which is precisely the fantasy fulfillment of desire [*l'accomplissement fantasmatique du désir*]" (*DF* 356). Freud himself maintains that the compromise between the death-urge and the contrary instinct of self-preservation gives rise to the rhythm of human creativity and achievement; but in Lyotard's account, this rhythm finds a material and local manifestation in the scansion or oscillation of poetic language. Moreover, Lyotard's account of oscillation is as applicable to the joking process as it is to the poetic process, thanks to the substitutive nature of joking as response to obstacle. But a more radical reading of Freud, as I have suggested in chapters 3 and 4, would read all human undertaking as "aesthetic" or "poeticized," insofar as human social life and achievement are both "textual" and "perverse," something other than simple biological function, entailing intersubjective "play" of human being in and for the Other.

Thus, the association of the aesthetic with Freud's account of the comic process entails a reflection on teleology, for the comic and the aesthetic/literary/poetic share their substitutive nature, their status as deflections from goals dictated by biological needs.

In other words, whereas authoritative, nonpoetic discourse aims to demonstrate clearly, the aimless aesthetic mode tends to complicate, overdetermine, and equivocate (Lyotard: "The poetic text may have no pretensions to Truth" [*DF* 282]). I have argued then throughout this study that the aesthetic is fundamentally perverse, if we accept Freud's notion of perversion as a libidinally motivated activity that deflects/alters the original aim, lengthening the path to the final aim. Lyotard's reading of poetry as antitruth seems to suggest that "Truth" is the Imaginary shortest distance between two points; the aesthetic allows for Symbolic (per)/(di)versions.

For Freud, of course, perversion in its extreme manifestation becomes fetishism ("Fetishism," 1927) in which the intermediate sexual object not only becomes the substituted aim but also functions to veil or even deny the reality of the original object. (For Freud, the veiled original object is the woman's genitals, the [absent] phallus, so that the fetish object serves to veil and to deny the reality of "castration.") Thus, fetishism, like the joke, represents a compromise between desire and reality since the purpose of the fetish object is to preserve the illusion that the phallus is present, in a perverse fiction that is also a substitutive gratification.

This equation between the poetic and the perverse is reinforced by Freud's own characterization of the work of art as a veiling of libidinal or egotistic impulse, which not only makes the writer's own egotistical fantasy palatable to the reader but actually bribes the reader with the lure of formal pleasure. (Freud: "The writer bribes us by the offer of a purely formal—that is, aesthetic—pleasure in the presentation of his fantasies. This increment of pleasure which is offered us in order to release yet greater pleasure from deeper sources in the mind is called an incitement premium, or technically, 'forepleasure'"

["Creative Writers and Daydreaming," 1908, *SE* 9:15]).

Thus the reader of poetry is in a position analogous to that of the joke's hearer, seduced by form and enticed into a diversion from unequivocal meaning. And by accepting the bribe of pleasure, the reading Other is implicated in the textual cover-up. An understanding of the joking process, then, can aid the critic in investigating the artifice of the aesthetic act. For the critic is always a voyeur of sorts, who lifts the veil to expose "the poet's secret": the means by which a writer acts as an accomplice to the unconscious, implicating the not-so-innocent bystander in the transaction. By a metaphoric substitution, a sleight of hand fostering a kind of imposture (one word for another), the poet performs the literary *Ankleidung* that is essential to the aesthetic act.

Thus even if all human communication is aesthetic and excessive in nature because of the human desire that motivates it, there is perhaps still a certain specificity to the literary act. Blanchot seems to suggest that *la parole plurielle* solicits its own derailment, pleasurably and comically, whereas other acts of communication aim at achieving authority, directness, unequivocal truth, or maximum efficacy. If it is only a question of aim or modality that separates the aesthetic from the nonaesthetic, something may well be lost: the illusion of the purity, nobility, or magic of literary activity understood as a kind of sacred rite (as in the notion of "art for art's sake" or the concept of the poet as inspired seer). But something may be gained in this postmodern demystification as well, whereby all literature is engaged in a perpetual conversation about desire. The postmodern text is perhaps less concerned with disguising losses than with celebrating gains, proliferating possibility in a comic vision, which may transform human regress into human progress, human need into human desire, unworking distinctions between art and life, aesthetic and useful language, along the way.

Postmodern sublime-ation

But if everything is poetic or textual (cry the arbitrators of taste in dismay), what happens to standards? What is the difference between literature and plain language? How may the postmodern "sliding" be stopped and meaning be affixed? What keeps us from sliding into an aesthetic abyss where one meaning is as good as another, where the endless endgame rules out any judgments, including the ethical judgments upon which social action must be grounded? These are difficult questions to be sure, and they bring us back to the question of the nature of postmodern aesthetics. In *The Postmodern Condition* (77–81), Lyotard associates postmodern aesthetics with the notion of the sublime, and dissociates postmodernism from the notion of taste or even beauty. This involves a repudiation of Kant's definition of the aesthetic—as the tasteful, beautiful, and useless motivated by a "purposiveness without purpose" exempt from the concerns of real life. Postmodernist aesthetics (writes Lyotard) are more like a manifestation of the Kantian sublime: a mixture of pain and pleasure deriving from a sense of unattainable, from the intuition of something infinite that cannot be represented. For Lyotard, then, the postmodern aesthetic is less gratuitous than impossible; it may be summed up as the "presentation that something unrepresentable exists." (Again, Beckett's work provides an example of this impossibility, motivated as it is by the compulsion to express "nothing," the inexpressible.) But in dispensing with the notion of gratuity in favor of the notion of unrepresentability or impossibility, we do not get out of the postaesthetic impasse: even if Beckett's art is not considered as separate from real life, it may nonetheless still be read as a lesson in navel contemplating—as a representation of the futility of action or as a staging of infinite regress, a paralyzed downward spiral suspended in ahistorical time.

It is at this point that I think psychoanalysis may intervene, suggesting that the Symbolic Order, while infinite, is anything but regressive; indeed, it is the task of the oedipal Other to stop infinite regress, aimed at sublime Imaginary bliss, by diverting desire into exterior social channels. This is the thrust, for instance, of Neil Hertz's reading of the role of the oedipal Father vis-à-vis the sublime: it is he who institutes limits and enables progress, upward and outward, by saying "no" to regress.[2] My own reading of Freud through Lacan has tried to suggest that the role of the oedipal Other is not necessarily a paternal function, but may be understood as the obstacle posed by social necessity, the presence of an audience for every one of our comic roles, or even as the presence of the real obstacles that thwart our every desire. This argument depends on another crucial insight in Freudian theory: the obstacle not only deflects or rechannels desire but it actually changes its character (as when the promise of biological satisfaction underlying the joker's "wooing talk" is transformed into the social pleasure of sharing the object of desire by "joking talk"). In other words, Freud's comic theory may transform a gratuitous aesthetic of infinite regress into a driving aesthetic of infinite progress: Freud's aesthetic is not a regressive cult of the pure and the beautiful; it is instead a function of excess, prolongation, diversion, drive.

Nor is Freudian sublimation a matter of simple repression of desire. It is closer to perversion—the diversion of a desire altered by obstacle, a desire that is the motor of all human action and achievement. (As Freud writes in *Beyond the Pleasure Principle,* "It is the difference between the amount of pleasure which is demanded and that which is actually achieved that provides the driving factor that will permit of no halting. . . . The backward path that leads to complete satisfaction is as a rule obstructed by the resistances which retain the repressions" (36). In Freud's account, the potential for infinite regress (into bliss or death) becomes the sublime capacity—or compulsion—for progress. Like Kant's sublime, Freud's aesthetic is infinite. Like Kant's aesthetic, it is disinterested, deflected from major vital need. But it is also always the exercise of infinite interest in the Other as audience, as object, as next subject in the joking chain. It is Didi's performance for Gogo, and for us. It is Godot as interested Other, unattainable but in attendance.

The Aesthetic Nature of the Comic: Rethinking "Gratuity"

> What they say of jokes is true of literature too: it's the way you tell it that matters.
>
> Terry Eagleton, *Walter Benjamin: or Towards a Revolutionary Criticism,* 143

The poetics of the comic

These reflections on the comic nature of Freud's aesthetic seem to bring us back to our initial query: what is comic about literature, and just how do the comic and the aesthetic intersect? Blanchot, Derrida, Lyotard and company would seem to concur that the comic is an instance of the poetic or literary, as an overdetermined or metaphoric mode of discourse open to the ambiguity of figural expression.

But postmodern writing also seems to suggest that the inverse statement is true, that poetic or literary language is somehow comic. For, as we have seen, postmodern writers emphasize that literary language is a playful entertainment relying on *double entendre.* While it is obviously not the case that all literature elicits laughter—which is perhaps a functional definition of the comic—it does at least seem to be true that the unworked textuality characteristic of a certain postmodern text is consistently comic in register, insofar as it points to the fundamental laughability of a certain self-satisfied, authoritative discourse. In other words, the unworked text stages an open-ended comic circuit where none of the participants—reader, writer, or critic—may have the last word.

Yet even this "conclusion"—that there can be no conclusion to the unworked transaction—cannot serve as a final say. Even if we concede the "excessive" or "aesthetic" nature of textuality, we readers nonetheless seem compelled to go on questioning the text, looking for some applicability, use, or value, some way of inserting the lessons of *écriture* into our own experience and practice. This is no easy task, especially since the lesson of the literary and theoretical avant-garde in France and elsewhere often seems to be the apprenticeship in a kind of social paralysis. The last scene of Ionesco's *Le nouveau locataire* is a typical example: the "hero," having spent the preceding scenes making the move into a new apartment, allows himself to be buried under his own possessions, a mountain of objects, the "trappings" of modern life. Entombed by the spoils of his labor, he merely pulls the ladder in after him and turns out the light. But Ionesco's "moving" scene poses a challenge to those who witness it: are we, like the new tenant, to become mere placeholders, zeros "couched" in aesthetic language? Like Hamm, are we content to throw in the towel, conceding the endgame? Or like the Orator in the final scene of *Les chaises* (Ionesco), must we relapse into infantile prattle, having learned that it is impossible to mean anything?

Deconstructing the tower of babble

This kind of questioning of certain postmodern postures may also underlie much of the current distrust of the post-structuralist phenomenon in literary and critical circles, since some critics have responded to the "deconstruction" of literary and philosophical texts as an all-out assault on meaning itself, or as at best a self-indulgent exercise in solipsism. One of the most mordant attacks is Eagleton's pastiche of Derrida, which serves as epigraph to his chapter on Marxism and deconstruction in the aforementioned study on Walter Benjamin. (A sample: "Dare I die deary da? Da dare die did, Die Derider. Didiwriter. Dadadidididididada. Aaaaaaaaaaaaa . . . Der i da [Oedipal Fragment]."). Significantly, Eagleton makes his (maliciously funny) point by exploiting the comic device of allusion, in a tendentious joke whose point is comprehensible only to those initiated in the discourse he is attacking.

While we may question the fairness of Eagleton's jibe, we must share his concern over the future and function of literature and criticism.[3] For the debate over the relevance of deconstructive criticism is perhaps merely the most recent version of a much older debate around the issue of the obligation and efficacy of the literary text vis-à-vis the society that produces it, and the corollary question of the relationship of literary practice in all its forms to real life. Is the aesthetic endgame a deadend?

In one form or another, these questions have engaged many of the most influential writers and theorists of our century.[4] Ionesco and Kenneth Tynan fought it out in a heated published exchange (the *"controverse londonienne"* reproduced in Ionesco's *Notes et contre-notes*), with the former arguing for the purity of the work of art and its exemption from didactic or ideological functions. The surrealists broke over a related question—the issue of the servitude of art to radical politics (discussed in Breton's *La position politique du surrealisme,* 1935)—and in the heydey of existentialism, Sartre took on many of the leading intellectuals of the day over the question of *engagement.* There are even echoes of the question of artistic gratuity in the well-known quarrel between Barthes and Picard (during the 1960s), although with a different political inflection, since in that case the partisan of textual or aesthetic independence, at least as concerns literary conventions or standards (Barthes), is also a writer concerned with the political valence of the literary text (*Le degré zéro de l'écriture*); while the proponent of the positivist argument for the connection of the textual process with life or realistic representation (Picard) is an advocate of universal and timeless (hence apolitical) criteria for the evaluation of the text.[5]

In our own day, even in those literary circles where there is consensus about the political relevance of art, there is disagreement concerning the political valence of the avant-garde, especially the Continental absurdist "anti-literature" of the 1950s and 1960s, and the poststructuralist tendency prevalent in the last three decades. On the one hand, Marxist critics like Eagleton, in the tradition of Sartre, bemoan the solipsism of certain texts, both literary and theoretical; on the other hand, writers like Julia Kristeva (who has herself drawn on Marxist-feminist-psychoanalytic concepts) have praised the inherent subversive capacity of the avant-garde as an essential component of "revolutionary" art.[6] (This dialogue is itself an echo of the Brecht-Lukacs debate about the revolutionary function of the avant-garde, discussed at some length in Eagleton's book on Benjamin.) Like other writers of Eastern European origin (Kundera and Milosz are two examples), Kristeva argues for the simultaneously subversive and liberating qualities of the ("dialogic" or "polyphonic") literary act: social transformation will be forecast and facilitated by the poet, who possesses a special kind of radical voice, or social memory.[7] (This confidence in the poet is reflected, for instance, in the following lines by Milosz: "You have wronged a simple man. . . . Do not feel safe, the poet remembers/you can slay one, but another is born/The words are written down, the deed, the date" ["You Who Wronged"]).

Thus, the current debate over the nature and responsibility of the aesthetic act (and about the alleged estrangement of the aesthetic from "serious needs") restages a familiar controversy about writers and writing: is the poet a Priest or an Everyman; the leader of an inspired rite performed for an elite few (in the tradition of Mallarmé, who believed that art compensates us for the poverty of lived experience, and that poetry is full or "remunerated" language), or the voice of a collective appeal, the scribe of history, whose work is a response to real societal needs (in the tradition of writers like Aragon or Milosz)? Both of these views, oddly enough, are recognizable heirs of the Romantic tradition that fostered two counterposed views of the poetic tradition (poet as vessel of inspired truth and poet as legislator of humankind); both views were reflected in the surrealist debate over the autonomy of art, its exemption from dogma or party line. It is not surprising, then, that the latest version of the debate should be taking place in Marxist critical circles around the question of the political ramifications of postmodernism.[8]

This debate is of particular interest for our consideration of the comic process, especially since (as I have suggested in chapter 2) the comic mode has long been the focus of a similar discussion in which partisans of the referential theories have argued for the social utility of the comic mode, emphasizing the instrumental nature of the process as a tool of enlightenment or socialization, while partisans of the idea of an absolute, innocent, or disinterested comic mode have insisted on the poetic nature of a process exempt from partisan uses. As I have tried to suggest, such a distinction and the resulting debate is perhaps itself a habit of a certain logocentric bias when it comes to evaluating aesthetic issues. For the distinction between these points of view is a shaky one, since one can argue that even the most disinterested laughter works to consolidate the social norms it pretends to ignore, and conversely, that the most convential referential comic processes may sometimes work to subvert societal norms and conventions when the ridicule is directed against the powers that be.

Indeed, the "posting" of a third perspective on the comic process, as a postmodern allegory of *écriture* (itself already an allegory of human subjectivity), is intended to expose the highly problematic nature of the traditional distinction between comic categories. The postmodern text acts to reveal the assumptions upon which these distinctions are grounded: the bias in favor of binary logic and the tendency to cast human values and experience in the form of binary oppositions (right/wrong; truth/error; inside/outside; male/female; complete/incomplete), and the bias in favor of teleological or goal-oriented thought and action (which emphasizes closure and efficacity). A rethinking of these habits is central to the efforts of both psychoanalytic and poststructuralist literary criticism, which work to erode the very ground upon which questions of logic and teleology are posed. It is even perhaps this erosion of the logocentric bias that is responsible for the emergence of the postmodern comic, a self-deconstructing mode that works thanks to its own contradictions (whereas earlier comic writing, conforming to binary logic, has tended to cover up the internal contradictions of the process, masquerading as *either* a referential/utilitarian process *or* as an absolute/poetic process). Indeed, the aesthetic post-comic is at once a textual phenomenon or characteristic—as manifested in the Beckett texts studied here—and a reinterpretation of the comic process itself as an effect of desire. This reencounter of the comic process, I have argued, necessarily supplants the binary absolute-referential distinction with an understanding of all comic texts as infinite entertainments (and all infinite entertainments as comic texts), whose punch line is always already purloined and passed on by desire.

Service non compris? The "gratuity" of the Beckettian waiter

Perhaps, then, a similar operation needs to be performed on the two apparently counterposed views of literature/criticism outlined above (as, on the one hand, a potentially liberating and socially useful activity, and, on the other hand, a compensatory ritual, not subject to the privations of real life) in order to answer at least some of the charges of solipsism to which an aesthetic reading of the literary process is vulnerable. After the endgame, we need to determine not only how to ground our practice as critics and readers but also how to inform that critical practice with the lessons of the postmodern comic.

The first question—that of grounding critical practice—is already being addressed by contemporary critics of many stripes, and is the subject of lively debate among critics in this country who have been influenced by poststructuralist and psychoanalytic theory. The political aesthetics, for instance, of Barthes, Foucault, and de Man, as well as of some representatives of the "Yale School" of the 1970s, are all problematic for different reasons, and all continue to be cited by opponents of poststructuralism as examples of how deconstruction can go wrong, being appropriated by the Right.[9] But other critics (the likes of Barbara Johnson, Jonathan Arac, Gayatri Spivak, Michael Ryan, Stephen Melville) have made an effort to temper the sometimes idealist bent of poststructuralism with reference to Marxian and Lacanian theories of collectivism, ideology, and subjectivity, and hence to examine the ideological valence of the postmodernist aesthetic. The most successful of the efforts at grounding deconstruction in a political perspective (Jameson, Ryan) make extensive use of psychoanalytic (Jameson), Marxist (Ryan, Althusser), and feminist theory (Spivak, Jardine, Johnson, Felman) to analyze the interaction between writer, reader, and society.[10]

This effort, in my view, must be continued and expanded—particularly as concerns the integration of a feminist perspective with a psychoanalytic or poststructuralist one—in response to the challenge posed by the aesthetic or unworked text. For the superimposition of political and psychological categories causes both bodies of theory to emerge transformed. The politicization of psychoanalytic theory by feminists and others, for example, entails a reevaluation of the notion of the individual subject and the individual unconscious, henceforth considered a social construct (and for the feminists, a construct in which notions of gender play an important role). For these theorists, subjectivity is not just the province of the individual but must also be considered as a collective (hence political) category of agency and an effect not just of the individual's "desire" but also of ideology. This is perhaps the most important ramification of Lacan's doctrine of the decentered subject: if the unconscious is a function of the Other(s), it may be considered a political construct rather than an effect of individual psychology.

This transcoding of Freudian and political concepts could also prove useful in addressing the question of the gratuity of the aesthetic comic and of the postmodern text in general. For instance, the elaboration of the concept of writing as diversion/perversion—seeking a substitutive satisfaction of desire in a displaced object—might focus on the fetishistic nature of the text, as an art object upon which both reader and writer cathect. This focus could in turn permit the analysis of the ideological valence of that cathexis, determining where the individual's investment—as desire or wish—intersects with real conditions, becoming a vested interest in the exercise of power.

Or the study of text as symptom or as gratification of desire, in the Freudian tradition, could be brought to bear on specific tropes like metaphor and metonymy, by making use of Freud's contrast between *perversion* and *neurosis* (in the *Three Essays on Sexuality*, 1905) to elucidate the aesthetic nature of the "perverse" literary act and to make clear just how the textwork differs from neurotic symptom. This difference is an important one when it comes to evaluating the efficacity or political potential of the gratuitous text, for the distinction between perversion and neurosis hinges on the question of the gratification of desire. (Freud claims, in *Three Essays* [31], that perversions gratify libidinal drives while neuroses repress them.) Recast in political terms, this distinction could be useful for considering the social ramifications of the postmodern text. The Kantian elitist tradition of art, which holds that art is pure, separate from real concerns, could be considered a "neurotic" response that tries merely to substitute aesthetic activity for real action, which it scorns; the "perverse" poststructuralist aesthetic, on the other hand, would tend to see art as a long-circuit in the face of an obstacle, capable of deriving an altered gratification. (One view sees the text as an evasion of reality, a simple symptom, while the other sees the text as an altered, deflected, or creative response to reality, a response to real conditions.) At any rate, Freud's own theory on perversion, when applied to the artistic process, tends to undercut the notion of the aesthetic as the province of genius or poetic privilege since the upshot of Freud's comic theory (of perversion as long-circuit) is that all human activity is to some degree perverse and aesthetic,[11] a displacement of desire. Freud's treatment of the passing of the Oedipus complex, which suggests that every finding of a love-object is a refinding of the original maternal object, may be read as a comic solution of a fundamentally tragic situation (the original object may be a model for the present one, but the first object itself is lost; in fact, it is the essential nature of sexual desire to be displaced onto substitute objects that double for the always already lost original). This kind of emphasis on the primal divorce or doubling is even more pronounced in Lacanian theory, which emphasizes the notion of splitting [*Spaltung*] as the origin of the divided ego. Reflected in the mirror (of the *stade du miroir*), the original lost object is in some sense the alienated ego itself, which as Imaginary construct, has by definition never been whole or identical to itself.[12]

This tragic psychoanalytic vision of irremediable original scission, however, has a comic aftermath: the excess quotient of desire may become the motor for action and for creative social solutions. Excess aesthetic desire, in other words, is that which defines our human being and motivates the "excessive" social urge to reach out and to create for others (this is what Marx calls "species being,"[13] and what existentialism sees as the transcendence of the *pour soi* resulting in social obligation or *engagement*). A certain postmodern writing reflects this good news: the "anti-aesthetic" impulse of postmodernism (to cite the title of Hal Foster's collection of essays on postmodernism)[14] is actually only a resistance against a certain elitist, imploded aesthetic. A rereading of the term *aesthetic* through Freud's theory may permit us to see the aesthetic side of human endeavor as a social construct, and even perhaps encourage us to reconsider the boundaries between art and work, in order to avoid using the aesthetic as a justification for noninvolvement. In other words, Freud's aesthetic may help us to deconstruct the boundaries between literary activity and real life: writing is work, hence, part of life, and life is a social web (as Derrida is suggesting when he claims that "there is nothing outside the text"). This is at least one of the punch lines that a postmodernism of resistance, rather than reaction, may want to purloin from Freud's comic theory.

Future moves: the "ends" of the game

An examination of the perverse nature of textuality as social diversion is only one of many possible ways in which a psychoanalytic/poststructuralist theory of writing might help to unwork (or "deconstruct") ideological assumptions about aesthetic activities. There is no reason that a mingling of Freudian and materialist theory should not yield a continued emphasis on art as, on the one hand, a symptom of real social conditions (such as patriarchy), and on the other hand, as a kind of blueprint for derepressive and liberating human activity (as suggested in the best of Marcuse's insights, his concept of libidinized work in *Eros and Civilization* [1955]). Of course, such an aesthetic of work is possible only in a postscarcity society that has presumably succeeded in surmounting "vital needs," such as need for food and shelter. But the idea is already present in Freud's utopic account of human activity and progress (in the final passage of *Beyond the Pleasure Principle*) as a kind of creative and productive response to desire (as the death-drive). Freud's analysis already seems to deconstruct a too-strict binary opposition between the pleasures of play and work. (On the other hand, this kind of strict distinction clearly underlies the elitist aesthetics of high modernism, touting the purity of a hermetic art accessible only to the initiated.) As in Marcuse's eroticized view of work, however, Freud's account of human societal creation presupposes the satisfaction of vital needs—the task of politics and social organization—so that the untrammeled aesthetic processes to which he refers in *Jokes* and elsewhere may ensue. In a sense, political solutions precede aesthetic ones in Freud's view (indeed, this is the gist of his impassioned humanist argument in his late essay "Why War?" [1933]). And postmodern strategies of reading may help us to follow Freud's lead, deconstructing the ideological assumptions that blur even our most aesthetic vision so that the unworked text may be called into social play.

Thus, one "conclusion" to be drawn from this reading of the unworked postmodern text as a comic phenomenon—the conclusion that the comic is somehow poetic—might also serve as an indication of the derepressive potential of the comic mode. Comic texts will doubtless continue to do what they have been doing for centuries (through satire, parody, and related techniques): that is, they will continue to question social convention by criticizing existing institutions and to expose repressive or automatic habits of thought. But the "post"-comic mode may do more than just criticize the status quo; it may actually help deconstruct the assumptions that ground repressive ideologies such as patriarchy or ethnocentrism, unworking their intellectual authority. Through its alliance with poetic modes of expression, the post-comic may actually provide a transformed vision of reality, activating a profoundly poetic memory of the past and a profoundly poetic vision of the future (as in the magical realism of Latin American writers such as Luisa Valenzuela, Isabel Allende, Gabriel García Márquez; or the profoundly comic and poetic vision of Milan Kundera; or the most lyric moments in Ionesco's work). As Kundera reminds us in the opening lines of *The Book of Laughter and Forgetting,* the struggle of human beings against repression may be metaphorized as "the struggle of memory against forgetting," the struggle to retain the lessons of history. In the case of a single individual, of course, the derepressive function of psychoanalysis may be considered an analogous struggle to retrieve the experience and lessons of the past. The derepressive work of the poetic figure may aid in this "comic" process of "rediscovery of something familiar" (one of Freud's jokework techniques) by making ordinary discourse permeable to the intrusion of censored or "forgotten" material of all kinds. Of course, the comic mode has always done exactly that, granting a license to express what is forbidden. But unlike traditional comic forms like satire, the postmodern comic not only unworks external authority but also renounces its own pretension to authority, inviting a self-questioning, owning up to the inevitability of its own implication in what is being criticized. The postmodern comic, to put it in psychoanalytic terms, is an aesthetic acknowledgment of the lessons of the countertransference.

The postmodern text does what Freud was unable to do (with Dora and others): it concedes that there is no value that is not influenced by one's position and stakes in the game. But this is not equivalent to saying that values should not be held or do not have real effects in real life. On the contrary, the postmodern text encourages the kind of critical spirit that enables social criticism and permits human beings to make judgments and take action, even while acknowledging the potential for error that haunts the most scrupulous actions and judgments, the blindness to our own interest that may shadow the most "self-evident" (perhaps a little *too* evident?) insights.

These, then, are some possible "conclusions" to be drawn from the assertion that the comic is poetic. The corollary conclusion, that the poetic or literary is comic (that there is something comic about the structure and function of the text), might serve as a kind of injunction to humility when it comes to evaluating the vocation and function of literature. For the comic structure of the textual transaction is a structure in which, by definition, the power of one participant acts to limit the power of the others, and thus may serve to undercut the notion of the poet as Priest, or the notion of the literary text as a sacred rite affording a sanctuary or escape from real life.

Both "conclusions" are potentially liberating, insofar as they suggest an antidote to the illusion of absolute power, gratification, efficacity (or a monopoly on Truth). All of these illusions may be fostered by a certain conception of literature as pure aesthetic vision, "innocent" of real concerns. The postmodern vision is double vision (or triple, or quadruple), which entails a blurring of the distinction between play (the aesthetic or disinterested) and work (the necessary and interested). Interestingly, this lesson, already implicit in Freud's own comic theory of sublimation and deferral—that our love may coincide with our work—is not unlike Marx's concept of species being: both posit human being as a function of excessive desire, a surplus that obliges us to create and construct for other social beings, in excess of the requirements of need. For if the comic endgame sometimes seems to border on an exercise in self-absorbed contemplation, it also always poses a kind of challenge, implicating the reader in its game (*"à toi de jouer"*). Among the many punch lines that we may purloin from Freud (lines that he purloined from the poets, with whom he credits the discovery of the unconscious) is the one-liner that intellectual work, however aesthetic, is life, not just a reflection or representation of it.

It may finally be up to us as readers to determine whether

the unworked text is to remain out of work—a pretext for idle reflection having little bearing on our social practice—or whether we will take a "tip" from Beckett's "waiters," and adopt a comic position that allows us to scrutinize our own reading and writing and to see that even the most aesthetic of plays is endlessly performed with and for the Other.

NOTES

Preface

Unless otherwise indicated, all translations throughout this study are my own.

1. There are, of course, other important postmodern and poststructuralist theorists—such as de Man, Barthes, Foucault, Kristeva—who are not treated in detail here, in part because of considerations of length; but also because some of the concepts of these writers in particular, it seems to me, are open to appropriation by the kind of solipsistic postmodernism against which I argue here. (In the case of Barthes, this is true only for the late works, which seem to represent a turning from the activist or political engagement of his earlier work.) Moreover, the work of the figures I focus on—Bataille, Lacan, Lyotard, Derrida, and Blanchot—is somewhat more exemplary of the kind of "ludic" or comic tonality I want to associate with a progressive "postmodernism of resistance."

2. On this question, see the collection edited by Hal Foster, *The Anti-Aesthetic: Essays on Postmodern Culture* (Port Townsend, Wash.: Bay Press, 1983).

Opening lines

Maurice Blanchot, *L'entretien infini* (Paris: Editions Gallimard, 1969) 233.

Jacques Derrida, *L'écriture et la différence* (Paris: Editions du Seuil, 1967) 370.

Jacques Lacan, "Fonction et champ de la parole et du langage en psychanalyse," *Ecrits* I (Paris: Editions du Seuil, 1966) 148.

Julia Kristeva, *Polylogue* (Paris: Editions du Seuil, 1977) 40.

Terry Eagleton, *Walter Benjamin or Towards a Revolutionary Criticism* (London: Verso Editions, 1981) 170.

Hélène Cixous, "Le rire de la méduse," translated in *New French Feminisms*, Elaine Marks and Isabelle de Courtivron, eds. (New York: Schocken Books, 1981) 257.

Samuel Beckett, *Fin de partie* (Paris: Editions de Minuit, 1957) 33.

Eugene Ionesco, *Notes et contre-notes* (Paris: *Idées*-Gallimard, 1966) 175.

Stuart Schneiderman, *Jacques Lacan/The Death of an Intellectual Hero* (Cambridge: Harvard UP, 1983) 37.

Lacan, "Une lettre d'amour," *Feminine Sexuality: Jacques Lacan and the école freudienne,* ed. Juliet Mitchell and Jacqueline Rose (New York: W. W. Norton, 1982) 157.

1. Introduction: A Comic Contagion

1. See, for instance, Shirley Nelson Garner, Claire Kahane, and Madelon Sprengnether, eds., *The (M)Other Tongue* (Ithaca: Cornell UP, 1985); and Alice Jardine, *Gynesis* (Ithaca: Cornell UP, 1985).

2. Geoffrey Hartman, *Criticism in the Wilderness: The Study of Literature Today* (New Haven: Yale UP, 1980) 9.

3. Michel Foucault, *The History of Sexuality,* trans. Robert Hurley (New York: Vintage Books, 1980). Originally published as *La volonté de savoir* (Paris: Gallimard, 1976).

4. The notion of "transcoding" is borrowed from Fredric Jameson's work, especially *The Political Unconscious: Narrative as Socially Symbolic Act* (Ithaca: Cornell UP, 1981).

5. Paul de Man, "The Rhetoric of Temporality," *Blindness and Insight* (Minneapolis: U of Minnesota P, 1983) 187–228. Originally published by Oxford UP, 1971.

6. Frank Lentricchia, *After the New Criticism* (Chicago: U of Chicago P, 1980).

7. See, for instance, Annie LeClerc's *Parole de femme* (Paris: Grasset, 1974).

2. Posting the Modern (Casing the Comic)

1. In *The Anti-Aesthetic: Essays on Postmodern Culture,* ed. Hal Foster (Port Townsend, Wash.: Bay Press, 1983) 130.

2. "Le facteur de la vérité," in *Ecrits* I (1966), translated as "The Purveyor of Truth," in *Yale French Studies* 48 (1973), *French Freud,* ed. Jeffrey Mehlman.

3. In *Blindness and Insight* (Minneapolis: U of Minnesota P, 1983) 142–65.

4. Berman has since published an explicit and mordant attack on postmodernism, titled "Why Modernism Still Matters," *Tikkun* 4.1 (January/February 1989) 11–14 and 81–86.

5. Owens's citation is quoted from Gregory Ulmer's article, "The Object of Post-Criticism," in Foster, The Anti-Aesthetic, 95.

6. A shorter version of this article first appeared in *Structuralist Review* 1.3 (Summer 1979).

7. Practically every major thinker since Aristotle has contributed to the debate over the sources and the uses of the comic mode; thus I have not undertaken a complete review of the theories consulted here. But for a partial listing of the works consulted in the process, see the bibliography at the end of the text, "A Selected List of Theoretical Works on the Comic."

8. For my own reading of the "modern" and "postmodern" elements of Baudelaire's comic theory, which I see as an anticipation of Freud's theory, see my "Baudelaire and Freud: The Poet as Joker," in *Literature and Psychoanalysis*, ed. Maurice Charney (Rutherford, N.J.: Fairleigh Dickenson UP, 1987).

9. See Frank Lentricchia's study of de Man in *After the New Criticism* (Chicago: U of Chicago P, 1980).

3. Freud's Bottom Line: Jokes and Their Relation to the Aesthetic

1. The activities of dreaming and writing are discussed, respectively, in *The Interpretation of Dreams* (1900), *Standard Edition* 4–5, and in "Creative Writers and Daydreaming" (1908), *Standard Edition* 9.

2. Samuel Weber, *The Legend of Freud* (Minneapolis: U of Minnesota P, 1982).

3. Lacan deals with this relation in "La direction de la cure et les principes de son pouvoir," *La Psychanalyse* 6 (1961): 149–206.

4. Freud writes: "In one group of these jokes the technique consisted in focusing our psychical attitude upon the sound of the word instead of upon its meaning. . . . It may be suspected that in doing so we are bringing about great relief in psychical work and that when we make serious use of words we are obliged to hold ourselves back with a certain effort from this comfortable procedure" (119).

5. Freud insists on the scheming nature of the jokework, which disguises forbidden thought to outwit censorship: "Here the jokes are once again expressing their original nature by setting themselves up against an inhibiting and restricting power, which is now the critical judgment" (133).

6. *Three Essays on the Theory of Sexuality*, trans. James Strachey (New York: Basic Books) 16.

7. See Laplanche and Leclaire's *La vie et la mort en psychanalyse* (Paris: Editions du Seuil, 1976).

8. Indeed, it is this voluntary aspect which is the constituent element of humor, that subspecies of the joke in which we rise above a threaten-

ing situation by making light of it or by making fun of ourselves.

9. Jeffrey Mehlman, "How to Read Freud on Jokes: The Critic as *Schadchen*," *New Literary History* 6.2 (Winter 1975): 439–61.

4. Lacan's Purloined Punch line: Joke as Textual Paradigm

A shorter version of this chapter first appeared in *Modern Language Notes* 98.5 (December 1983) and was reprinted in *Lacan and Narration*, ed. Robert Con Davis (Baltimore: Johns Hopkins UP, 1984 and 1986), and in *Contemporary Literary Criticism: Modernism Through Post-Structuralism*, ed. Robert Con Davis (New York: Longman, 1986).

1. Gregory Ulmer, "The Object of Post-Criticism," in *The Anti-Aesthetic: Essays on Postmodern Culture*, ed. Hal Foster (Port Townsend, Wash.: Bay Press, 1983) 83–110.

2. Jacques Derrida, *La carte postale* (Paris: Flammarion, 1980) 317.

3. *Ecrits* I (Paris: Editions du Seuil, 1966), translated in *Yale French Studies* 48 (1976): 39–72. All page numbers refer to this translation.

Epigraph: Translated in *Feminine Sexuality*, eds. Juliet Mitchell and Jacqueline Rose (New York: W. W. Norton, 1982) 137–61.

4. Freud, "The Dissolution of the Oedipus Complex" (1924), *Standard Edition* 19: 173.

5. See Section V of the *Interpretation of Dreams* for Freud's discussion of the dramatic technique of *Oedipus Rex*.

6. *Beyond the Pleasure Principle* appears in volume 18 of the *Standard Edition*. However, I prefer John Rickman's translation (*A General Selection from the Works of Sigmund Freud* [New York: Doubleday-Anchor, 1957] 141–68), and page numbers refer to that edition.

7. Anthony Wilden, *The Language of the Self* (New York: Dell Publishing Co., 1975).

8. For a discussion of Lacan's Symbolic register, see Wilden 249–70.

9. Freud, "Two Principles of Mental Functioning," *SE* 12: 215.

10. "The Floating Signifier: From Lévi-Strauss to Lacan," *Yale French Studies* 48 (1972): 17.

11. Roman Jakobson, "Two Aspects of Language and Two Types of Aphasic Disturbances," *Fundamentals of Language* (The Hague: Mouton, 1956) 55–56.

12. In "L'Instance de la lettre dans l'inconscient," *Ecrits* I, Lacan elaborates on Saussure's linguistic theory, recasting the relation of signifier and and signified (S/s) as formulae representing the processes of metaphor and metonymy.

13. *Yale French Studies* 55/56 (1977), reprinted as *Literature and Psychoanalysis: The Question of Reading: Otherwise*, ed. Shoshana Felman (Baltimore: Johns Hopkins UP, 1982) 280–300.

14. In Felman (note 13) 11–52.

15. Lacan on *Hamlet,* Felman 17.

16. See, for instance, Fredric Jameson's "Imaginary and Symbolic in Lacan: Marxism, Psychoanalysis, and the Problem of the Subject," Felman 338–95; and Leo Bersani's *The Freudian Body: Psychoanalysis and Art* (New York: Columbia UP, 1986).

17. See Barbara Johnson's "The Frame of Reference: Poe, Lacan, Derrida," in *Yale French Studies* 55/56 (1977): 243.

18. See Freud's "Fetishism" (1927), SE 21: 149.

19. For a series of "postmodern" readings of Freud's "Fragment of an Analysis of a Case of Hysteria" (1905), see *Diacritics* 13.1 (Spring 1983), *A Fine Romance: Freud and Dora.*

Epigraph: Feminine Sexuality: Jacques Lacan and the école freudienne, eds. Juliet Mitchell and Jacqueline Rose (New York: W. W. Norton, 1982) 134.

20. For a discussion of pronouns as "shifters," see Wilden 179–85.

21. Cited from Sharon Willis, "A Symptomatic Narrative," *Diacritics* 13.1 (Spring 1983): 48.

22. "French Feminism in an International Frame," *Yale French Studies* 62 (1981): 154–84.

23. "Female Paranoia: The Case for Psychoanalytic Feminist Criticism," *Yale French Studies* 62 (1981): 204–19.

24. See Julia Kristeva, *Desire in Language,* ed. Leon S. Roudiez (New York: Columbia UP, 1980).

5. Outwitting the Dialectic: Comic Negativity

1. In addition to the works already cited, see Jean-François Lyotard and Jean-Loup Thébaud, *Just Gaming* (Minneapolis: U of Minnesota P, 1985); first published in French as *Au juste* (Paris: Christian Bourgois, 1979).

2. See Julia Kristeva, *Desire in Language: A Semiotic Approach to Literature and Art,* trans. Thomas Gora, Alice Jardine, and Leon Roudiez (New York: Columbia UP, 1980).

3. Paul de Man, *Blindness and Insight* (New York: Oxford UP, 1971).

4. See, for instance, the collection edited by Jonathan Arac, *Postmodernism and Politics* (Minneapolis: U of Minnesota P, 1986).

Epigraph: Cited in Stephen Melville's *Philosophy Beside Itself* (Minneapolis: U of Minnesota P, 1986) 34.

5. Although in the article that Melville cites, Derrida is discussing the philosophical rather than the political ramifications of deconstruction, his recent explicit anti-apartheid activism has had to confront this issue as it pertains to political "positions" (the subject of his *Positions* [Paris: Edi-

tions du seuil, 1972]). And of course the recent revelations concerning de Man's writings for a collaborationist publication have been the occasion for some rather painful soul-searching as well. See Derrida's "Like the Sound of the Sea Deep within a Shell: Paul de Man's War," *Critical Inquiry* 14.3 (Spring 1988).

6. Melville is citing here from a published interview with Derrida: "Entre crochets," *Digraphe* 8 (April 1976): 97–114.

7. In *L'écriture et la différence* (Paris: Editions du Seuil, 1967) 369–407. Hereafter *EG.*

8. "La double séance" appears in *La dissémination* (Paris: Editions du Seuil, 1972) 201–317. Hereafter *DS.*

9. Derrida, for example, characterizes Foucault's work on madness as Hegelian, in spite of its "revolutionary" perspective on reason ("Cogito et historie de la folie," *EG,* 51–97).

10. See Rainer Nägele, "The Scene of the Other: Theodor W. Adorno's Negative Dialectic in the Context of Poststructuralism," *Postmodernism and Politics,*, ed. Jonathan Arac (Minneapolis: U of Minnesota P, 1986) 91–111.

11. Kristeva discusses the term in "Bataille, l'expérience et la pratique," in *Bataille,* ed. Barthes et al. (Paris: UGE-10/18, 1973) 267–301.

12. Bataille, quoted from *October* 36 (*Georges Bataille*) (Spring 1986): 61.

13. Bataille, *October* 36: 53, 73.

14. Page numbers refer to the Gallimard edition, 1957.

15. Bataille, *L'expérience intérieure* (Paris: Gallimard, 1943).

16. Derrida, *EG* 372.

17. "Hegel, la mort, et le sacrifice," *Decaulion* 5, cited by Derrida, *EG* 378.

18. *October* 36: 51.

19. *La dissémination,* 201–317.

20. Lacan discusses Frege's concept of integers in the writings of 1966, and in the papers published as *Cahiers pour l'analyse* (May 1966).

21. In the *Three Essays on Sexuality* (1905), and the essay "Fetishism" (1927).

22. Lacan discusses metaphor and metonymy, and their relation to repression and *désir,* in "L'instance de la lettre dans l'inconscient," *Ecrits* I (Paris: Editions du Seuil-Points, 1966) 249–89.

23. Barthes, "Les sorties du texte," *Bataille* (Paris: UGE-10/18, 1973) 62.

24. Cited by Derrida, *EG* 386.

25. Sollers, in *Bataille* 36 n24.

6. The Infinite Entertainment: Blanchot's "Unworked" Text

1. It is interesting that Blanchot's use of the term *continuity* is diametrically opposed to Bataille's use of the same term. For Blanchot, continuity is associated with the rationality of the Logos; for Bataille, continuity implies the loss of any such rationality, in the erotic act.

2. See, for instance, Le Clerc's *Parole de femme* (Paris: Grasset, 1974) and Irigaray's *Speculum de l'autre femme* (Paris: Editions de Minuit, 1974).

3. This recalls Derrida's writing on the "ne-utrality" of a "negativity" which refuses to cooperate with the dialectic (EG 402).

4. Freud underlines the aggressive component of identification in *Totem and Taboo* (1912), in which he speaks of the "introjection" of the other in an act of cannibalism; and in "Mourning and Melancholia" (1917), in which he speaks of depression as a raging against the introjected image of the Other.

5. In his 1912 essay "The Dynamics of Transference," Freud states that at least four persons are involved in every analytic session—since the patient's parents are also present in an emotional sense.

6. This is the *Anlehnung* [laying on] discussed in the *Three Essays on the Theory of Sexuality* (1905).

7. In commenting on the urge to excess, Blanchot asks: "Now is it not the case that nothing, in this sameness, comes down to the same [*ne revient au même*], except the return itself; and that the affirmation of the return leads one to affirm at once both difference and repetition, hence the non-identity of the same?" (*EI* 411).

8. Freud's comic technique of "condensation with modification" might also be considered an example of "repetition with difference."

9. "The Unconscious," *Yale French Studies* 48 (1972): 151–68.

7. Beckett's Aesthetic Play: The Comic Text *En Souffrance*

1. Freud's view of literature as substitutive deflection of the writer's desire is set out in "Creative Writers and Daydreaming" (1908). Cast in rhetorical terms, this same circuitous movement is the focus of Peter Brooks's classic essay on metonymy as the motor of plot, and of Lacan's study of Hamlet as comic figure who is never where he is supposed to be at the right time. Both essays appear in *Literature and Psychoanalysis: The Question of Reading: Otherwise,* ed. Shoshana Felman (Baltimore: Johns Hopkins UP, 1977, 1980).

2. From Samuel Beckett and Georges Duthuit, "Three Dialogues" (hereafter *TD*), *Samuel Beckett: A Collection of Critical Essays,* ed. Martin Esslin (Englewood Cliffs, N.J.: Prentice-Hall, 1965) 16–22.

3. Interestingly, Frank Lentricchia writes of de Man's aesthetic project

in similar terms (*After the New Criticism* [U of Chicago P, 1980] 41): "Literature earns its value by imaging forth the negative truth of human failure; human being as failing."

4. See Lyotard's *Discours, figure* (355–56) for a discussion of literary forms as obstruction to credence in the literary event. Stephen Melville also treats the question of literary "absorption," in *Philosophy Beside Itself: On Deconstruction and Modernism* (Minneapolis: U of Minnesota P, 1986) 10–13.

5. This portion of the essay first appeared in *Structuralist Review* 1.3 (Summer 1979).

6. For a more detailed treatment of the Schema L and its avatars, see Anthony Wilden's *Speech and Language in Psychoanalysis* (Baltimore: Johns Hopkins UP, 1981) 160–62.

7. All page references, unless otherwise noted, are to the French version of *En attendant Godot* (Paris: Editions de Minuit, 1952); the translations are my own.

8. In French, the construction "*en*" + present participle has two meanings: the first is "while" (as in the popular sense of "*en attendant*": in the meantime, while waiting); the second is "by" (as in the proverb "*On devient forgeron en forgeant*": one becomes a smith by practicing the trade).

9. Lyotard and others have associated Kant's notion of the sublime with the aesthetics of the modern and the postmodern (see Lyotard's *The Postmodern Condition* 77–81). Lyotard considers modern and postmodern aesthetics to be derived from the "sublime" intuition of something that is beyond the limits of expression.

10. For a psychoanalytic treatment of the "sublime" as proliferation, and of the role of the oedipal Father in limiting the sublime, see Neil Hertz's "The Notion of Blockage in the Literature of the Sublime," *Psychoanalysis and the Question of the Text,* ed. Geoffrey Hartman (Baltimore: Johns Hopkins UP, 1978).

11. In *Murphy* (1938), the character is actually straitjacketed, and refers to his padded cell as "the little world" [*le petit monde*].

12. All references, unless otherwise noted, are to the French version of *Fin de partie* (Paris: Editions de Minuit, 1957); all translations are my own.

13. Published in English as "My Chances/*Mes Chances:* A Rendezvous with Some Epicurean Stereophonies," *Taking Chances: Derrida, Psychoanalysis, and Literature,* ed. Joseph Smith and William Kerrigan (Baltimore: Johns Hopkins UP, 1984) 1–32. In this essay, Derrida deconstructs the dichotomy between chance and determinism in Freud.

14. And of course, Freud's joke is a chance encounter of sorts, a confrontation with unconscious desire, which emerges spontaneously as a reaction to an exterior situation. In fact, Freud argues that all humor

relies on chance connections and contrasts with unconscious material. It is perhaps this connection with unconscious chance that made the subject of humor so fascinating to the surrealists.

8. Postaesthetics: After the Endgame

1. The concept of "steady work" as lifelong commitment to progressive activism is the subject, for instance, of Irving Howe's *Steady Work: Essays in the Politics of Democratic Radicalism* (New York: Harcourt, 1963).

2. Neil Hertz, "The Notion of Blockage in the Literature of the Sublime," Hartman 62–85.

3. For two treatments of the debate on the political valence of "postmodernism" and "deconstruction," see Frank Lentricchia's *Criticism and Social Change* (Chicago: U of Chicago P, 1983), and the collection of essays titled *Postmodernism and Politics,* ed. Jonathan Arac (Minneapolis: U of Minnesota P, 1986).

4. See Lentricchia, *After the New Criticism* (Chicago: U of Chicago P, 1983) for the debate on "aesthetic criticism."

5. The politics of Barthes's work are problematic. Whereas his early work is politically aware, even "Marxist" in approach, the highly subjective and lyric work of his last years has a troubling tone. (I am thinking of his advocacy of a certain "bliss of the averted gaze" in *The Pleasure of the Text* (1975); it is this emphasis that leaves Barthes open to the kind of reading that Cook and Kroker give him in *The Postmodern Scene,* as one of the representatives of "the death of the social" discussed in the opening chapter of this book. So even though much of Barthes's work seems profoundly comic, in the sense that I use the term—dealing with the notions of disguise and the erotic nature of the text—I have chosen not to focus on his work as an example of a progressive "postmodernism of resistance." Still, for a reading of Barthes's "humor" that does not cast his work in an anti-social light, see Candace D. Lang's *Irony/Humor* (Baltimore: Johns Hopkins UP, 1988), Chapter 6 ("Barthes: *Ecrire le Corps*").

6. Julia Kristeva, *Desire in Language: A Semiotic Approach to Literature and Art,* ed. Leon S. Roudiez (New York: Columbia UP, 1980).

7. Kristeva, *Polylogue* (Paris: Editions du Seuil, 1977).

8. See, for instance, Michael Ryan's *Marxism and Deconstruction: A Critical Articulation* (Baltimore: Johns Hopkins UP, 1983); Frank Lentricchia's *Criticism and Social Change* (note 3); Jonathan Arac's collection Postmodernism and Politics (note 3); Terry Eagleton's *Criticism and Ideology* (London: New Left Books, 1976); Edward Said's *The World, the Text, and the Critic* (Cambridge, Mass.: Harvard UP, 1983); and the Spring 1982 issue of *Diacritics* (for articles on Althusser, Macherey, and others).

9. For my own reservations about Barthes, see note 5 above. My objections to the "aesthetic" politics of Hartman and the Yale School are

expressed in my article with Alexander Argyros, "Aesthetic Criticism Reassessed: Hartman's Contagious Orbit" *Diacritics* 16.1 (Spring 1987). And on de Man, see the heated discussion in *Critical Inquiry* 15.4 (Summer 1989), an issue devoted to the question of whether de Man's "deconstructionist" theory is necessarily of a piece with his anti-Semitic wartime journalism. In any case, I want to argue here that even if postmodernism/poststructuralism may be open to appropriation by reactionary or quietist ideology, or even if individual "poststructuralists" may have engaged in reprehensible activities, poststructuralism may *also,* or alternately, be read as a profoundly social and progressive "text"; not only is poststructuralism not inherently reactionary, as some contend, but it is potentially progressive and engaging.

10. In addition to the works mentioned in note 5 above, see Fredric Jameson's *The Political Unconscious: Narrative as Socially Symbolic Act* (Ithaca: Cornell UP, 1981); Louis Althusser's *Lenin and Philosophy,* especially the essay on "Freud and Lacan" (London: New Left Books, 1971); and the essays in *Yale French Studies* 62 (1981), *Feminist Readings: French Texts/American Contexts.*

11. Indeed, one could argue that according to Freud's own terms, human sexuality itself is always in a sense perverse or aesthetic, since it is always distinct from, and in excess of, biological need. Freud maintains in the *Three Essays* that even in its first manifestations (whereby the infant desires the mother quite separately from the desire for food), sexuality is always already a kind of supplement, a "laying on" [*Anlehnung*] to the biological process of the satiation of hunger.

12. On "splitting" and the "narcissistic constitution of the ego" in Lacanian theory, see Anthony Wilden's *The Language of the Self* (Baltimore: Johns Hopkins UP, 1984) 168–72, 190–91.

13. "Species being" is discussed in the *Economic and Philosophical Manuscripts* (1844).

14. Foster, *The Anti-Aesthetic.*

SELECT BIBLIOGRAPHY

The following list contains works cited or referred to in the text as well as works of immediate relevance to the topic. Most of the cited references are widely available versions in the original language (with the exception of the texts by Freud, where the reference is to the Strachey translation in the *Standard Edition*). Whenever possible, information about available translations is given also. Works dealing primarily or specifically with comic theory—including most of those referred to in chapter 2—are in the separate bibliography which follows.

Abraham, Nicolas, and Maria Torok. *L'écorce et le noyau.* Paris: Flammarion, 1978.

Althusser, Louis. *Lénine et la philosophie.* Paris: Maspero, 1969. *Lenin and Philosophy and Other Essays.* Trans. Ben Brewster. London: New Left Books, 1971.

Arac, Jonathan. *Postmodernism and Politics.* Theory and History of Literature 28. Minneapolis: U of Minnesota P, 1986.

Arrabal, Fernando. *Fando et Lis. Théâtre I.* Paris: Christian Bourgois, 1968.

Barthes, Roland. *Essais critiques.* Paris: Editions du Seuil, 1964.

———. *Le plaisir du texte.* Paris: Editions du Seuil, 1974. *The Pleasure of the Text.* Trans. Richard Miller. New York: Hill and Wang, 1975.

———. *S/Z.* Paris: Editions du Seuil, 1974. *S/Z.* Trans. Richard Miller. New York: Hill and Wang, 1974.

Barthes, Roland, et al. *Bataille.* Paris: Union Générale d'Editions-10/18, 1973.

Bataille, Georges. *L'érotisme.* 1957. Paris: Union Générale d'Editions-10/18, 1974.

———. *L'expérience intérieure.* Paris: Gallimard, 1943.

———. "Hegel, la mort, et le sacrifice." *Decaulion* 5 (1955): 21–43.

———. *La littérature et le mal.* Paris: Gallimard, 1957.

———. *Madame Edwarda.* Paris: Pauvert, 1966.

———. *Oeuvres complètes.* Paris: Gallimard, 1970. 10 vols.

———. *La part maudite.* Paris: Editions de Minuit, 1967.

———. *Writings on Laughter, Sacrifice, Nietzsche, Un-Knowing.* Special issue *October* 36. Trans. Annette Michelson, with essays by Rosalind Krauss, Annette Michelson, and Allen S. Weiss. (Spring 1986): 3–154. Cambridge, Mass.: MIT P, 1986.

Baudrillard, Jean. "The Ecstasy of Communication," Trans. John Johnston. In Foster 126–34.

———. *Oublier Foucault.* Paris: Editions Galilée, 1977. *Forget Foucault.* Trans. Nicole Dufresne. New York: Semiotext(e), 1987.

Beckett, Samuel. *En attendant Godot.* Paris: Editions de Minuit, 1952.

———. *La dernière bande de Krapp.* Paris: Editions de Minuit, 1960.

———. *Fin de partie.* Paris: Editions de Minuit, 1957.

———. *Murphy.* Paris: Editions de Minuit, 1947.

———. *Watt.* 1953. New York: Grove Press, 1959.

Beckett, Samuel, and Georges Duthuit. "Three Dialogues." *Samuel Beckett: A Collection of Essays.* Ed. Martin Esslin. Englewood Cliffs: Prentice-Hall, 1965, 16–22.

Bellemin-Noël, Jean. *Vers l'inconscient du texte.* Paris: Presses Universitaires Françaises, 1979.

Berman, Marshall. *All That Is Solid Melts Into Air.* New York: Simon and Schuster, 1982.

———. "Why Modernism Still Matters." *Tikkun* 4.1 (January/February 1989): 11–15, 81–86.

Bersani, Leo. *The Freudian Body: Psychoanalysis and Art.* New York: Columbia UP, 1986.

Blanchot, Maurice. *L'entretien infini.* Paris: Gallimard, 1969.

———. *L'espace littéraire.* Paris: Gallimards-Idées, 1955.

———. *The Gaze of Orpheus and Other Essays.* Trans. Lydia Davis. Barrytown, N.Y.: Station Hill Press, 1981.

———. *La part du feu.* Paris: Gallimard-NRF 1949.

Booth, Wayne C. *A Rhetoric of Irony.* Chicago: U of Chicago P, 1974.

Breton, André. *Position politique du surréalisme.* Paris: Editions du Sagittaire, 1935. J. J. Pauvert, 1962 and 1971.

Brooks, Peter. "Freud's Masterplot: Questions of Narrative." In Felman 280–300.

Charney, Maurice. *Literature and Psychoanalysis.* Rutherford, N.J.: Fairleigh Dickenson UP, 1986.

Chasseguet-Smirgel, Janine. *La sexualité féminine.* Paris: Payot, 1964.

Cixous, Hélène. "Le rire de la méduse." *L'arc* (1974): 39–54. "The Laugh of the Medusa." Trans. Keith Cohen and Paula Cohen. In Marks and de Courtivron 245–64.

Culler, Jonathan. *On Deconstruction: Theory and Criticism after Structuralism*. Ithaca: Cornell UP, 1982.

Davis, Robert C., ed. *Contemporary Literary Criticism: Modernism Through Post-Structuralism*. New York: Longman, 1986.

———, ed. *Lacan and Narration*. Baltimore: Johns Hopkins UP, 1984, 1986.

Deleuze, Gilles. *Différence et répétition*. Paris: PUF, 1969.

Deleuze, Gilles, and Félix Guattari. *L'anti-Oedipe*. Paris: Editions de Minuit, 1972. *Anti-Oedipus: Capitalism and Schizophrenia*. Trans. Robert Hurley, Mark Seem, and Helen R. Lane. New York: Viking, 1977.

de Man, Paul. *Allegories of Reading: Figural Language in Rousseau, Nietzsche, Rilke, and Proust*. New Haven: Yale UP, 1979.

———. *Blindness and Insight: Essays in the Rhetoric of Contemporary Criticism*. 1971, 1983. New York: Oxford UP, 1971. Theory and History of Literature 7. Minneapolis: U of Minnesota P, 1983.

Derrida, Jacques. *La carte postale: de Socrates à Freud et au-delà*. Paris: Flammarion, 1980.

———. "Coming into One's Own." In Hartman 114–48.

———. *La dissémination*. Paris: Editions du Seuil, 1972, 201–317. *Dissemination*. Trans. Barbara Johnson. Chicago: U of Chicago P, 1981.

———. *L'écriture et la différence*. Paris: Editions du Seuil, 1967. *Writing and Difference*. Trans. Alan Bass. Chicago: U of Chicago P, 1978.

———. "Le facteur de la vérité," *Poétique* 21 (1975). "The Purveyor of Truth," *Yale French Studies* 52 (1975): 31–113.

———. *Glas*. Paris: Galilée, 1974.

———. "Ja, ou le faux bond." *Digraphe* 11 (March 1977): 83–121.

———. "Like the Sound of the Sea Deep within a Shell: Paul de Man's War." *The Sociology of Literature*. Ed. Priscilla Parkhurst Ferguson, Philippe Desan, and Wendy Griswold. Special issue *Critical Inquiry* 14.3 (Spring 1988).

———. "Pas." *Gramma* 3–4 (1976).

———. *Positions*. Paris: Editions de Minuit, 1972. *Positions*. Trans. Alan Bass. Chicago: U of Chicago P, 1981.

Eagleton, Terry. *Criticism and Social Change*. London: New Left Books, 1971.

———. *Walter Benjamin: Or Towards a Revolutionary Criticism*. London: Verso Editions, 1981.

Fages, Jean-Baptiste. *Comprendre Jacques Lacan*. Paris: Privat-Pensée, 1971.

Felman, Shoshana, ed. *Literature and Psychoanalysis. The Question of Reading: Otherwise*. Baltimore: Johns Hopkins UP, 1977, 1980.

Flieger, Jerry Aline. "Baudelaire and Freud: The Poet as Joker." *Literature and Psychoanalysis*. Ed. Maurice Charney. Rutherford, N.J.: Fairleigh Dickenson UP, 1987.

———. "Entertaining the Ménage à Trois: Psychoanalysis, Feminism, Literature." *Psychoanalysis and Feminism.* Ed. Richard Feldstein and Judith Roof. Ithaca: Cornell UP, 1989.

———. "The Purloined Punch Line: Joke as Textual Paradigm." *Lacan and Narration.* Ed. Robert C. Davis. Special issue of *Modern Language Notes* 98.5 (December 1983): 941–67.

Flieger, Jerry Aline, and Alexander Argyros. "Aesthetic Criticism Reassessed: Hartman's Contagious Orbit." *Diacritics* 16.1 (Spring 1987).

Foster, Hal, ed. *The Anti-Aesthetic: Essays on Postmodern Culture.* Port Townsend, Wash.: Bay Press, 1983.

Foucault, Michel. *La volonté de savoir.* Paris: Editions Gallimard, 1976. *The History of Sexuality: Volume I: An Introduction.* Trans. Robert Hurley. New York: Vintage Books, 1980.

Freud, Sigmund. *The Standard Edition of the Complete Works of Sigmund Freud.* 24 vols. Trans. James Strachey. London: Hogarth, 1955, and New York: W. W. Norton, 1961.

———. *Beyond the Pleasure Principle* (1920). Vol. 18.

———. *Civilization and its Discontents* (1930). Vol. 21.

———. "Creative Writers and Daydreaming" (1908). Vol. 9.

———. "Delusion and Dream in Jensen's *Gradiva*" (1906). Vol. 9.

———. "The Dissolution of the Oedipus Complex" (1924). Vol. 19.

———. "The Dynamics of Transference" (1912). Vol. 12.

———. "Female Sexuality" (1931). Vol. 21.

———. "Fetishism" (1927). Vol. 21.

———. "Formulations on the Two Principles in Mental Functioning" (1911). Vol. 12.

———. "Fragment of an Analysis of a Case of Hysteria" (1905). Vol. 7.

———. *Group Psychology and the Analysis of the Ego* (1921). Vol. 18.

———. "Instincts an their Vicissitudes" (1915). Vol. 14.

———. *The Interpretation of Dreams* (1900). Vol. 4–5.

———. *Introductory Lectures on Psycho-Analysis* (1916–17). Vol. 15–16.

———. *Jokes and their Relation to the Unconscious* (1905). Vol. 8.

———. *Moses and Monotheism* (1939). Vol. 23.

———. "Mourning and Melancholia" (1917). Vol. 15.

———. "Negation." ["Die Verneinung"] (1925). Vol. 19.

———. "On Narcissism: An Introduction" (1914). Vol. 14.

———. *The Psychopathology of Everyday Life* (1901). Vol. 6.

———. "Remembering, Repeating, and Working Through" (1914). Vol. 12.

———. "Repression" (1915). Vol. 14.

———. "Some Psychological Consequences of an Anatomical Distinction Between the Sexes" (1925). Vol. 19.

———. "The Splitting of the Ego in the Process of Defense" (1938). Trans. James Strachey. *The International Journal of Psychoanalysis* 22

(1941). (Unfinished essay not included in the *Standard Edition.*)
———. *Three Essays on a Theory of Sexuality* (1905). Vol. 7.
———. *Totem and Taboo* (1912). Vol. 13.
———. "The Uncanny" (1919). Vol. 17.
———. "The Unconscious" (1915). Vol. 14.
Gallop, Jane. *The Daughter's Seduction.* Ithaca: Cornell UP, 1982.
Garner, Shirley Nelson, Claire Kahane, and Madelon Sprengnether. *The (M)Other Tongue: Essays in Psychoanalytic Interpretation.* Ithaca: Cornell UP, 1985.
Gaudin, Colette, et al., eds. *Feminist Readings: French Texts/American Contexts. Yale French Studies* 62 (1981).
Habermas, Jürgen. "Modernity—An Incomplete Project." In Foster 3–15.
Hartman, Geoffrey. *Criticism in the Wilderness: The Study of Literature Today.* New Haven: Yale UP, 1980.
———. ed. *Psychoanalysis and the Question of the Text.* Baltimore: Johns Hopkins UP, 1978.
Hegel, G. W. F. *Hegel's Phenomenology of Spirit.* Trans. A. V. Miller. Oxford: Oxford UP, 1977.
Hertz, Neil. "The Notion of Blockage in the Literature of the Sublime." In Hartman 62–85.
Howe, Irving. *The Idea of the Modern in Literature and the Arts.* New York: Horizon Press, 1967.
Hyppolite, Jean. *Genesis and Structure of Hegel's Phenomenology of Spirit.* Trans. Samuel Cherniak and John Heckman. Evanston: Northwestern UP, 1974.
Ionesco, Eugene. *Notes et contre-notes.* Paris: Gallimard-Idées, 1962.
———. *Théâtre complet.* 4 vols. Paris: Gallimard-NRF, 1962–1978.
Irigaray, Luce. *Ce sexe qui n'en est pas un.* Paris: Editions de Minuit, 1977. *This Sex Which Is Not One.* Trans. Catherine Porter. Ithaca: Cornell UP, 1985.
———. *Speculum de l'autre femme.* Paris: Editions de Minuit, 1974. *Speculum of the Other Woman.* Ithaca: Cornell UP, 1985.
Jakobson, Roman. "Two Aspects of Language and Two Types of Aphasic Disturbances." *Fundamentals of Language.* The Hague: Mouton, 1956. 55–82.
Jameson, Fredric. "Imaginary and Symbolic in Lacan: Marxism, Psychoanalytic Criticism, and the Problem of the Subject." In Felman 338–395.
———. *The Political Unconscious: Narrative as Socially Symbolic Act.* Ithaca: Cornell UP, 1981.
Jardine, Alice. *Gynesis: Configurations of Woman and Modernity.* Ithaca: Cornell UP, 1985.
———. "Toward a Transatlantic Feminism." *Yale French Studies* 62 (1981).

Johnson, Barbara. "The Frame of Reference: Poe, Lacan, Derrida." In Felman 457–505.

Kojève, Alexandre. *Introduction to the Reading of Hegel.* Trans. James H. Nichols, Jr. New York: Basic Books, 1969.

Kristeva, Julia. "Bataille, l'expérience et la pratique." *Bataille.* Roland Barthes, et al. Paris: Union Générale d'Editions-10/18, 1973.

———. *Desire in Language: A Semiotic Approach to Literature and Art.* Ed. Leon S. Roudiez. Trans. Thomas Gora, Alice Jardine, and Leon S. Roudiez. New York: Columbia UP, 1980.

———. *The Kristeva Reader.* Ed. Toril Moi. New York: Columbia UP, 1986.

———. *Polylogue.* Paris: Editions du Seuil, 1977.

Kroker, Arthur, and David Cook. *The Postmodern Scene: Excremental Culture and Hyper-Aesthetics.* New York: St. Martin's Press, 1986.

Kurzweil, Edith, and William Phillips. *Literature and Psychoanalysis.* New York: Columbia UP, 1983.

Lacan, Jacques. *Ecrits.* Paris: Editions du Seuil-Points, 1966, 1971.

———. "Desire and the Interpretation of Desire in *Hamlet.*" In Felman 11–52.

———. "Kant avec Sade." *Critique* 191 (1963): 291–313.

———. *Le séminaire livre XX: encore.* Paris: Editions du Seuil, 1975.

———. *Le séminaire sur "La Lettre volé." Ecrits* I, 19–75. *Seminar on the Purloined Letter.* Trans. Jeffrey Mehlman. *Yale French Studies* 48 (1976); 39–72.

Lang, Candace D. *Irony/Humor.* Baltimore: Johns Hopkins UP, 1988.

Laplanche, Jean. *Vie et mort en psychanalyse.* Paris: Editions du Seuil, 1976. *Life and Death in Psychoanalysis.* Trans. Jeffrey Mehlman. Baltimore: Johns Hopkins UP, 1976.

Laplanche, Jean, and Serge Leclaire. "L'inconscient." *Les Temps Modernes* 183 (July 1961): 81–129. Trans. *Yale French Studies* 48 (1976): 151–68.

Laplanche, Jean, and J.-B. Pontalis. *Vocabulaire de la psychanalyse.* Paris: PUF, 1967.

Le Clerc, Annie. *Parole de femme.* Paris: Grasset, 1974.

Lentricchia, Frank. *After the New Criticism.* Chicago: U of Chicago P, 1980.

———. *Criticism and Social Change.* Chicago: U of Chicago P, 1983.

Lewis, Philip. "The Post-structuralist Condition." *Diacritics* 12 (Spring 1982).

Lyotard, Jean-François. *La condition postmoderne: rapport sur le savoir.* Paris: Editions de Minuit, 1979. *The Postmodern Condition: A Report on Knowledge.* Trans. Geoff Bennington and Brian Massumi. Theory and History of Literature 20. Minneapolis: U of Minnesota P, 1984.

———. *Des dispositifs pulsionnels.* Paris: Union Générale d'Editions, 1973.

———. *Discours, figure.* Paris: Editions Klincksieck, 1971.

———. "Re-writing Modernity." *Substance* 54 (1987): 3–9.

Lyotard, Jean-François, and Jean-Loup Thébaud. *Au juste.* Paris: Christian Bourgois, 1979. *Just Gaming.* Trans. Wlad Godzich. Theory and History of Literature 20. Minneapolis: U of Minnesota P, 1985.

Macksey, Richard, and Eugenio Donato, eds. *The Structuralist Controversy.* Baltimore: Johns Hopkins UP, 1972.

Marcuse, Herbert. *Eros and Civilization.* New York: Random House, 1955.

Marks, Elaine, and Isabelle de Courtivron, eds. *New French Feminisms.* New York: Schocken Books, 1981.

Marx, Karl. "The Meaning of Human Requirements." *The Economic and Philosophical Manuscripts of 1844.* Trans. Martin Milligan. Ed. Dirk J. Struik. New York: International Publications, 1973.

Mehlman, Jeffrey, ed. *French Freud: Structural Studies in Psychoanalysis. Yale French Studies* 48. Millwood, New York: Kraus Reprints, 1976.

———. "How to Read Freud on Jokes: The Critic as *Schadchen.*" *New Literary History* 6.2 (Winter 1975): 439–61.

Meltzer, Françoise, ed. *The Trial(s) of Psychoanalysis.* Special issue of *Critical Inquiry* 13.2 (1987): 215–413. Chicago: U of Chicago P, 1987.

Melville, Stephen W. *Philosophy Beside Itself: On Deconstruction and Modernism.* Theory and History of Literature 27. Minneapolis: U of Minnesota P, 1986.

Mitchell, Juliet, and Jacqueline Rose, eds. *Feminine Sexuality: Jacques Lacan and the école freudienne.* Trans. Jacqueline Rose. New York: W. W. Norton, 1982.

Mitchell, W. J. T. *Critical Inquiry* 15.4 (Summer 1989). (Issue devoted to the question of de Man's wartime writings.)

Moi, Toril. "The Missing Mother: The Oedipal Rivalries of René Girard." *Diacritics* 12.2 (Summer 1982): 21–31.

Montrelay, Michèle. *L'ombre et le nom: sur la féminité.* Paris: Editions de Minuit, 1977.

Nägele, Rainer. "The Scene of the Other: Theodor. W. Adorno's Negative Dialectic in the Context of Poststructuralism." In Arac 91–111.

Nietzsche, Friedrich. *Beyond Good and Evil.* Trans. Helen Zimmern. New York: Macmillan, 1924.

———. *The Gay Science.* Trans. Walter Kaufmann. New York: Random House, 1974.

Owens, Craig. "The Allegorical Impulse: Toward a Theory of Postmodernism." *October* 12 (1980).

Poe, Edgar Allan. "The Purloined Letter," in *Great Tales and Poems of Edgar Allan Poe.* New York: Pocket Library, 1951.

Rimmon-Kenan, Shlomith, ed. *Discourse in Psychoanalysis and Literature.* London: Methuen Books, 1987.

Ryan, Michael. *Marxism and Deconstruction: A Critical Articulation.* Baltimore: Johns Hopkins UP, 1982.

Said, Edward. *The World, the Text, and the Critic.* Cambridge, MA: Harvard UP, 1983.
Schneiderman, Stuart. *Jacques Lacan: The Death of an Intellectual Hero.* Cambridge, MA: Harvard UP, 1983.
Schor, Naomi. "Female Paranoia: The Case for Psychoanalytic Feminist Criticism." *Yale French Studies* 62 (1981): 204–19.
Smith, Joseph H., and William Kerrigan;, eds. *Taking Chances: Derrida, Psychoanalysis, and Literature.* Baltimore: Johns Hopkins UP, 1984.
Spivak, Gayatri. "French Feminism in an International Frame." *Yale French Studies* 62 (1981): 154–84.
Staten, Henry. *Wittgenstein and Derrida.* Lincoln: U of Nebraska P, 1984.
Ulmer, Gregory. "The Object of Post-Criticism." In Foster 83–110.
Weber, Samuel. *The Legend of Freud.* Minneapolis: U of Minnesota P, 1982.
Wilden, Anthony. *The Language of the Self.* (Translation and commentary on Lacan's "Champ et fonction du langage dans la psychanalyse," *Ecrits* I.) New York: Dell, 1975. Baltimore: Johns Hopkins UP, 1984.
Willis, Sharon. "A Symptomatic Narrative." In *A Fine Romance: Freud and Dora.* Spec. issue *Diacritics* 13.1 (Spring 1983).
Wittgenstein, Ludwig. *Philosophische Untersuchungen. Philosophical Investigations.* Trans. G. E. M. Anscombe. New York: Macmillan, 1953.

A Selected List of Theoretical Works on the Comic

Aristotle. *Poetics.* Trans. S. H. Butcher. London, 1886, Section V.
———. *Problems.* Trans. Barthélemy-Saint-Hilaire. Paris, 1891, Chap. 2–xxv, Chap. 11–xiii, Chap. 28–viii.
Bain, Alexander. *The Emotions and the Will.* 2nd ed. London: Longmans, 1865.
Baudelaire, Charles. "De l'essence du rire: et généralement du comique dans les arts plastiques." *Curiosités esthétiques.* Paris, 1855.
Benayoun, Robert. *Anthologie du nonsense.* Paris: J. J. Pauvert, 1957.
Bergson, Henri. *Le rire.* Paris: Félix Alcan, 1900.
Boileau-Despreaux, Nicolas. *L'art poétique.* 1674.
Breton, André. *L'anthologie de l'humour noir.* Paris: J. J. Pauvert, 1966.
Courdaveaux, Victor. *Le rire dans la vie et dans l'art.* Paris, 1875.
Darwin, Charles. *The Expression of the Emotions.* London, 1872.
Descartes, René. *Des passions de l'âme.* 1649, chap. 3.
Dewey, John. "The Theory of Emotion." *Psychological Review.* (Nov. 1894).
Dugas, Léon. *Psychologie du rire.* Paris, 1902.
Eastman, Max. *The Sense of Humor.* New York: C. Scribner's Sons, 1921.
Groos, C. *Die Spiele der Merschen.* Jena, 1899.
Hazlitt, William. *Lectures on the English Comic Writers.* London, 1819.

Hecker, Ewald. *Die Physiologie und Psychologie des Lachens und des Komischen.* Leipzig, 1873.

Hegel, Georg W. F. *Aesthetik.* 1835. Trans. F. P. B. Osmaston. London, 1920.

Hobbes, Thomas. *Leviathan.* 1650, chap. 6.

Kant, Immanuel. *Critique of Aesthetic Judgment.* 1790. Trans. James Meredith. Oxford Press, 1911.

Lamennais, Félicité Robert de. *Esquisse d'une philosophie.* Paris: Pagnerre, 1840.

Lang, Candace D. *Irony/Humor.* Baltimore: Johns Hopkins UP, 1988.

Lessing, Gotthold Ephaim. *Hamburgische Dramaturgie.* Hamburg, 1764.

Lipps, Theodore. *Komik und Humor.* Hamburg, 1898.

McDougall, William. *Social Psychology.* 1909; rpt. Boston: John W. Luce, 1960.

Meredith, George. *An Essay on Comedy.* Westminster, 1898.

Nietzsche, Friedrich. "The Soul of Artists and Authors." *Human, all-too-Human: A Book for Free Spirits.* Edinburgh: T. N. Foulis, 1910.

Nohain, Jean. *Histoire du rire à travers le monde.* Paris: Librairie Hachette, 1965.

Pagnol, Marcel. *Notes sur le rire.* Paris: Nagel, 1947.

Parisot, Henri. *Le rire des poètes.* Paris: Editions P. Belfond, 1969.

Penjon, Albert. "Le rire et la liberté." *Revue Philosophique* 36 (Aug. 1893).

Plato. *Dialogues.* Trans. Jowett. New York: C. Scribner's Sons, 1907.

Renouvier, Charles. *La nouvelle monadologie.* Paris: A. Colin, 1899.

Ribot, Théodule. *La psychologie des sentiments.* Paris, 1902.

Richter, Jean-Paul. *Vorschule der Aesthetik.* Hamburg, 1804.

Schauer, Otto. "Uber das Wesen der Komik." *Archive für die Gesämte Psychologie* 18 (1910).

Schopenhauer, Arthur. *The World as Will and as Representation.* Leipzig, 1819. Trans. Haldane and Kemp.

Sidis, Boris. *The Psychology of Laughter.* New York: F. Appleton, 1919.

Spencer, Herbert. "The Physiology of Laughter." *Essays* 2. London, 1901.

Spinoza, Baruch. *Ethics.* Trans. R. H. M. Elwes. 1833.

Smith, Willard. *The Nature of Comedy.* Boston: Gorham Press, 1930.

Sully, James. *An Essay on Laughter.* London, 1902.

Valéry, Paul. *Mon Faust.* Paris: Gallimard, 1948.

Vischer, F. T. *Aesthetik.* 3 vols. Leipzig, 1846–1851.

Ziegler, J. *Das Komische.* Leipzig, 1899.

INDEX

Absolute comic (*comique absolu*), 33–35, 39–49, 68–69, 147–48, 172, 178–79
Absolute Knowledge, 18–19, 28, 32, 132, 137, 144–46, 161, 169. *See also* Dialectic
Absorption, in art, 201–2, 241
Abstract negativity. *See* Negativity
Active state (vs. passive), 111, 113; and libido, 118–19, 243–44; and male gender, 109, 118–19; and play, 95, 97, 228
Aesthetic(s), 101, 151, 213, 218; elitist ("art for art's sake") 23–24, 107; of failure (Beckett) 197–204; Freud's definition of, 58–59, 94; *Godot* as, 197–208; and jokes, 69–70, 90; Kantian, 107, 222; of maintained desire, 176–78, 197–204; and perversity, 76, 84; and play, 58–59; and poetry, 242–45; postmodern, 19, 167, 189, 193–94; social implications of, 206–8, 225–28, 233–39; 245–59
Affirmation, 133, 136, 156, 169, 183, 184, 188, 228
Aftermath, 3, 29, 32, 47, 84, 146, 165, 170, 178–79, 255. *See also* Excess
Aim (*Tendenz*): of absolute comic, 40; aesthetic ("aimless"), 224, 237; deflection from biological, 74, 75, 90,107; fetishistic, 107; in innocent and tendentious jokes, 58, 66, 69–71, 78; poetic, 242–46; poststructuralist ("aimless"), 131, 135–38, 143, 145; of referential comic, 35–36. *See also* Butt of joke; Goal; Purpose
Allende, Isabel, 193, 257
Allusion, 50, 60, 87, 147–49, 248. *See also* Joke technique
Alter ego, 20, 101, 105, 149, 171–72, 210, 222. *See also* Other, the
Althusser, Louis, 253
Ambiguity, comic, 59–62, 110, 144, 216, 231, 247
Analysis (psychotherapy), 112, 119, 132, 146, 161, 205, 217, 222, 236, 257
Anchorage (*points de capiton*), 215–16, 231
Anlehnung. *See* Laying on
Anouilh, Jean, 11
Arac, Jonathan, 27, 252
Arrabal, Fernando, 179
Attention, 57, 80, 90, 91, 101–2, 110, 111, 127, 172, 204, 207, 208, 214, 220, 221. *See also* Absorption; Ideational mimetics

Band (*bande*), 128–29, 209
Barthes, Roland, 4, 26, 53, 122, 125, 163, 249

Bataille, Georges, 7, 11–13, 53, 177–79, 200–204, 214; *Conférences sur le Non-Savoir*, 138; on eroticism, 43–50, 59, 67–68, 71–77, 100, 112; "Hegelianism" of, 129–54; *L'érotisme*, 133, 135, 138, 140, 141–43; *L'expérience intérieure*, 133–35; on transgression, 160–65; *See also* Erotic; Master; Negativity, Sovereignty; Transgression
Baudelaire, Charles (*De l'essence du rire*), 7, 13, 15, 30, 33–43, 45, 53, 58, 60, 63, 68–69, 129, 134–35, 141–42, 147–48, 155, 171–72, 179
Baudrillard, Jean, 22, 23, 26–30, 121–22
Béance (gap). *See* Stigma; Wound
Beckett, Samuel, 3, 7, 8, 10, 13–15, 20–21, 47, 50, 52, 128, 150, 179, 182, 185, 194, 245, 252, 259, chapter 8 passim; *Endgame* (*Fin de partie*), 223–34; *Murphy*, 197, 218; *Three Dialogues*, 198–200; *Waiting for Godot* (*En attendant Godot*), 197–222; *Watt*, 193, 197, 211, 232
Belief. *See* Absorption; Credulity
Bergson, Henri, 38, 78, 218
Berman, Marshall, 24, 25
Betweenness (*l'entre-deux*), 150, 174
Bewilderment and illumination, 59, 65, 92, 113, 183. *See also* Joke technique
Bind (double), 59, 60, 127–32, 136, 140, 143, 147, 164, 209–12, 237
Blanchot, Maurice, 4, 7, 9, 11–13, 17–21, 30–37, 43–48, 50–53, 59–63, 72, 130, 146, 165–93, 197–98, 202–14, 218, 222–25, 230–37, 240, 244, 247, chapter 6 passim; *L'entretien infini*, 4, 12, 21, 30–31, 50, 61, 132, 166–94, 202–4, 207, 223. *See also* Discontinuous theater; *Parole littéraire*; *Troisième rapport du neutre*
Bond, binding, 88, 90, 92–96, 105, 112, 113, 129, 208, 210, 212, 227
Booth, Wayne C., 12, 14
Brecht, Bertolt, 10, 203, 250
Breton, André, 38, 249
Brooks, Peter, 104, 107
Butt of joke, 64, 69, 80, 82, 91, 94, 98, 109–12, 116, 121, 139, 150, 175

Castration, 106, 107, 109, 142, 161–63, 174, 217, 243
Censorship (joke and dream), 57, 64, 67, 70, 71, 77, 156, 158, 241
Chain: signifying, 162, 182, 213, 215, 239; social, 91, 108
Chance, 12, 31, 38, 127–28, 134, 140, 190, 225–28, 233
Chatter, Heideggerian (*rumeur*), 52, 183, 185, 212, 224, 231
Cheating (*tromperie*), 43–47, 132, 136, 141, 160, 193. *See also* Bataille; Comedy, naive; Eroticism
Cixous, Hélène, 9, 11, 18, 21
Coleridge, Samuel Taylor, 112, 202
Comedy: classic, 36, 221; of manners, 37; naive (Bataille's "*naïve comédie*" of transgression), 44, 46, 75, 136, 141, 144, 146, 160, 174–75, 203
Comic: definition of, 11–13; of superiority; 35, 58, 82, 98, 154; theory, 7, 13, 30, 33, 37, 49, 54, 57, 67, 74, 81, 187, 246, 254, 255, chapter 3 passim; victim, 37, 41, 76, 81, 82, 134, 172, 202, 214. *See also* Butt of joke
Comic lending; 79, 81, 82, 150, 202, 221, 222. *See also* Ideational mimetics
Comic Other, 42, 82, 83
Commedia, 148, 151
Communication, 18, 22, 23, 26, 27, 54, 112, 121, 122, 160, 168, 172, 185, 190, 210, 234, 244. *See also* Chain, signifying; Identification
Compulsion. *See* Death-drive; Repetition
Condensation, 59–65, 71, 80, 103, 156, 158, 238. *See also* Joke technique
Continuity, 12, 23, 29, 45, 46, 132–

34, 137, 141, 148, 149, 166, 168, 173, 178, 202
Cook, David, 26
Countertransference, 112, 146, 177, 214, 257
Credulity, 17, 19, 28–29, 130, 201

Darwin, Charles, 18
Death-drive (death impulse, death instinct, *Thantatos*), 6, 19, 44, 99, 101, 141, 142, 177–78, 181, 187, 228, 242, 256
Deleuze, Gilles, 125
Delusion, 37, 40, 102, 172, 203
De Man, Paul, 4, 12–16, 24, 25, 28, 33, 39–41, 85, 125, 126, 145, 169, 252; *Blindness and Insight*, 25
Demand (*demande*), 72, 100, 106, 110, 176–78, 179, 224, 229, 246
De-monstration, 85–86, 120, 125
Denegation (*Verneinung*). *See* Negation
Denial, 24, 25, 28, 107, 122, 163. *See also* Negation
Derrida, Jacques, 8, 9, 17, 18, 28, 50, 51, 61, 72, 85–86, 109–10, 125–32, 136–42, 144–52, 164, 169, 187–91, 226–28, 233, 241, 248; *La dissémination*, 50, 191; "La double séance," 50, 62, 129, 147–51, 187–88; *L'écriture et la différence*, 125–46; *Pas*, 133
Designation, 61, 95, 153, 155, 158, 159, 162, 164, 183, 191
Desire (*désir*): Beckett's theater as emblem of, 200–214, 217, 221–34; Blanchot's desire of the Other (*le troisième rapport du neutre*), 171–90; comic as symptom of, 4–12, 14, 15, 17, 19, 57, 81, 84; 91–100; for death or ending (*la petite mort*), 43, 141–44, 149; deflected from biological aim, 67, 71, 75–78, 91–100; as excess, 29, 47, 171; intersubjective circuit of, 83, 88, 91–100; 102–14, 117–22; in language, 117–22, 102–14, 146, 150–63, 165, 167; literature of, 31, 200–214, 217, 221–34; for meaning, 52, 61; object of, 68, 89, 147; sexual, 72, 87; social implications of, 235–38, 241–46, 252–58. *See also* Demand; Need
Detour, 22, 39, 50, 74, 89–90, 99–100, 104–6, 164, 170, 180, 185, 186, 202, 212, 223, 237. See also *En souffrance*; Long-circuit
Dialectic, Hegelian, 10, 18, 28, 32, 34, 43–51, 61, 125, 129–34, 137–40, 146, 150, 151, 154, 160, 161, 164–71, 175–78, 183, 188, 208, 210, 222, 224
Diderot, Denis, 22
Difference, 32, 86, 176, 193, 240; between self and Other, 171, 173, 188, 200; maintenance of, 173, 176, 180, 188–90, 200; and repetition, 180–83, 186, 215, 227; sexual, 117–19, 128
Discontinuous theater, 202–4, 207, 215
Displacement, 60, 63–65, 79, 80, 103, 156, 238; of desire, 106–7, 111, 161–63, 253–54. *See also* Fetish; Joke technique
Dissemination, 167, 228, 271
Donato, Eugenio, 125
Dora, case of, 87, 112, 132, 257
Double meaning (*double entendre*), 5, 50, 60, 61, 105, 136, 157, 194, 207, 210, 217, 224, 247
Double-talk, 34, 51, 146, 167, 187, 217, 224; as wordplay, 73, 159
Dream, dreamwork, 6, 11, 57, 60, 64, 71, 76, 93–98, 132, 140, 149, 151, 152, 183, 193, 232; fulfillment of desire by, 156–60, 163, 174, 201, 241
Duck-rabbit, Wittgenstein's, 62
Dugas, Léon, 41, 43
Dupe, comic. *See* Butt of joke
Duplicity, 6, 34, 40, 51, 61, 167, 187
Duras, Marguerite, 52, 182

Eagleton, Terry, 9, 10, 247–50
Écriture. *See* Writing
Ego, 174, 177, 205–6, 255; consti-

Ego (*cont'd*)
tution of, 79–83; *See also* Alter ego; Superego
En souffrance, 50, 120, 188, 197, 202, 207, 210, 225, 231, 234
Erotic, eroticism: Bataille's theory of, 30, 43–50, 100, 112, 128–41, 173, 177, 200–203; Blanchot's concept of, 180; Freud's theory of, 141–51; joke as, 59–78, 97; literature and, 93; Lyotard's theory of, 154, 160–63; theater and, 200–203, 214, 223
Error, 97, 125–28, 134–40, 145, 164–66, 180, 209, 211, 227–28, 237, 251, 258
Excess (surplus): in Beckett's theater, 206, 209, 211, 220–29, 232–34; of desire, 10, 68, 72, 84, 100–103, 107, 110, 146, 176–79; eroticism/pleasure as, 46–53, 115, 135; Freud's aesthetic of, 246–47, 255, 258; laughter as function of, 38, 41, 146; of meaning, 32, 61, 77, 143; overdetermined language as, 161, 164–65; 237–44; postmodernism as, 25–26, 29, 84, 182–84; of reason, 169–70
Existentialism, 168, 249, 255

Faltering (*chavirement*), 100, 141
Fantasy, 112, 147–48, 151, 219, 242–43
Farce, 9, 10, 87, 108, 110, 121, 132, 135, 140, 141, 147; motto of (*A trompeur, trompeur et demi*), 108, 110–11, 119, 139, 225, 229
Felman, Shoshana, 253
Feminism, feminist theory, 4, 9, 13, 18, 54, 114–19, 122, 131–32, 168, 217, 249, 253
Fetish, fetishism, 86, 106, 107, 111, 120–22, 161, 163, 242–43, 253
Figure (figural language), 17, 71, 95, 104–5, 151–61, 181, 237, 240–41, 257. *See also* Metaphor; Metonymy; Poetic; Poetry; Synecdoche; Trope
Flaw, comic, 34, 82, 255
Foreclusion (*Vorwerfung*), 161–63
Forepleasure, 112, 244
Forgetfulness, forgetting (*oubli*), 25, 169, 182, 212, 231, 257
Fort-da, 95–97, 152, 181, 188, 229, 233
Foster, Hal (*The Anti-Aesthetic: Essays in Postmodern Culture*), 27, 121, 137, 201, 244, 250, 255, 258
Foucault, Michel, 4, 7, 15, 24, 26, 28, 125, 126, 142, 168, 252
Fragment (*parole fragmentaire*), 26, 50, 149, 165, 167, 176–79, 183, 187, 248
Freud, Sigmund, 7–9, 11–20, 29, and aethetic pleasure, 101, 176, 200–204, 238, 246–47, 254–55; *Beyond the Pleasure Principle* (repetition compulsion), 6, 19, 44, 94–100, 104, 140–43, 184, 242, 246, 256; comic theory, 37–39, 43, 53–54, chapter 3 passim, 147–59; death instinct (and repetition compulsion), 48, 101, 105, 143–45, 177–78, 181, 184, 228, 242; Dora, case of, 87, 112, 132, 257; dream theory of, 6, 11, 57, 60, 64, 71, 76, 93–98, 132, 140, 149–52, 156–60, 163, 174, 183, 193, 201, 232, 241; father's role in, 217–18; and feminism, 132; *Jokes and Their Relation to the Unconscious*, 57–84; 157–59, 179–80, 212, 238; joke theory of, 57–84, 85–93, 179, 212, 214–20, 224, 227; Lacan's return to, chapter 4 passim; *Moses and Monotheism*, 231, 256; on myth, 231–32; on negation, 159–165; oedipal triangle of, 23, 102, 105, 126, 175, 177, 205, 213, 236, 246; on perversion, 174, 255; on play (*fort-da*), 94–97, 152, 181, 188, 229, 233, 243; and social interaction, 246, 253–59; on symptom, 106–7, 174; *Three Essays on the Theory of Sexuality*, 72, 75, 106, 109, 163, 177,

254; *Totem and Taboo*, 79, 216; on veiling (*Ankleidung*) 242–43; *Why War?* 256; on writers and writing (*Creative Writers and Daydreaming*), 6, 93–94, 100, 102, 151, 198, 243–44

Game (play), 9, 14, 31, 235, 238; in Beckett, 14, 182, 197–207, 211–16, 223–36; of chance, 127; children's 69; erotic, 43–47, 67–68, 132, 136, 144; Freud's (*fort-da*), 60, 93–98, 152, 181–88, joke as, 68, 71, 74–75, 78, 90; intersubjectivity as, 53–54, 78, 108–10, 177, 180, 257; language, 21, 126, 240; poetry as, 191–94; poststructuralist 126–32, 163–67, 182–89; as social paradigm, 256–59; theatrical, chapter 7 passim; of writing (*jeu de l'écriture*), 12, 52, 104, 108, 182–89, 193
Gender, 108–21, 253
Genet, Jean, 20, 193
Giraudoux, Jean, 11
Goal: aesthetic as divorced from, 69, 243, 251; of Beckett's characters, 207, 212, 216; death as, 99, 101, 172, 184, 187; of dialectic, 145; Hamlet's 105–6; of joke, 49, 70, 90, 180, 230; of literature, 47, 198. *See also* Aim; Purpose
Godot (character), 210–14
Gratuity, 235, 237, 245–49, 252, 253

Habermas, Jürgen, 24, 28
Hamlet, 22, 104–6, 162
Hartman, Geoffrey, 4
Hecker, Ewald, 206
Hegel, Georg Wilhelm Friedrich, 17, 18, 32, 41, 46, 129–46, 152–53, 164–65, 168–70, 179. *See also* Dialectic
Heidegger, Martin, 168, 185, 209
Hertz, Neil, 246
History (*histoire*): end of, 9, 18, 20, 169; as farce, 237; forgetting (repression) of, 25–26, 257; poet and, 250; poststructuralist view of, 125–27, 178; as tale (*histoire*), 226–28
Hobbes, Thomas, 37
Hommelette, 20
Howe, Irving, 25–27
Humor, 78, 217–20; *L'humour noir*, 7, 38, 227
Hymen, 62, 149, 150
Hysteria, 106, 109

Ideational mimetics, 78–83, 91, 150, 172, 202, 214, 221
Identification: Blanchot's concept of, 171–73, 190; comic, 39, 47, 79, 82–83, 214; Freudian, 82–83, 101–2; with poet (imaginary), 108, 221–22; in theater, 201–2, 214
Illusion, 149–50, 189–90; of ego, 39–40, 102, 172; of light (Blanchot), 175; of literary purity, 139–41; 202, 217–18; of phallic power, 243–44. *See also* Imaginary
Imaginary, the (*L'imaginaire*), 39–41, 101–8, 112–16, 140, 172–73, 179, 189, 205, 209–11, 213, 221–22, 243, 246, 255
Interminable cure, the, 16, 200, 222, 236, 237
Intersubjectivity, 8, 53, 88, 89, 93, 94, 101, 103, 106, 113, 178, 234–35, 246, 252–54. *See also* Freud; Lacan; Game; Joke(s); Joking triangle; Object; Oedipus; Text
Interval, 32–36; 39, 52, 153–54, 158, 162, 168, 171–72, 174, 181, 187–91, 193, 208, 215
Ionesco, Eugene, 8, 10, 51, 52, 179, 185, 193, 248–49, 257
Irigaray, Luce, 18, 115, 168
Irony, 12–16, 33, 40–41
Iterability, 29, 179, 183

Jakobson, Roman, 103, 239
Jameson, Frederic, 8, 16, 19, 253
Jardine, Alice, 117, 253

Johnson, Barbara, 16, 20, 109, 252, 253
Joke(s): 212, 240; in Beckett, 212–22; bewilderment and illumination in, 175, 212, 220, 238–39, 247, 256; butt (object) of, 69, 80, 82, 91, 94, 110, 112, 116, 150; desire in, 179–80; difference from comic 79–81; as figural language, 157–59; Freud's theory of, 57–84, 157; innocent, 58–59, 69–70, 73; Lacan's theory of, 87–122; as narrative paradigm, 87–124; negation in, 157–59; obscene, 66, 90, 154; tendentious (obscene), 58, 65–70, 73, 80, 89, 93, 141, 248; and the unconscious, 238–39. *See also* Comic lending; Joke technique; Joking triangle
Joke technique, jokework, 6, 10, 11, 59, 60–64, 71–80, 93, 103, 212–215, 238. *See also* Bewilderment and illumination; Condensation; Displacement; Regression
Joking triangle, 76–78, 91, 94, 98, 111, 118, 176, 212, chapter 4 passim
Jouissance, 95, 116, 174, 178
Joyce, James, 16

Kant, Immanuel, 18, 24, 38, 49, 59, 107, 131, 154, 184, 222, 233, 237, 245, 246, 254
Kerrigan, William, 5, 6, 14, 21, 198
Kristeva, Julia, 4, 7, 10, 116, 117, 125, 126, 130, 131, 170, 191, 249, 250
Kroker, Arthur, 26

Lacan, Jacques, 4, 7, 8–10, 13, 14, 17, 38–40, 51, 53, 63, 72, 79, chapter 4 passim, 125, 132, 140, 144, 152, 161–67, 172–77, 184–89, 246; *Ecrits*, 87, 101, 107, 119, 238, 239; the Schema L, 205, 206; *Seminar on the Purloined Letter*, 86–122, 226. *See also* Desire; Imaginary, the; Law; Mirror Stage; Misrecognition; Symbolic order
Laplanche, Jean, 101, 181, 239
Lapse, 25, 53, 127, 164, 228, 241, 248
Laughter (*le rire*), 7–10, 13, 31–39, 48–51, 57–59, 144–47, 165, 170, 220–22, 227, 247, 251; Baudelaire on, 33–43; control in, 77–82; greater (*le rire entier* or *le rire majeur*), 134–35, 140; lesser (*le rire mineur*), 134–35, 139, 141. *See also* Comic; Joke(s)
Law: patriarchal (in psychoanalysis), 85, 90, 96, 101–2, 105, 107, 112, 119, 121, 174, 216, 217; transgression of, 131, 133, 144. *See also* Symbolic order
Laying on (*Anlehnung*); 72, 177, 238
Le Clerc, Annie, 168, 181, 239
Lentricchia, Frank, 15
Libido, 68, 90, 91, 94, 109, 115, 118
Light: Blanchot's "reign of," 12, 19, 168; Blanchot's theory of, 170, 171, 175; of communication (Baudrillard), 23, 36; fragmented, 149. *See also* Interval; Reason; Transparent
Lipps, Theodore, 38, 59
Literature: Bataille's theory of, 200; Beckett's theory of 198–200, 232–33; Blanchot's theory of, 177, 179; 189–92, 197–98, 207, 218; of desire 31, 51, 151, 177, 203; Freud's theory of, 201, 222, 226; postmodern theory of 4, 11, 14, 47, 51, 238, 244–49, 258
Locus (in intersubjective circuit), 110, 113–17
Logocentrism, logos, 3, 4, 18, 125–28, 131, 167, 169, 187
Long-circuit, 74, 76, 78, 93, 100, 170, 177, 205, 213, 254. *See also* Detour; Schema L
Lyotard, Jean-Francois, 4, 7, 9, 13, 33, 83, 85, 121, 125–26, 130, 132, 151–65, 181, 185, 187, 190–

92, 201, 226, 237, 240–47; *Discours, figure*, 71, 152, 156, 181, 185, 187, 190, 201, 241–43; *Just Gaming* (*Au juste*), 226; on play; 95–99; *Postmodern Condition, The*, 16–19, 24–28, 245

McDougall, William, 41
Macksey, Ricahrd, 125
Mallarmé, Stéphane, 3, 47, 129, 147–51, 188, 191, 250
Marcuse, Herbert, 256
Márquez, Gabriel García, 193, 257
Marx, Karl, 25, 130, 237, 248, 249, 250, 252, 253, 255, 258
Masking, 68, 172, 181. *See also* Veil
Masochism, 47, 82, 141, 200
Master, mastery, 31, 131, 138, 139, 141, 146, 171, 189, 208, 209, 228
Master narrative, 88, 113, 120. *See also* Metanarrative
Meaning: in allegory 86; in Beckett, 199, 207, 215–17; as context, 85; death as loss of, 133, 135; desire in, 52, 61–64, 72; double or multiple 5, 37, 47, 51, 62–64, 72, 183–85, 228, 230; escape from (non-sense, absolute negativity), 53, 72, 135–38, 140–46, 163; "no" of (meaning) 153–57; in poetry, 238–48; stable or full, 14, 183; of symptom or trope, 106, 238–41, 244; unrooted or veiled, 180–88, 190–92; violation of (figure or wordplay), 80, 238–41, 163–166
Mehlman, Jeffrey, 81–84, 103, 107, 150
Melville, Stephen, 27, 128, 252
Memory, 149, 238, 250, 257. *See also* Forgetfulness
Meredith, George, 46
Metanarrative, 17, 18, 19, 28, 29, 126, 130. *See also* Master narrative
Metaphor, 9, 10, 12, 13, 17, 28, 75, 103–7, 181–84, 190, 238–41, 244, 247; in feminine sexuality, 113–17; paternal, 215–17; and repression or symptom, 161–62, 254
Metonymy, 103–7, 117, 254
Michaux, Henri, 20, 21
Milosz, Czeslaw, 250
Mimesis, 28, 47, 78, 147–48, 169
Mirror stage (*Stade du miroir*), 39, 101, 172
Mise-en-abîme, 63, 132, 149, 164
Misrecognition (*méconnaissance*), 40, 102, 107, 113, 173, 222
Mitchell, Juliet, 114–17
Modernism, 16, 17–19, 20–54, 85, 122, 169, 233, 256
Molière, Jean-Baptiste Poquelin, 22
Mother: in genesis of play, 95–96, in *Hamlet*, 105; loss of, 142, 181; as object of denial, 132, 140, 149, 152–58, 161; in oedipal theory, 92–96

Name of the Father, 9, 215
Narcissism, 79, 120
Narrative, 17, 18, 23, 26–29, 51–54, 71, 85–89, 91–94, 120, 152, 156; of desire, 117; identification, 102; plot in, 104, 106, 152, 156
Need, biological, 51, 58–59, 69, 72, 76, 90, 95, 101, 107, 176, 238, 246, 250; Lacan's formula for, 110, 176, 224, 243; opposed to desire, 178–80, 208, 229, 244; social, 252, 256, 258. *See also* Demand; Desire
Negation, 45, 126, 130, 132, 138–40, 142, 145, 154, 158, 161–64, 183, 188. *See also* Denial
Negativity: *négativité abstraite*, 131, 135, 138; *négativité sans emploi*, 130–33, 138, 144, 164, 178, chapter 5 passim
Neurosis, 95, 97–98, 106–7, 163, 254
Nietzsche, Friedrich Wilhelm, 25, 133, 137, 169
Nihilism, 126, 130, 169
Nonsense, 10, 37, 59, 64, 65, 91, 111, 146, 164, 238

Object: art, 28, 254; comic (or joke), 34, 36, 41, 62, 66, 76, 78, 80–83, 89–97; of desire (sexual object), 68, 72, 75, 89–97, 105–6, 111, 141, 147, 162, 173–79, 181, 211–14, 246, 254; displaced, 173–79, 211–14, 253; female (mother), 106, 114–15, 142; fetish, 86, 120, 121, 152–64, 243; lost or missing, 111, 142, 152–55, 200, 255; Other as, 82, 89–97, 141, 205–6; poetic, 20; postmodern (allegorical), 80–86; substitute, 96, 107, 149, 161, 255; word as, 159, 162–64
Obstacle (to desire), 62, 66, 73–78, 89, 91, 99–102, 105, 107, 151, 163, 171, 201–4, 246, 254; in Beckett, 213, 216; in poetry, 241–42
Oedipus, oedipal theory, 18, 23, 77, 174–77, 205, 211–14, 231, 236, 246–48, 254, chapter 4 passim
Originality, 29, 85
Other, the (otherness), 32, 39, 41, 63, 81, 82, 83, 91, 101, 107, 110, 117, 139, 141–42, 144, 157, 163–65, 232, 259; Blanchot's concept of, 171–96; Godot as, 204–22
Overdetermination, 6, 53, 60, 63, 164, 206
Owens, Craig, 28, 121

Paradigmatic axis, 103, 239
Paradox, 62–63; in Beckett, 207, 209, 216–20, 224; of chance, 228, 232, 241–42; of desire, 149–50, 153, 180–85; of farce, 110; literary, 192, 201; of negation, 155, 158, 162; of transgression, 136–40, 142–44
Parody, 26, 225, 256
Parole d'entendement. *See* Understanding
Parole de raison. *See* Reason
Parole littéraire (Blanchot), 31–34, 47–51, 59, 183, 189, 191–92, 212
Parole pleine, 40
Passivity, 83, 97, 98, 109, 111, 113, 118, 149
Penjon, Albert, 38
Petit objet a, 174. *See also* Object; Schema L
Phallocentrism, 115, 126
Phallus, 110, 113, 115, 116, 217, 243
Plato, 49
Play, play-acting. *See* Game
Pleasure: aesthetic (poetic, textual), 72, 84, 164, 183, 189, 241–46, 256; death and, 111, 134, 141–42, 178; of game, 191–92; joking, 52, 57–60, 63–70, 72–78, 81, 84, 90–101, 112, 122, 154, 241–46; in laughter, 49, 59; sexual (*jouissance*), 72, 95, 105, 174; woman's 115–16, 126, 178
Plural speech (*la parole plurielle*), 31, 186, 230
Poe, Edgar Allan, 9, 109, 111, 120, 121
Poetic, the, 151, 155–56, 160, 181–92, 227, 231, 237–47, 250–51, 256–58
Poetry, techniques of, 131–34, 147, 163, 179–82, 185, 189–91, 201, 224, 232–33, 237, 239–45, 250
Ponge, Francis, 20, 21, 159
Positivism, positivity, 18, 24, 28, 43, 129, 130, 169
Postmodernism: characteristics of, 29–30; as comic text, chapters 1 and 2 passim; as death of social, 27; defined, 24–28; as intensification of modernism, 27; politics of, 11, 15, 19, 23, 24, 25, 27, 128, 249–56; and poststructuralism, chapter 5 passim; of reaction, 27; of resistance, 27, 29, 121, 233, 234, 255
Poststructuralism, 4, 28, 122, 125–28, 140, 252, chapters 5 and 6 passim
Presentability, 16, 245
Primary process, 6, 71, 103, 156, 158, 165, 191, 237, 238, 241. *See*

also Condensation; Displacement; Dream; Joke technique; Regression; Unconscious, the
Progress: and desire, 244–46, 256; metanarrative of, 17–19, 28, 125
Proust, Marcel, 16, 150
Psychosis, 162–63
Pun, 8, 10, 20, 21, 31, 37, 60–63, 70, 80, 128, 149, 155, 156, 164, 187, 206, 209, 239, 240
Punch line, 8, 10–11, 61, 63, 64, 74, 76, 80, 83–85, 88, 91–93, 97–99, 103, 111, 113, 147, 178, 217, 226, 236
Purpose, joking, 58–59, 65–66, 69–73, 76, 78, 84. *See also* Aim; Goal; Joke

Queneau, Raymond, 20, 21, 52, 159, 182

Realism, realistic literature, 202–4, 226, 249, 257
Reality: "continuous" or seamless, 166, 171; denial of, 162–63, 233, 243; language as response to, 94–99, 152–59; mastery of, 14, 38, 50, 141
Real (Lacanian), 4, 9; reality, 96, 99, 117, 162, 201, 202
Reason: in Beckett, 227, 233; excess of, 183–84, 224–25; ideological reign of, 19, 125–39, 144; and nonsense, 10, 24, 32–34, 42; opposition to (in joking), 42, 59–65, 161–69, 241; and referential comic, 37–38, 53; and speech (*parole de raison*), 32–34, 43–46, 132
Referential comic (*comique significatif*), 13, 33–42, 49, 63, 68, 69, 135, 171, 172, 175, 251
Regression, 60. *See also* Dream; Joke technique
Repetition: as affirmation, 169; comic, 83, 232; compulsion 6, 19, 92–100, 235; desire as motor of, 178–82; with difference, 186, 188, 215–16, 227; *écriture* as, 86; Freud's theory of, 92–100, 242; of history, 237, in literature, 32, 47–52, 104; of pleasure 72, 142
Representation, inadequacy of, 199. *See also* Mimesis; Presentability
Repression (*Verdränung*), 11, 67, 100, 101, 103, 107, 115, 127, 142, 157, 161–63, 239–40, 246, 257
Residue, 3, 25–29, 32, 34, 47, 48, 138, 140, 150, 176, 179, 224, 227, 229. *See also* Aftermath; Excess; Trace
"Return to Freud," Lacan's, 22, 92, 117, 119
Ritual, 77, 79, 136, 181, 200, 201, 216, 252. *See also* Erotic; Sacred; Transgression
Rogue, comic, 109, 139, 175. *See also* Butt of joke
Rose, Jacqueline, 114–17
Roussel, Raymond, 192, 193

Sacred, 133–35, 154, 241, 244, 258
Sacrifice, 41–45, 67–68, 75, 79, 84, 105, 133–42, 146, 147, 155, 179, 200–203, 214, 216
Sarraute, Nathalie, 52
Satire, 256, 257
Schema L, 177, 205
Schopenhauer, Arthur, 38, 49
Schor, Naomi, 115–17
Seminar on the Purloined Letter, The, 86, 87, 106, 108, 120, chapter 4 passim
Shifters, 113
Short-circuit, 73, 77, 92–94, 100, 105, 120, 122, 170, 173, 205, 241
Signified, 71, 162
Signifier, 85, 116, 117, 121, 162, 176, 215, 217, 238, 239; occulted, 239
Silone, Ignazio, 235
Smith, Joseph, 5, 6, 14, 21, 198
Sovereignty, 133, 137–40, 163, 179
Space, spacing (*espacement*), 23, 71, 121, 153–58, 162, 164, 186–87,

Space, spacing (*cont'd*)
190, 199; between self and other, 176, 180; three-dimensional (theatrical), 204, 211, 214, 219, 227, 230, 232
Spencer, Herbert, 38
Spivak, Gayatri, 115, 117, 252–53
Splitting (*Spaltung*), 39, 254
Stein, Gertrude, 182, 183
Stigma, 10, 43, 47, 91, 97, 109, 110, 113, 147, 213. *See also* Wound
Structural machine, 9, 86, 120
Subjectivity, 4, 8, 9, 18, 22, 30, 39, 54, 86, 88, 89, 101, 113, 116–19, 127, 251–53. *See also* Intersubjectivity
Sublimation, 142, 238, 246, 258
Sublime, the, 39, 40, 134, 218, 219, 245–46
Superego, 214
Superiority, comic of, 1–53, 58, 63–65, 82, 83, 98, 134–35, 139, 154, 221
Surrealism, 3, 7, 12, 190, 227, 249, 250
Symbolic order, 67, 79, 86, 95, 102, 103, 105–8, 112–20, 162, 173, 174, 189, 205, 209–13, 217, 221–22, 243, 245
Symptom, 95, 99, 169–70, 200, 253–55; Beckett on, 208, 210, 213, 225; Blanchot on, 169–76, 184; feminine, 106–9, 113–14; joke or laughter as, 7, 10–12, 77, 81, 84, 88, 120, 134, 200; postmodern, 3, 5, 9, 29, 30; of repression, 161; sexuality as, 142; speech as, 32, 153. *See also* Desire; Figure; Neurosis
Synecdoche, 104, 117, 241
Syntagmatic axis, 103, 239

Terminology, 11–13, 134, 137, 230
Text: Beckett's theatrical, 197–234; comic, 59, 71–74, 197–234; and intersubjectivity and 101–6, 113–22; postmodern, 3–17, 20–23, 30, 47–53, 57, 84, 165; as social circuit, 27, 235–59; and textuality 84–89, 93, 150–51, 155; unworked, 4, 30, 31, 166–94, 197
Theatrical pact (willing suspension of disbelief), 112, 202, 221
Third term (*en tiers*), 102, 171, 173, 204, 206, 222; outsider as, 66, 76, 77, 205, 214, 230
Trace, 6, 10, 83, 88, 132, 147, 148, 150, 186, 192–93
Transcoding, 8, 49, 106, 121, 162, 253
Transference, 10, 112, 177, 214, 229
Transgression, 12, 44–52, 65–71, 75, 84, 112, 169, 170, 179, 180, 203, 216–220, 238–42; dialectic, 131–47, 151–60, 163–65. *See also* Erotic
Transparent, transparency, 23, 34–36, 61–62, 87, 102–4, 108, 111, 113, 117–18, 158–59, 168, 171–75, 190. *See also* Light
Triangle, 77, 80, 89, 93, 94, 112, 115, 176, 177, 204–5, 213–14, 236
Trickery, trickster, 20, 43, 44, 52, 64, 80, 111, 175, 193, 239
Troisième rapport du neutre, 174, 176, 200
Trope, 17, 71, 103, 104, 117, 157, 191, 227, 237–39, 254. *See also* Figure
Truth; disguised, in joke, 75, 92–93, 112, 217; and error (Bataille), 140, 145–48; failure of, 47, 231; ideology of, 18, 19, 23, 166–71, 175, 208, 243–44, 250–51, 258; poetic, 185–89

Ulmer, Gregory ("The Object of Post-Criticism"), 85–87, 120–21, 150
Unconscious, the, 6, 14–19, 48, 53, 57, 59, 81, 84, 87–88, 103–7, 116, 127, 156–57, 162, 165, 171, 177, 231; as alien, 211, 213; in the schema L, 187, 205; "structured like a language," 238–40, 244, 253, 258

Undecidability, 15, 61, 119, 127, 128, 224, 228
Understanding (*parole d'entendement*) 31, 32, 34, 35, 36, 60, 171, 172; *See also* Light; Reason

Veil, veiling (*Ankleidung*) 59, 76–79, 84, 92–94, 101–2, 105, 111–12, 114, 191–94, 198, 201, 217, 228, 233, 240, 243–44
Verneinung. *See* Negation
Victim, comic. *See* Butt of joke
Violation, 44, 46, 66, 68, 70, 71, 74, 109, 156, 238
Vischer, F. T., 48
Visibility, 23, 35, 171. *See also* Light
Voyeurism, 73, 118

Weber, Samuel, 63
Wilden, Anthony, 101
Wish fulfillment, 71, 84
Wit, 12, 13
Woman (in Freudian and Lacanian theory) 22, 54, 66, 67, 75, 90, 106, 112–20, 243
Wooing talk, 66, 71, 89, 92, 179, 246
Wordplay. *See* Double-talk; Figure; Pun
Wound (*béance*), 51, 53, 98, 128, 142, 164. *See also* Flaw, comic; Stigma
Writer, 148; Freud on, 93–96, 102, 243–44; postmodern, 16–18, 22, 85–87, 192–93, 240, 247–50, 253; and reader, 3, 14, 21, 84, 112–13, 238, 257; and society, chapter 8 passim
Writing: Bataille's theory of (*écriture majeure et mineure*) 139, 145; Beckett on, 197–200, 232–36; and desire, 29, 57, 202–3; feminine, 113, 116; fragmentary, 177; game of, 104–6; mad game of (*Le jeu insensé d'écrire*), 183–86, 192; postmodern, 3–7, 17, 20–22, 30, 62–63, 182, 202–3, 247–59; postmodern theory of (*écriture*), 4, 12, 15, 72, 85–86, 113, 139, 145, 187, 189, 192, 235, 247–51; triangle of, 94

Designed by Martha Farlow

Composed by Graphic Composition, Inc., in Meridien

Printed by BookCrafters, Inc., on 50-lb. BookText Natural and
bound in Holliston Aqualite with Multicolor Textured endsheets

OPEN SHELF